Paths to Making a Difference:
Leading in Government

Revised Edition

By

Paul R. Lawrence
Ernst & Young LLP

Mark A. Abramson
Leadership Inc.

Contributors

Marc Andersen
Werner Lippuner
Aloha McBride
Robert Shope
Linda M. Springer
Donald L. Thomas

Ernst & Young LLP

ROWMAN & LITTLEFIELD PUBLISHERS, INC.
Lanham • Boulder • New York • Toronto • Plymouth, UK

Published by Rowman & Littlefield Publishers, Inc.
A wholly owned subsidiary of The Rowman & Littlefield Publishing Group, Inc.
4501 Forbes Boulevard, Suite 200, Lanham, Maryland 20706
www.rowman.com

10 Thornbury Road, Plymouth PL6 7PP, United Kingdom

British Library Cataloguing in Publication Information Available

Library of Congress Cataloging-in-Publication Data

The first edition of this book was previously cataloged by the Library of Congress as
follows:

Lawrence, Paul R., 1956–
Paths to making a difference : leading in government / [edited by] Paul R. Lawrence
and Mark A. Abramson
    p. cm.
    Includes bibliographical references.
    1. Government executives—United States. 2. Political leadership—United States.
    I. Title.
    JK723.E9 P39 2011
    352.60973—dc23
    2011034768

ISBN: 978-1-4422-1307-4 (cloth : alk. paper)
ISBN: 978-1-4422-1308-1 (pbk. : alk. paper)
ISBN: 978-1-4422-1309-8 (electronic)

Printed in the United States of America

CONTENTS

Acknowledgments

In undertaking a three-year project, there are numerous people to thank for their valuable assistance over the project's length. We want to first thank the Ernst & Young LLP professionals who participated in the project by joining us on our interviews and reviewing the manuscript. We want to thank Marc Andersen, Werner Lippuner, Aloha McBride, Robert Shope, Linda Springer, and Donald Thomas for their support and valuable assistance.

We want to thank the support team that assisted us in the production of the book. Lauren Verdery at Ernst & Young LLP provided valuable assistance throughout the entire project, including coordinating the project with the firm. We want to thank Lucia Barzellato, Les Brorsen, Mark Bushell, Cheryl Overby, Stephen Seliskar, Eboni Thomas, and Karon Walker from Ernst & Young LLP. The project received valuable support and advice from the now-retired Greg Schoen of Ernst & Young LLP. Special thanks to Philippe Peuch-Lestrade and Uschi Schreiber, previous and current Ernst & Young Global Government and Public Sector Leaders.

We want to thank Suzanne Glassman and Philip Kent for the photographs that appear throughout the book. We want to thank Ashley Johnson, who worked with us in summer 2011 while we were making our final push to complete the first edition of the book. In summer of 2012, we were ably assisted by Sean Heffernan who worked closely with us on the preparation of the revised edition. We received invaluable assistance from Linnae Vaughn throughout the entire project.

The book could not have been completed without our top-notch production team at FIREBRAND. We want to thank Sandy Jones, Effie Metropoulos, and Scott Rodgerson for their hard work on this project. We want to especially thank Sandy Jones for making numerous revisions throughout the layout and editing stages of the production process. We want to thank Effie Metropoulos for her excellent editing skills and for achieving the difficult goal of consistency in a 262-page volume.

We want to thank Jon Sisk and Darcy Evans at Rowman & Littlefield for their valuable assistance. We have enjoyed working with Jon over the years on numerous books.

Last but certainly not least are the 32 individuals who agreed to be featured in this book and who gave us a substantial amount of their time. It is a true understatement to say that there would have been no book without their participation. In addition, we want to thank their staffs for working closely with us in scheduling our interviews and reviewing our final product.

We learned that each of the participants is ably supported by thoughtful and energetic staff members who assist them in accomplishing their organization's mission: Rebecca Adelman, James Anderson, Janet Arneson, Jennifer Arvantis, Michael Barre, Andrea Bleistein, Terrence Bogans, Linda Bonney, Miles Brundage, Megan Byrnes, Jeff Carter, Marcia Davies, Karen Duncan, Stephen Dunwoody, Catherine Early, Stephanie Fine, Paige Fitzgerald, Warren Flatau, William Glavin, Andrew Gumbiner, Denise Herbert, Linda Holland, Thomas Irwin, Charlyn Isaac, Beth Jones, Dennis Jones, Bartel Kendrick, Dottie Lee, Jennifer Lee, Thomas Lillie, Debra Livramento, Rose Lusi, Amit Magdieli, Chad Maisel, Brittney Manchester, Charles McLeod, Dawn Mimes, Dixi Moody, V. Gabriela Morales, Peter Pappas, Grace Ramdat, Jennifer Rankin Byrne, Belinda Rawls, Gareth Rees, Lucy Salah, Emily Schwartz, Melissa Schwartz, Roslyn Sellars, Yolanda Sharpe, Nadia Shepherd, Alexandra Sova, Joel Spangenberg, Garth Spencer, Ben Stein, Jen Stutsman, Carol Thomas, Maria Thomas, Laura Thrower, Lucas Tickner, Lynda Tran, Sedelta Verble, Krishanti Vignarajah, Cheryl Walker, Matthew Warshaw, Lily West, Deidre Wilkinson, Demetriss Williams, Maureen Wood, and Katie Yocum.

Part One

The Job of the Political Executive

Chapter One

The Selection and Preparation of Political Executives

The Selection and Preparation
of Political Executives

What We Set Out To Do

In the spring of 2009, we launched an ambitious project. Would 32 top political executives in the newly formed Obama Administration—some of whom
had not yet arrived—be willing to meet with us for interviews over their first 18
months in office? Our goals were both to track their learning curves and to understand more about their journeys as political executives during the first term of an
administration. By starting at the beginning of an administration, we would have
the opportunity to see their early experiences firsthand and continue the conversation throughout their tenure. In undertaking a series of interviews, we sought to
capture the challenges facing political executives as they were experiencing them.

Our goal was to capture the experience of political executives in real time
while it was fresh. The reality is that there is high turnover among political executive positions. We wanted to capture their insights so that they might be shared
with future political executives. There is a clear need to better document the experience of political executives so that lessons can be learned and shared.

In January 2013, a new group of political executives will arrive in Washington,
either to join the Obama Administration or to begin a new administration. This
book is designed to assist them in making the transition from their previous position into government. For first-timers in the federal government, the transition can
indeed be daunting. We trust that this book will make it less daunting and provide
appointees with practical advice on their journey into the halls of government.

We believe that effective political executives are key to the success of both a
new administration and of government as a whole. In many ways, political appointees are the "quarterbacks" of government. They call the plays (with some help from
their coaches at the White House and at Department headquarters). Their organizations look to them for leadership. There is no doubt that the career civil service is
essential to government's effectiveness in delivering programs and services to the
American people, but the political executives to whom civil servants report are the
people who steer the ship. We were eager to learn more about their experiences.

Another goal of this book is to provide useful insights to the Office of
Presidential Personnel (OPP). The job of the OPP is to select the nation's top political executives—a crucial task. The book also offers OPP another way to think
about the political positions it is filling. Previous books on Presidential appointee
positions have been organized by Department or around policy clusters (health,
defense, natural resources). We offer a framework organized around the management challenges facing those who accept each type of position. The job specs for
a producer (described in Chapter Six), a regulator (described in Chapter Eight),

or a Deputy Secretary (described in Chapter Five) are dramatically different. The desired professional backgrounds and other requirements for each type of position are also different.

What We Would Like Future Political Executives to Know

We learned much from our 100 hours of interviews with top political executives during the last three years. Based on these conversations, we would like to share the following lessons with future executives.

Lesson One: Accept the right job. Of the 32 political executives we interviewed, we believe that all were, in fact, in the right job. We were impressed by how well their backgrounds matched the positions for which they were selected. To be candid, we had not expected to find such a high batting average. Sometimes in the Presidential appointment process, individuals do not get their first, second, or even third choice. Thus, in the past, some appointees have ended up in positions that did not fit their backgrounds well.

We were impressed that nearly all the executives described undertaking their own due diligence prior to accepting the position which they had been offered. Many devoted significant time to seeking advice and knowledge about the position. This due diligence was often undertaken in their free time while they were still in another position. They wanted to be sure that the job was indeed right for them. Generally, while it might be tempting to accept a Presidential appointment, it is important to be cautious about accepting a position which might not be the right fit.

Lesson Two: Get agreement on job expectations. Once a political executive is selected for the right position, it is crucial that he or she get agreement on the expectations for the job. One aspect of government is that there is a (relatively) clear chain of command up the ranks. It is important to understand the expectations for the position from those higher in the chain. Many of the political executives profiled in this book clearly knew what was expected of them—often, they were charged with implementing a Presidential priority, such as the Recovery Act. In other cases, expectations are less clear. The need for agreement on expectations is especially crucial when the position requires a close, personal relationship, such as that between a Secretary and the Deputy Secretary.

Lesson Three: Select a path to follow. We noticed a clear pattern among those interviewed. Many had consciously selected a path to pursue during their tenures. For some, it was a management path that would lead to strengthening their organizations. For others, it was a special initiative path that might include a Presidential priority. For still others, it was a policy path in which they pursued policy changes. While some executives followed several paths simultaneously, the more successful executives appear to have continued on their main paths. There is no right or wrong answer as to which path a political executive should pursue. What is crucial is the selection of a path and a focus on completing it and accomplishing the desired goal at the end of the road.

We were frankly surprised that so many of the political executives we interviewed came into their positions with specific plans and goals that they wanted to accomplish. Over the period in which we met with them, we were also impressed that few, if any, had forgotten their plans. While our conversations changed due to new events, the conversations about their plans remained on target.

It is easy in government for political executives to become captives of their inboxes and to be reactive to events and requests for their time. It is easy to keep busy as a political executive in government. The challenge is accomplishing both an individual's mission and the agency's goals and priorities. In reflecting on the potential impact of political executives, Seth Harris, Deputy Secretary of Labor, says, "The challenge is whether you are going to leave 'footprints in concrete' or 'footprints in the snow.'"

What We Would Like the Office of Presidential Personnel to Know

Lesson One: All jobs are not the same. We decided that it would be useful to cluster the positions studied in this book around the type of functions to be performed in the position. While it may be readily apparent that being a government scientist is different from being a regulator, which is different from being a producer, we continue to find across government many examples of the presumption that all jobs are the same and a smart person can fill any of them. This is not the case.

Lesson Two: Identify the right set of experiences for the job. To us, the most compelling part of OPP's job is deciding upon the set of experiences most needed in a specific position at a specific point in time. There is no doubt that nearly everyone on the long list for a Presidential appointment is clearly qualified, in the sense of having a distinguished professional career and impressive educational credentials. But the key question is whether the person has the right set of experiences for a specific job at the point in time when she or he is selected.

One example is the White House decision in 1998 to change the set of experiences sought for the head of the Internal Revenue Service (IRS). Throughout its history, the IRS had a distinguished tax lawyer as its head. In 1998, a decision was made to look for a business executive who may or may not have had a legal background, but who would be able to manage the information technology challenges then facing IRS. The right set of experiences had changed for IRS.

In this book, one of the best examples of the White House deciding on a new set of desired experiences for a position is the selection of Michael Bromwich to take over the Minerals Management Service (MMS) in the Department of the Interior in the aftermath of the Deep Horizon crisis in the Gulf of Mexico. Instead of sticking with the traditional set of energy and natural resources experience for MMS, a decision was made to recruit an executive with crisis management and turnaround skills. In addition, at that point in the history of MMS, it was appropriate (and perhaps necessary) to select an individual who had *not* had previous experience with the energy industry.

Lesson Three: Experience matters. After coming to agreement on the right set of experiences, realizing the importance of experience cannot ever be overestimated. In the discussion above, we focused on determining the right set of experiences for a specific moment in an organization's history. After that determination is made, finding people with that right set of experiences is crucial.

An additional challenge for the OPP is anticipating problems ahead of time and making selections partly based on the question, "What type of individual and what type of experience would be necessary if the agency faced a major crisis?" In the case of the Mine Safety and Health Administration, Administrator Joe Main had the experience to deal with the Upper Big Branch mine explosion. Main recalls, "I've lived through these experiences before, so I knew what to expect … My experiences earlier in my career were crucial."

The Importance of Orientation Activities for Political Executives

During our interviews, we learned that new political executives are eager to receive useful information and insights about operating in Washington. We observed a clear need for orientation activities at the departmental or agency level, in addition to activities organized by the Office of Presidential Personnel in the White House (Lawrence and Abramson, 2010a).

The orientation of political appointees has long been an issue of importance to new administrations. Amendments to the Presidential Transition Act of 2000 provided $1 million for each new administration to provide orientation for its new appointees. Both the Clinton Administration (without the funding provided by the 2000 Transition Act) and the George W. Bush Administration conducted a series of orientation sessions for their appointees. The Obama Administration has undertaken a series of activities as well.

In a 2010 report, *Ready to Govern: Improving the Presidential Transition,* the Partnership for Public Service concluded that too little attention is paid—and insufficient resources are devoted—to preparing and training political appointees (Partnership). In a survey of departing political executives conducted in 2008, the last year of the George W. Bush Administration, the National Academy of Public Administration and the Partnership for Public Service found that nearly 45% of those responding to the survey reported that they had received no orientation and that 33% of those responding rated the orientation they did receive as only somewhat effective (17.2%), not very effective (12.5%), or very poor (3.1%) in effectiveness (DeSeve).

Our interviews support this finding and clearly demonstrate the desire for orientation services. One political executive tells us, "I wish there had been a boot camp, *Washington 101*. That would have been helpful. A boot camp would have told me how to navigate in Washington, including working with the Hill." Political executives do receive numerous briefing books at the start of their tenure, but these books don't provide much advice on the navigation challenge. Nearly all those interviewed express a desire to better understand the workings of Congress and the Office of Management and Budget (OMB).

The orientation efforts by the White House are very worthwhile. But more are needed. In *addition* to the ongoing White House efforts, "on-boarding" initiatives should be launched in each Department to accommodate the specific orientation needs of its new political executives. Many private-sector and public-sector organizations have such on-boarding programs, which can serve as models for a political executive on-boarding program. There are three key advantages to an on-boarding program located in each Department or agency:

- **Speed.** Departments and agencies can provide orientation on a rolling schedule as soon as possible after the appointees arrive.
- **Customization.** Political executives come to their positions with different backgrounds and expertise. Those who come from the Hill obviously do not need to be briefed on the workings of Congress.
- **Small groups.** Each Department and agency (or perhaps groups of Departments) can put together small groups, perhaps 10–12 new appointees, for orientation sessions on specific topics.

The challenge is made even more daunting by the rolling nature of the political appointment process. All appointees do not arrive at the same time. Confirmation dates for the 21 individuals profiled in the first edition of this book who required confirmation by the U.S. Senate ranged from April 2009 to December 2009. Eight arrived in the April–June time period, eight arrived in July and August, and five arrived in the October–December time period. The rolling nature of the appointments process requires that on-boarding activities be ongoing and that all political appointees receive some type of orientation during the first month of their tenure.

Based on our interviews with new political executives, we developed the following recommendations on implementing on-boarding programs for political executives.

Recommendation One: The Chief Operating Officer (COO) of each Department should create a small unit (one or two people) within his or her office to assume responsibility for the on-boarding of new political executives. Placement of this function in the office of the COO, usually the Deputy Secretary, would give both prestige and credibility to the initiative.

Recommendation Two: The COO's on-boarding team would meet with each new political executive shortly after confirmation (political executives are limited in the activities they can undertake prior to confirmation). The on-boarding team would undertake a series of activities for small groups of newly confirmed appointees which are tailored to their specific orientation needs. The team would also facilitate informal meetings for new political executives with those political executives who were confirmed earlier and have been in the Department or agency longer.

Recommendation Three: The Congressional Research Service, part of the Library of Congress, should be asked by the Office of Presidential Personnel to conduct background sessions on the inner workings of Congress and on how to work effectively with the legislative branch. The Office of Management and Budget should be tasked by the Office of Presidential Personnel to conduct a series of seminars on the budget process and working with OMB. As noted earlier, nearly all those interviewed wanted to know more about Congress and OMB.

The Road Ahead

There is clearly a demand for orientation on the part of new political executives. Based on our interviews with political executives newly appointed to the Obama Administration, there is a clear need to increase the supply of orientation activities. The need can be met by each Cabinet Department and independent agency developing its own unique orientation in addition to those being provided by the White House. New political executives deserve no less.

Chapter Two

The Role of the Political
Executive as Builder

The Role of the Political Executive as Builder[*]

What do executives do? How do they spend their time? What do they leave behind after their tenure? To answer these questions, we interviewed 32 top political executives in the Obama Administration (as described in Chapter One).

We found that executives can be described as builders. Our interviews focused on how each of the 32 executives spent their time and energy. Their activities included:

- Building organizational capacity
- Building strong processes
- Building relationships
- Building credibility and visibility

While we had anticipated an emphasis on building organizational capacity and capability, we were surprised at the importance executives place on building relationships and building credibility. While relationships and credibility are important for executives in all sectors, they take on additional importance in the public sector.

Building Organizational Capacity

A consistent theme from our interviews is the importance of getting the right people into the organization and improving the organization's internal operations. While it has become a cliché in recent years, people are the organization's most important asset, according to all the executives interviewed. This is especially true in government where "knowledge work" and "knowledge workers" are the norm. The federal government is widely credited with having the most educated workforce in the nation.

Daniel Poneman, Deputy Secretary of the Department of Energy, describes the importance of people in his organization. "The Department is all about its people. It's a great organization that depends on a good esprit de corps," he explains. "The people I work with are glad to be here. They have engaging work."

Because of the importance of people to the successful accomplishment of the Department's mission, Poneman devotes a significant amount of his time to people issues facing the Department. "I've worked on ensuring that we have a process for getting good people into the Department and then retaining them once they are hired and are here," says Poneman.

According to Poneman, hiring is only one part of the personnel challenge. "[Hiring] is just the front edge," he explains. "Our mission is evolving, and we need to continue to provide career paths that are exciting so we not only attract but retain talent."

[*] This chapter is based on material that was originally published in the *Public Manager,* Summer 2012, and is used with permission from the *Public Manager.*

Government science executives also emphasize in our interviews the importance of people. While many of the science agencies have world-class equipment and facilities, science organizations are about people, many interviewees say.

"The Energy Information Administration (EIA) is all about its people—federal employees and contractors," says Richard Newell, former Administrator of EIA. "It is a people organization. We have 370 federal employees with about 200 contractors. We need to keep them and attract new people. I'm pleased that people in our community are asking me about whether there are any new positions at EIA."

Patrick Gallagher, Director of the National Institute of Standards and Technology (NIST), is very clear about his deep commitment to the institution. "I want to create an environment conducive for our scientists," he says. "We have world-class scientists here. Our job is all about attracting people—hiring and then retaining them. Retaining people is always a challenge because they can make three or four times more money anywhere else, either in the academic community or [private] industry. Not only am I impressed that NIST has three Nobel Prize winners here, I'm more impressed that all three have stayed."

During his confirmation hearings, Arun Majumdar, the first Director of the Advanced Research Projects Agency-Energy (ARPA-E), told Senate committee members that people were one of the five core values instrumental to ARPA-E. In describing his early days at ARPA-E, Majumdar tells us, "I started recruiting people. I wanted to get the right people. Putting together your team is critical. As a new agency with special hiring authorities, we had the flexibility to recruit outside of the civil service system. People didn't have to wait for six months. We have proved that good people will come here. We were able to get nearly all the people we wanted."

Nearly all those interviewed are very aware of the need to prepare for the forthcoming retirement wave among their civil servants. William Taggart, former Chief Operating Officer (COO) of the Office of Federal Student Aid (FSA) in the Department of Education, tells us, "Nearly 20 percent of [our employees] will be eligible to retire in the next five years. We had only 975 people, with headcount falling, while our workloads were up 200 percent in some cases. It was clear that we needed to hire more staff to perform tasks that were deemed as 'inherently governmental.' We needed to hire the right people, with the right competencies, who knew how to work in a team-based environment."

Reflecting on his experience at the Department of Labor, Seth Harris, Deputy Secretary, says, "Improving management in the Department is a real challenge. We needed to improve the Senior Executive Service (SES) and develop an ever-stronger corps of SES members. We needed to define what it means to be an elite manager in the SES and what skills they need. We needed to do more skill development. I'm not just talking about training, I mean skill development. We also worked on individual performance measures and better SES evaluations."

A key part of building organizational capacity is changing the culture of the organization. Rafael Borras, Under Secretary for Management at the Department of Homeland Security (DHS), describes this challenge. "There is the cultural part

of my job which is less about policies," says Borras. "Culture and priorities interact with each other. We have many agencies (in DHS) which have their own history. We needed to get them to interact with each other and interact differently with
each other. We want to change people's DNA, not just to change their minds."

Inez Tenenbaum, Chairman of the Consumer Product Safety Commission,
also recognizes the importance of cultural change as part of building organizational capacity. Tenenbaum says, "We are trying to create a new culture here and
get people to change the way they are doing business. We want to create a culture
of excellence. We want to bring in new talent and get new people."

Building Strong Processes

Along with building organizational capability, the executives we interviewed focused on the internal operations and processes of their organizations.
David Hinson, National Director of the Minority Business Development Agency
(MBDA), quickly realized that enhancing organizational capability and agency
processes would be a major priority for him.

"I tried to get the agency more focused," Hinson recalls. "I wanted to begin
to quantify the results of the agency. I wanted to change the tone of the organization. I've been trying to get all of us to work together. We tended to work in silos
before I arrived."

Seth Harris faced both people and process issues in his role as COO at Labor.
"We had to improve the business practices of the Department," asserts Harris. He
concluded that the Department needed to launch a new strategic planning process. Harris also realized that, together with the strategic planning process, the
Department needed new performance measures. "The Department was measuring the wrong things," says Harris. "The measures were typically internal, and
we were not measuring outcomes. The Department had focused on outputs and
process measures previously. We realized that measuring outcomes is incredibly
hard, but absolutely essential."

A major characteristic of the Producers described in Chapter Six is their relentless focus on the inputs and outputs of their organizations. "We understand
our inputs and outputs at PTO," says David Kappos, Director of the United States
Patent and Trademark Office (USPTO). In attacking the challenge of reducing the
paperwork backlog, he knew it was important to track the agency's progress—to
provide transparency for the public and a management tool inside the organization.

"The USPTO has a critical role to play in our economic recovery," Kappos
told us in 2010. "That's why people really care about the backlog, which hinders
innovation and economic growth. In response, we set specific targets. Our goal
is to get the backlog under 700,000. We haven't been under that figure for many
years. The goal is to get it down to a backlog of 325,000. That would be about
70 dockets per examiner, which is about right … we set 699,000 for FY 2011.

Getting under 700,000 would be a major accomplishment."

He accomplished the goal in June 2011 when patents pending fell to 695,086. Since then, they have continued to fall and reached an all-time low in August 2012 when patents pending dipped to 623,168. Kappos created the PTO Dashboard, which is updated monthly on the agency's website to track progress on key performance indicators, such as patents pending.

A similar backlog problem faced Allison Hickey, Under Secretary for Benefits in the Department of Veterans Affairs. Much of the growth in backlog was due to an increase in both the number of claims and complexity of the claims. In order to improve the process, the Veterans Benefit Administration (VBA) began to treat less complex claims differently than more complicated claims. VBA created "express lanes" for certain claims. "We are able to push these less complicated claims through at a faster pace," describes Hickey. "If we can do this, there will be less work on the front end. We can get less complicated claims through which will then allow us to spend more time on tougher, more complicated claims. We are trying to manage our throughputs."

A similar emphasis on improving processes is seen at the Transportation Security Administration under Administrator John Pistole. After his arrival in June 2010, Pistole quickly came to the conclusion that his agency needed to change the way it was operating. "We had been using a one-size-fits-all approach," says Pistole. "But I knew it didn't have to be this way. As an FBI agent, I would get on a plane with special treatment. So I knew we were already treating people differently. I knew that there were many possibilities of doing things differently."

Building Relationships

For these executives, building relationships means reaching out to key stakeholders and partners both inside and outside of Washington, D.C. David Hinson of MBDA and Ray Jefferson, former Assistant Secretary of Labor for Veterans' Employment and Training Services (VETS), adopted similar external strategies to achieve their missions.

"I spent a lot of time during my first year on the road building relationships," Hinson recalls. "You need to build good relationships with corporate America. Building these relationships is crucial."

In describing his strategy for VETS, Jefferson explains, "We want to create partnerships ... to find employment opportunities for veterans."

Both Hinson and Jefferson developed working relationships with the Chamber of Commerce, among many other organizations, in support of their different missions: assisting minority businesses and assisting veterans to find employment opportunities.

In addition to their work with the private sector and non-profit organizations, David Hinson and Ray Jefferson spent a significant amount of time working

Building Relationships:
Three Conversations to Have Right Away
By Linda M. Springer

The list of people seeking an audience with newly appointed heads of federal agencies fills up quickly from the moment of confirmation. Included in this list are stakeholders within the agency who have executed this drill before and are prepared with briefing materials. Congress, the media, and other government-focused groups are also anxious to engage.

While it's gratifying to realize so many people are following you and your organization's work, it's also quickly apparent that accommodating the seemingly endless suppliers of advice and insights must be prioritized. Those who direct policy and fund your agency's mission at both ends of Pennsylvania Avenue are obvious recipients of your attention. There are others, both inside of and external to the agency, who should also be high on the list of an astute leader. Based on my experience in government, there are three conversations that I recommend new political executives begin in the earliest days of their tenure.

Conversation One: The Inspector General (IG)

Newly appointed leaders can be victims of a lack of candor from well-intentioned subordinates who want to start off their relationship with a positive tone. Agency heads are no exception. There is one executive in your agency, however, who will provide you an unvarnished assessment of the landscape upon which you have entered—the Inspector General. It's the IG's job to assess and report on the integrity, efficiency, and effectiveness of your organization. That knowledge will quickly give you a sense of performance strengths and weaknesses and help you understand the organization for which you are now responsible. A healthy relationship with the IG will also foster an ongoing channel for staying informed and setting a tone of accountability during your tenure. In fact, the resources of the Office of the Inspector General are able to assist at your request in understanding issues, activities, and problems in the agency.

Remember, any past skeletons that emerge during your period of service have the potential to hijack your agenda, take up your time, and distract your team. It's wise to learn about any vulnerabilities in advance. A top-to-bottom review with the Inspector General as you enter office will go a long way toward empowering you to be a proactive, responsible leader.

Conversation Two: The Chief Financial Officer (CFO)

Budgeting and funding at federal agencies is likely to be significantly different from what a new agency head coming from outside government has experienced. Even those with financial backgrounds will need to be briefed to better understand the basics of federal financial management. The nexus between policy and your agency's budget will permeate discussions with both the White House, particularly the Office of Management and Budget, and Congress. To become articulate in advocating for the funding required by your organization to execute its mission, it's important to come under the tutelage of your Chief Financial Officer early on. The CFO will help you understand the timeline and multi-step processes associated with the budget. Key players and their roles (including yours), terminology, and legal requirements will all be covered in your conversation with the CFO.

A side benefit of this conversation is the relationship that will develop between you and the Chief Financial Officer. Like the IG, the CFO's role in the agency's fiscal accountability is well-established. Your early association with the CFO provides a visible endorsement of the importance of fiscal accountability and sets a high standard for financial management in your agency.

Conversation Three: Staff in Agency Field Offices

Approximately 85 percent of the federal workforce is located outside the metropolitan Washington area. Even smaller agencies are likely to have employees with remote duty stations. Other arrangements, such as telework, add to the challenge of maintaining a high level of employee engagement. As the agency head, you are responsible for leading all of your associates, not just those in your building. This will require a dedicated effort to initiate and maintain visible relationships with your team. They want and need the opportunity to interact with you, hear your plans, and offer input and support. Your employees are proud of their contributions to the agency's mission and they want you to share in that pride. Visiting field offices will show associates that they are not forgotten and that you value their work and insights.

Successful field office interactions are characterized by appreciation and listening. Your employees don't expect you to be an immediate expert in what they do, but hope you will be in a learning mode. You must be inspiring, approachable, and above all, sincere—they will know if you are just going through the paces. Your associates may not always agree with your policy decisions, but they won't forget that their new leader made them a priority right from the start.

Keep Talking—Early and Often

The clock is ticking on your tenure from the moment you take the oath of office. These early conversations are foundational to your reputation as the agency head, but they are just the beginning. Continued interaction with each of these constituents will prove mutually beneficial and support the common mission to which you and they are committed.

with other government agencies. Both MBDA and VETS were created to serve as "spurs" and leaders in government for their respective missions. Hinson and Jefferson had to carve out roles and activities in which their agencies could contribute in a crowded field of numerous agencies, all of whom have some piece of the action in their policy area.

Building relationships also includes enhancing relationships between an organization's own employees. Bill Taggart made employee engagement one of his top priorities. "Many of the staff worked at FSA an average of 18 years but did not feel valued by senior management," Taggart says. "I held several town hall meetings to get the employees' unfiltered feedback. They had a lot on their minds and were very vocal. That meant to me that they cared about the organization. It would have been much worse if I had been met with silence. It was essential for me to help the employees to feel better about the organization. I decided to get them involved in developing a new vision, mission, and core values for the organization. More than 200 employees participated in the process and helped to develop a new working relationship between the FSA employees and the COO."

Jonathan Adelstein, Administrator of the Rural Utilities Service in the Department of Agriculture, also emphasizes employee engagement. "I worked closely with the career staff here to make revisions in (procedures for our) second funding round. I wanted their buy-in and inspiration," he explains. "I wanted to know their ideas. We shared ideas and got different opinions on various options for round two. I believe in listening to staff. We had a very collegial relationship; it was not top-down. We had an ongoing dialogue."

All those interviewed also recognize that building relationships with members of Congress and their staffs is crucial. In explaining his strategy, Arun Majumdar says, "I tell them what I do. I like to explain our agency in layman's terms. I try to make it easy for them to understand and talk to them in terms of impact and savings, while giving them the big picture. It's been a pleasant and enjoyable experience to work so closely with Congress. I'm from California and have never worked with Congress before. You need to spend time with them. They need to trust you. That takes time and you have to devote ongoing meetings to them."

Equally important to those interviewed is fostering relationships with the White House and the Office of Management and Budget (OMB). OPM Director John Berry says, "I wanted to develop a good relationship with OMB, which I have done. I work closely with OMB on all our initiatives. I've also engaged the White House on many initiatives, such as our activities on improving work life and veterans' hiring. We worked hard on building our relationship with the White House."

When Rafael Borras arrived at the Department of Homeland Security, the Department had been on the Government Accountability Office's High Risk List since 2003. Hence, one of the major challenges facing Borras was enhancing the Department's reputation and evaluations with its oversight organizations. Rafael Borras says, "Our efforts have helped enhance our conversations with the Government Accountability Office and other oversight groups. We come back with a plan now when we have a problem we are trying to solve and a way to measure our progress."

While it is easy to focus on external stakeholders, Congress, and the Office of Management and Budget, Linda Springer, former Director of the Office of Personnel Management, cautions that political executives must also spend time with key colleagues in their own Department. She strongly recommends that political executives spend time and get to know their Inspector General, Chief Financial Officer, and staff in agency field offices (see *Building Relationships: Three Conversations to Have Right Away* on page 18).

Building Credibility and Visibility

David Hinson links improvements in the internal operations of his agency to its image both inside and outside the Department of Commerce. "I had to build credibility for the agency," Hinson says. "I wanted to show people what we were capable of doing. This required that we improve the skill sets of the agency. We had to make clear our expectations on training. I looked at everybody in the agency and decided what new capabilities we needed."

Many executives were surprised by the low visibility of their agencies. As Under Secretary for Economic Affairs in the Department of Commerce, Rebecca Blank worked to boost visibility by finding opportunities in which economic analysis could contribute to policy making in the Administration.

"We increased the visibility of the Economic and Statistics Administration in the White House," Blank says. "We are now getting more requests to do studies. The staff here is available to do this work and is enjoying getting involved in current issues and doing deep analysis. They like having new products and reports. These reports have generated requests from other parts of government to do similar studies."

Another way in which leaders and organizations can enhance credibility is an effective response to well-known external events. The U.S. Geological Survey faced a series of natural disasters in a two-year period, including the Haiti earthquake in January 2010, the Iceland volcano in March 2010, and the Japanese earthquake of March 2011. USGS's effective response to the increased number of natural disasters had positive impacts inside the agency, as well as outside the organization. Marcia McNutt, Director of the U.S. Geological Survey, states, "I think we increased the stature of the agency, increased our visibility and our name recognition. We received much attention in 2010 and were on the front pages of many newspapers. We made a contribution in 2010. We were involved in responses to the earthquakes and volcanoes. It showed our diverse expertise in many areas. I think all the increased attention also helped inside the agency. It showed the relevance of the agency and it started people within the agency to think about things that we can do that they never imagined before."

Enhancing an organization's credibility is especially critical when an executive takes over an agency that has recently faced a crisis or a scandal. In assuming the position of Director of the Minerals Management Service in the Department of the Interior (now reorganized into the new Bureau of Ocean Energy Management and Bureau of Safety and Environmental Management) in the aftermath of the Gulf Oil Spill in 2010, Michael Bromwich recalls a negative culture.

"The agency was suffering from years of negative publicity. There had been instances of corruption that had happened several years before. ... There was massive media attention given to the agency and many negative stories. ... We were the most heavily criticized agency in government when I started in June

2010, which did create a crisis mentality in the agency and in the Department of the Interior generally. We were being criticized in the media every day—every media outlet felt obliged to publish numerous critical pieces about the agency."

"Morale was as low as I've ever seen it in any organization," he continues. "There was a lot of tension in the agency, and a stream of negative commentary about it, including from inside the government. There was no end in sight to the negative publicity. I was very careful not to reinforce all this negative feedback by jumping on the bandwagon of criticism, but on the other hand I could not defend past acts of misconduct or lack of competence."

The Executive as Builder

Based on our interviews with political executives, we concluded that each found a path that they followed. Some followed what we call a policy path while others followed what we term a special initiative projects path.

We were surprised at the number who selected a management path aimed at strengthening their organization for the long term. We found leaders building, and in some cases rebuilding, their institution. The challenge they faced was finding the time and energy to devote to activities that would have payoffs in the long term, not the short term. They had to find time to build activities in the midst of immediate crises. They also had to resist the Washington temptation to devote nearly all their time to policy and not management issues.

We came away from our interviews with great admiration for those leaders in government who are now building institutions for the long term.

Chapter Three

The Role of the Political Executive as Manager

The Role of the Political Executive as Manager

Closely related to the role of political executive as builder, discussed in Chapter Two, is the role of political executive as manager. We emphasize the management role of the political executives profiled throughout this book because all too often, the management role may play second fiddle to the desire of a new political executive to play a policy role in government. In her essay *Advice to New Appointees: How to Influence the Policy Agenda* (see page 26), Linda Springer cautions that there might be fewer opportunities for the political executive to shape policy than they might have originally anticipated. Springer, however, does explain how political executives can help drive the policy agenda after they have gained a good understanding of how the process actually does work.

While there will be some opportunities for policy making as discussed by Springer, the reality is that the day-to-day life of a political executive is largely consumed with management-related tasks. This management role is crucial for the success of a political executive in accomplishing the mission of his or her organization and the President's agenda. Based on interviews for this book, we found that political executives face three major management tasks:
- Assessing the organization
- Achieving mission alignment
- Mastering metrics and measuring progress

Assessing the Organization

Many of the executives we interviewed spent their initial days on the job assessing their organization. David Stevens, former Commissioner of the Federal Housing Administration (FHA), tells us, "I spent my first days at FHA assessing the organization. I would go out into the field and talk with our staff. We held large staff meetings and an offsite planning retreat. I wanted to better understand the major issues facing the Department. I focused on what I thought I could accomplish and what would make a real difference."

During his initial assessment, Stevens says, "It became obvious to me that we needed to better manage risk. We needed a risk office and a chief risk officer. I felt FHA needed to go outside of the organization to recruit some top-notch Deputy Assistant Secretaries. We needed to recruit people with experience in credit risk, credit policy, and lending." Unlike several of the executives profiled in this book, Stevens concluded during his assessment of the organization that reorganization was not needed. "I decided," recalls Stevens, "that I didn't want to reorganize. So I put my efforts into assessing the talent already in the organization."

Assessments of the organization are especially crucial when a political executive arrives to find the agency in a firestorm of publicity, much of which is highly critical. David Strickland, Administrator of the National Highway Traffic Safety Administration (NHTSA), found himself in that situation when he arrived at NHTSA in the midst of the furor over the Toyota automobile recall. "When I got here in January (2010), there had already been a significant amount of work in progress on Toyota," recounts Strickland. "There was much work underway, including a study by the National Academy of Sciences and a research initiative with the National Aeronautics and Space Administration. My first task was to determine whether NHTSA was broken. Some people were saying that we had a broken culture here. I decided that they were wrong and that NHTSA was not broken. That decision was a risk I had to take, but I believed it. It turns out that I was right. The final analysis showed that NHTSA had done a fantastic job on the Toyota recall."

In some cases, problems find the new political executive without having to look very hard. Jonathan Adelstein, Administrator, Rural Utilities Services, recalls, "When I got here, I quickly found that we had a crisis in management regarding the information technology system we were using to accept applications for broadband projects. The process was in meltdown due to the unprecedented number of applications for loans and grants. RUS was working with another agency on application intake and it just wasn't working. It was a stressful situation in the beginning."

In addition, assessing the organization by visiting field organizations is an excellent tool for learning about the organization. Allison Hickey's early days at the Veterans Benefits Administration (VBA) in the Department of Veterans Affairs consisted of visits to employees in VBA regional offices. "I wanted to learn the VBA business and understand the process," recalls Under Secretary Hickey. "I wanted to see what they were doing and experience firsthand our claims processes and challenges. I did this for all lines of business. I wanted to understand our businesses."

Achieving Mission Alignment

Unlike David Stevens, Patrick Gallagher at the National Institute of Standards and Technology (NIST) concluded that reorganization was necessary for his organization. In Gallagher's perspective, the reorganization of NIST was not an end in itself but a crucial element of his strategy to change NIST's culture and to strengthen the organization to survive the fast pace of change in the 21st century. "The reorganization was never just about organizational structure or who reports to whom. It wasn't about boxes," he says. "It was about getting the organization better aligned. We wanted to get the right people and align them in the new organization. Alignment was our larger goal. We need to reset the agency."

Gallagher's management agenda was to move NIST away from an activity-based structure for the agency's laboratories, which were organized like a university.

Advice to New Appointees: How to Influence the Policy Agenda

By Linda M. Springer

A strong motivation for political appointees in coming to Washington is the opportunity to positively influence policy—to make a difference. Senior-level appointees may bring the expectation of setting a portion of the administration's agenda related to their agency's mission. This is particularly likely for a first-time appointee who hasn't experienced or operated within the government complex previously. In fact, the very characteristics that enabled executives to set and achieve goals in the private sector—decisive, directive, risk-taker—may actually undermine their prospects for success as government officials.

The new executive level appointee must distinguish whether he or she is in the driver's seat or is a passenger in the agenda-setting process. It is crucial to understand who really drives federal agency policy agendas and know the steps that newly appointed leaders can take to be influential contributors, regardless of their role.

Key Steps in Understanding the Policy Setting Process

Step One: Know what agenda has already been set

A new administration's agenda has its roots in the Presidential campaign. The candidate is surrounded by advisors that help establish key policy positions. These positions, particularly those with associated specific actions, are further developed during the post-election transition period where the focus expands to include implementation. Unless you are one of those pre-inaugural advisors, the foundation for part or all of your agency's agenda has already been set by someone else, at least directionally, prior to your invitation to join the administration as a political appointee. Needless to say, this is even more likely to be the case in a midterm or second-term appointment. Regardless of timing, the new political leader must be aware of relevant agenda items and related commitments for which he or she will be responsible before striking out in new territory to develop new policies.

Step Two: Know the opportunities to help shape policy

The newly appointed leader is expected to support the administration's agenda and needs to be quickly briefed on that agenda. However, the briefing process may be leveraged to reveal opportunities to provide policy refinements and other forms of influence. It may also become apparent that there are other initiatives the appointee has in mind that have not yet been considered. Fitting these new initiatives into the overarching direction and philosophy of the already articulated goals will increase the prospects that those suggestions will be favorably received. While the preexisting agenda will be a priority, the appointee may well be asked to drive this additional agenda.

Step Three: Know the relevant Executive Office of the President portfolios and develop relationships with key officials

Some of the President's closest agenda-setting advisors reside in organizations that are outside of the agency structure in the Executive Office of the President

(EOP). Several of these offices were established by Congress and have a statutory mission that includes policy development. A few examples are:
- Office of Management and Budget
- Council of Economic Advisers
- Office of Science and Technology Policy
- Office of the United States Trade Representative
- Council on Environmental Quality

The White House Office, itself an EOP entity, includes other central policy setting-offices including:
- Domestic Policy Council
- National Economic Council
- Office of Public Engagement and Intergovernmental Affairs

New political leaders would be well advised to learn more about EOP offices with portfolios related to the agency they will be serving, including key personnel. For more senior appointees, it may be appropriate or even anticipated that you reach out to those offices for a briefing. Establishing a trusted relationship could support the opportunity to contribute to shaping or suggesting additional policy initiatives.

Step Four: Know your agency's role in policy making and its go-to people

Newly appointed leaders should learn the historical and expected responsibilities of their agency or office. It's important to understand both policy establishment and administration roles. While these are considerations that should have been examined when contemplating an offer to serve, a validation of that initial research, particularly upon assuming the position, will inform your ability to drive and execute agendas for the administration. A related step is to identify and establish relationships with those in your agency that have held key responsibilities for carrying out its mission. The support of your go-to people will enable the responsiveness required to establish your reputation as a reliable member of the administration's policy-setting team.

Moving Forward

Political appointees, particularly those in leadership positions, need to remember they are part of a select team—the President's team. Their success will be closely associated with that of the administration in which they serve. Being in the know on the basics will serve as a foundation on which the political appointee can develop a position of influence in driving, as well as executing, the administration's agenda.

"In that structure, our managers acted much like chairs of academic departments," Gallagher recalls. "We wanted to move toward a mission approach."

The mission focus and reorganization were also part of Gallagher's goal to make NIST a better workplace and to enhance the agency's image among federal agencies and the research community. "NIST is a very special place," he says. "Researchers at NIST like their work and their mission. I wanted to restore the old sense of mission that [NIST's predecessor] the National Bureau of Standards had. Our efforts have brought more visibility to the organization."

Mastering Metrics and Measuring Progress

An important common theme among the political executives profiled in this book is the importance of numbers and metrics. David Kappos, Director of the United States Patent and Trademark Office (USPTO), says, "We understand our inputs and outputs at USPTO." In attacking the challenge of reducing the paperwork backlog at USPTO, Kappos knew it was important to track the agency's progress—both to provide transparency to the public and to use it as a management tool inside the organization.

"The USPTO has a critical role to play in our economic recovery," Kappos told us in 2010. "That's why people really care about the backlog, which hinders innovation and economic growth. In response, we set specific targets. Our goal is to get the backlog under 700,000. We haven't been under that figure for many years. The goal is to get it down to a backlog of 325,000. That would be about 70 dockets per examiner, which is about right … we set 699,000 for FY 2011. Getting under 700,000 would be a major accomplishment."

Kappos accomplished the goal in July 2011 when patents pending fell to 689,226. Since then, they have continued to fall and reached an all-time low in August 2012 when patents pending dipped to 623,168. Kappos created the PTO Dashboard, which is updated monthly on the agency's website to track progress on key performance indicators such as patents pending.

A similar situation faced Allison Hickey during her first year at VBA. One of the items she quickly identified as a major challenge to the agency was the lack of metrics to measure success. Hickey faced a large inventory of claims and a backlog. On top of the existing claims inventory and backlog of regular claims she found upon arrival, there were new Agent Orange claims to settle which required reallocating staff from processing other claims to complete the Agent Orange backlog. Over the last two years, VA received 260,000 claims from three new Agent Orange conditions which required a surge of over 37 percent of VBA's workforce to work on adjudicating these claims.

Metrics are now clearly high on the radar screen at the Veterans Benefits Administration. In September 2012, it announced that VBA had processed over one million claims for the third year in a row. In August 2012, VBA had its most productive claims processing period in history, completing a record 107,462 claims which surpassed the previous monthly record of 103,296 set in 2010. Hickey comments that the reduction is a testament to the dedication of VBA to meet the increasing needs of veterans. In the summer of 2012, VBA had 870,000 claims in its inventory. The claims backlog is defined as those claims that have been pending longer than the goal of 125 days.

The Challenge of Managing

The political executive has been likened to a juggler in that he or she must manage many balls in the air. Some of these balls will be policy balls and some will be related to management. While it is often easy to focus on policy, the political executive must devote sufficient attention to the management challenge. Richard Newell, former Administrator of the U.S. Energy Information Administration, says, "You have to walk a thin line between managing too much (micromanaging) and not managing enough. You have to know when to dig into detail and when not to dig in. But sometimes you have to dig in. You need to get your hands dirty and be willing to ask a lot of questions. You can't just go through the motions. You have to get into the details and go into the weeds."

Chapter Four

The Role of the Political
Executive as Innovator

The Role of the Political Executive as Innovator[*]

By Marc Andersen, Paul R. Lawrence, and Mark A. Abramson

Innovation is an important topic. All organizations want to do more of it, including the federal government. Everybody has a slightly different take on innovation and what it looks like.

In the private sector, innovation is somewhat easier to identify—a flashy new product that fulfills an unmet consumer need. Innovation is often discussed in the context of technology and technological innovations.

Based on our research over the last several years, we have found that innovation in government can most effectively be discussed by making the following distinction between types of government innovation:

- **Innovation from inside government,** when government employees seek to find new solutions and improvements in the delivery of traditional government activities
- **Innovation engaging the private sector in problem solutions**

Innovation from Inside Government

This type of innovation has received the most attention over the years. Since 1985, the John F. Kennedy School of Government's Innovations in American Government program has recognized nearly 500 innovation initiatives in federal, state, and local government. The Innovations awards program was created to foster increased attention in government to finding new ways to deliver services that address the nation's most pressing issues, and to reward and recognize those organizations that undertook new initiatives.

The challenge facing government has been in finding ways to institutionalize the quest for innovation. The bureaucracy has historically excelled at developing routines that can be repeated and duplicated. Thus, finding new routines (or new ways of doing business) has not been traditionally encouraged.

In the previous two chapters, we discussed the role of the political executive as builder and manager. In this chapter, we focus on the role of the political executive as innovator. During our interviews for this book, we found an increasing number of examples of the federal government's actively institutionalizing innovation.

At the Department of Veterans Affairs, an Employee Innovation Competition was created as part of the Department's Innovation Initiative (VAi2). The VAi2 program is significant because it created an ongoing process which could tap into the experience and expertise of its employees. Historically, employees have always had the

---

[*]   An earlier version of this chapter was published on the AOL Government website, May 9, 2012.

opportunity to volunteer ideas (e.g., the 20th century's employee suggestion box). What is different about the VAi2 program is that it organizes employee participation by identifying specific topics to improve care quality, access, and transparency in the delivery of programs to the nation's veterans (see *Innovation in Government: Creating VA's Innovation Initiative* on page 59 for a further discussion of this innovation initiative).

At the Department of Agriculture, innovation took the form of delivering a new program—Know Your Farmer, Know Your Food (KYF2). Instead of creating a new office, the Department organized an initiative through a cross-department task force, with every Agriculture agency represented. The concept was to involve the entire Department with participation from the many Agricultural components rather than locating the KYF2 program in a single office (see *Innovation in Government: Creating The Know Your Farmer, Know Your Food Program* on page 79 for a further discussion of this innovation initiative).

At the Department of Education, a new twist was developed on an old tool of government—the traditional grant. Instead of creating a formula grant program (in which every state receives funds), the Department used the grant instrument to create a nationwide competition in which only a limited number of states would receive funding based on the quality of their proposals to reform education in their states (see *Innovation in Government: Creating The Race To The Top Program at the Department of Education* on page 86 for a further discussion of this innovation initiative).

Engaging the Private Sector in Problem Solution

Innovation that engages the private sector appears to be expanding throughout the government.

Government is increasingly recognizing that in many cases, it does not have the solution to a problem that it is trying to solve or a product it is trying to develop. Thus, government is developing new ways to engage citizens, universities, corporations, and non-profits in problem-solving. During our interviews, we saw this approach in the following initiatives:

- The Challenge.gov website was created to be an online platform that government agencies can use to bring the "best ideas and top talent to bear on our nation's most pressing challenges." The website now contains over 175 challenges, many of which include monetary rewards.
- Similar to Challenge.gov, the VAi2 program is now running an Industry Innovation Competition in which it seeks ideas to be submitted in response to the Department's specified list of topics on which it is seeking innovation solutions.
- At the Department of Transportation, the Federal Highway Administration created its Every Day Counts program. FHWA is seeking to engage industry

in finding new ways to accelerate technology and innovation deployment, as well as to shorten project delivery time (see *Innovation In Government: Creating The Every Day Counts Program* on page 151 for a further discussion on this innovation initiative).

- At the Department of Energy, the Advanced Research Projects Agency-Energy (ARPA-E) was built on the model developed by the Defense Advanced Research Projects Agency (DARPA). ARPA-E is now engaging the private sector by soliciting concept papers in specified areas which are then reviewed, with full proposals requested for those who pass the initial review. Based on the full proposals, awards are made to develop technologies that are too risky for private-sector investment, but have the potential to identify disruptive energy technologies that can make current technologies obsolete.

In all of our interviews, we found government political executives wanting to ingrain the quest for innovation in their organizations—both for innovation driven within government and innovation engaging the private sector. In both quests for innovation, competition, recognition, and rewards are being used to solicit ideas.

Some leaders recognize that innovation is more than tactics. Arun Majumdar, former Director of ARPA-E, sums this up nicely when he tells us, "I want innovation to be the DNA of ARPA-E. It is part of our core strategy. Once you get people here, you have to give them the freedom to solve problems. So the key elements to creating a culture are getting talent, creating an open dialogue, and allowing people to realize their potential."

Part Two

Profiles in Political Leadership

Chapter Five

The Deputy Secretaries

Understanding the Job of the Deputy Secretary

The job of the Deputy Secretary[*] is one of the most important in government. With the passage of the GPRA Modernization Act of 2010, the position now has additional responsibilities for the management of Cabinet Departments. The job is also one of the toughest in government for several reasons:

- **The job is big—involving managing complex federal Cabinet Departments, many of which are "holding companies" for a diverse set of agencies.** For example, the Department of Commerce consists of 12 agencies and 10 staff offices.
- **There is often much ambiguity surrounding the responsibilities of the Deputy Secretary.** There is no single, agreed-upon model for the position. One Deputy Secretary tells us that after nearly two years in office, "The job of the Deputy Secretary is still a little unclear to me."
- **The success of the job frequently depends on the working relationship and comfort level between the Cabinet Secretary and the Deputy Secretary.** As one Deputy Secretary puts it, "There is always tension in the role between the Deputy Secretary and the Secretary. You need to gain trust."
- **The challenge of being "number two" in any organization is often a difficult one at best.** We are told by one Deputy Secretary, "I had never been a number two before, so this is a change for me. I didn't know how I would like being number two."

The Deputy Secretaries

Rafael Borras, page 44

Under Secretary for Management, Department of Homeland Security

William V. Corr, page 49

Deputy Secretary, Department of Health and Human Services

W. Scott Gould, page 54

Deputy Secretary, Department of Veterans Affairs

Seth D. Harris, page 61

Deputy Secretary, Department of Labor

David J. Hayes, page 65

Deputy Secretary, Department of the Interior

---

[*] This chapter also includes an Under Secretary position, held by Rafael Borras at the Department of Homeland Security.

Key Roles of the Deputy Secretary

Dennis F. Hightower, page 70

Deputy Secretary,
Department of
Commerce

Kathleen A. Merrigan, page 75

Deputy Secretary,
Department of
Agriculture

Anthony W. Miller, page 81

Deputy Secretary,
Department of Education

Thomas R. Nides, page 88

Deputy Secretary for
Management and
Resources, Department
of State

Daniel B. Poneman, page 92

Deputy Secretary,
Department of Energy

While there will always be some ambiguity and tension in the role of the Deputy Secretary, several key roles emerge from our interviews. The Deputy Secretaries profiled fulfill the following roles:
• Alter ego for the Secretary
• Chief Operating Officer (COO) of the Department
• Convenor
• Policy advisor
• Leader of departmental initiatives
• Crisis manager
• Liaison to stakeholders

Serving as an Alter Ego for the Secretary

One Deputy Secretary describes this function: "My major role is backing up the Secretary. We want to make sure that we make the best use of his time. I'm the back stop. I'm available across the board on many issues. Your job [as Deputy Secretary] is to serve the Secretary in whatever capacity he or she desires. I support the Secretary and focus on what is important to him. That has been my view from the first day I was here."

This role includes filling in for the Secretary when he or she is unavailable to attend key government meetings, and serving as "Acting Secretary" when necessary. As one Deputy Secretary tells us, "I have to be here when the Secretary is out."

Serving as the Chief Operating Officer (COO) of the Department

The role of a Department COO is clear. One Deputy Secretary reports that: "I work on the infrastructure of the Department. There are many actionable items and a bunch of moving parts. We need to work on many fronts." These fronts include working on the culture of the organization, as well as focusing on the people side of the Department. All of the Deputy Secretaries interviewed spend time working to strengthen their Senior Executive Service corps.

In addition to working with the departmental bureaucracy, Deputy Secretaries spend time on interagency committees, including the President's Management Council. In describing the COO role, one Deputy Secretary says, "My job is really a T-shape as I do a lot of collaboration across government with other agencies. It helps that I have a network of people I know across government. Then my job goes straight down the bureaucracy."

The concept of the Deputy Secretary serving as the COO of the Department is relatively new. The official designation of COO responsibilities dates back to an October 1993 Memorandum from President Bill Clinton establishing the President's Management Council (PMC) and asking each Department to designate a Chief Operating Officer. With a few exceptions (most notably the Department of the Treasury and the Department of Defense), Departments designated the Deputy Secretary as COO. In July 2001, President George W. Bush issued a Memorandum reestablishing the PMC and continuing the COO role.

In December 2010, Congress passed the GPRA Modernization Act of 2010 which codified the Chief Operating Officer role into law. The bill, signed into law by President Obama in January 2011, states that the COO shall be responsible for improving the management and performance of the organization and "achieving the mission and goals of the agency through the use of performance planning, measurement, analysis, regular assessment of progress, and use of performance information ..." In June 2011, President Obama issued an Executive Order implementing the GPRA Modernization Act. The Memorandum calls for the COO to be designated as the Senior Accountable Official responsible for leading performance and management reform efforts and reducing wasteful or ineffective programs.

The new law and Executive Order have the potential to change the role of Deputy Secretaries in government. One Deputy Secretary tells us, "I'll be interested in seeing the impact [of] the new GPRA law that says each Department must name a COO. The bill also establishes a new reporting relationship to the White House. It will be interesting to see how GPRA works and impacts the role of Deputy Secretaries."

Finally, the continued pressure to reduce spending has increased the time Deputy Secretaries spend on budget-related issues. Says one Deputy Secretary, "The budget is going to be a problem. Resources will become increasingly scarce in the future. I think we will continue to see reductions in the budget. We have been working long hours to come up with different budget scenarios. It's always more fun when you are budgeting for a good year, but management is tough and it is our job to make tough choices. We can manage our way through this. We will end up cutting some programs."

Serving as a Convener

Several of the Deputy Secretaries emphasized their role as "convener" of key decision-makers within their own Departments, and often key leaders from outside their Department. "The Office of the Secretary," says David Hayes, Deputy

Secretary of the Interior, "is the only place where everything comes together. Traditionally, the agencies have tended to work alone in the Department of the Interior. Integration can only happen when the Secretary, Deputy Secretary, and Assistant Secretaries get involved."

In describing his role at HHS, Bill Corr also emphasizes the importance of bringing people together to develop solutions and ensure continuous momentum. Corr says, "One key aspect of my job is to get the right people in the room, determine the decisions that need to be made and ensure that we not lose our focus on our goals."

Serving as a Policy Advisor

Because of their extensive careers inside and outside government, Deputy Secretaries bring a great deal of policy expertise and experience to their positions. This makes it natural for Deputy Secretaries to expect to play a policy role in the Department. Based on our interviews and observations of Deputy Secretaries in previous Administrations, the policy role varies dramatically from Department to Department.

In some cases, the Deputy Secretary may be asked by the Secretary to participate in the policy making process on a specific issue because of his or her expertise in that area. In other cases, a Deputy Secretary may be thrust into a policy making role because of the need for a strong individual to lead the policy making process. One Deputy Secretary tells us, "I had to step into the policy development and policy agenda-setting process. I ended up driving the policy process. So I had to do two and a half jobs for a while. This isn't the regular job of the Deputy Secretary."

There are no clearly defined lines between policy and implementation, as they often blend together and Deputy Secretaries naturally get involved in both. As one Deputy tells us, "It is a combination of both a COO role and a decision-making role. Reality is that you have to do some of both. The Recovery Act forced me to get involved in both policy and implementation."

In the past, some Deputy Secretaries may have been attracted to Washington for the chance to work on policy issues. Since Washington has always been more of a policy town than a management town, the policy side of the Deputy Secretary position has often been appealing to many appointees. Over time, however, the Deputy Secretary position has begun to swing more toward the management role and away from the policy role.

Serving as a Leader of Departmental Initiatives

When there is a high-priority initiative, the Secretary often asks the Deputy Secretary to take the lead. An initiative can either start within the Department and move to the White House or it can start at the White House and move to a Department for implementation. For example, the American Recovery and Reinvestment Act, passed by Congress in February 2009, quickly became an

Administration top priority. Deputy Secretaries in all Departments assumed some responsibility for oversight of the Act.

Serving as Crisis Manager

The Deputy Secretary often assumes the role of crisis manager. Bill Corr, Deputy Secretary of Health and Human Services, says, "A major difference be-tween my tenure in the Obama Administration and my time at HHS in the Clinton Administration is that the Department now has a critical emergency preparedness role. We now have emergency response capabilities for natural and man-made disasters that we did not have the first time I was here." During Corr's tenure, HHS confronted a series of emergencies during its first term: the H1N1 swine flu crisis, the Haitian earthquake, the Japanese tsunami, and the oil spill in the Gulf of Mexico.

David Hayes also faced a crisis at the Department of the Interior. "I was the operations lead for the Department on the Gulf Oil spill," Hayes says. "I spent every day—as did much of our team—from April 2010 to September 2010 on the oil spill … We were also involved in the response, the cleanup phase. We negoti-ated with BP every step of the way. I am proud of what we did."

Serving as Liaison to Stakeholders

In the past, many Deputy Secretaries were selected because of their relation-ship to specific stakeholder groups of a Department. The Deputy Secretary would then serve as the key liaison between the Department and that community. This responsibility often entails giving speeches to stakeholder groups and spending time on the road. In other cases, the Secretary might decide that he or she wants to take the lead in outreach. One Deputy Secretary reports, "When I came in, I thought I would just be doing management. But the Secretary wanted me to do more public outreach. So I ended up with a mixed portfolio. Part of my time was on public policy. Part of it was interfacing with the public. The rest of my time was on management."

The Ebb and Flow of the Deputy Secretary's Role

There is an ebb and flow between various roles over the course of a Deputy Secretary's tenure. One Deputy Secretary remarks, "We started out on manage-ment and we spent a lot of time on that during our first year. That was very im-portant. Then the Secretary asked me to play a greater role in another area. There are also the unexpected events which nobody can predict. So you must learn to live with this ebb and flow and you have to be ready to respond to unanticipated events."

Setting Expectations for the Deputy Secretary

The Deputy Secretaries we interviewed emphasize that there is no one-size-fits-all job description for a Deputy Secretary. The job is highly dependent on the relationship between the Secretary and the Deputy Secretary. But it does appear that administrations can do a better job in setting expectations for the position. Based on observations of previous Deputy Secretaries in both Democratic and Republican administrations, unmet expectations can decrease effectiveness in the job. A Deputy Secretary might accept the position expecting to work on policy and be surprised or disappointed to end up doing management.

To effectively accomplish an organization's mission, it is crucial that the Secretary and the Deputy Secretary (and perhaps the Office of Presidential Personnel) come to a fully understood agreement on expectations for the job of the Deputy Secretary—which of the roles described above will be fulfilled by the Deputy Secretary. Agreement on expectations by all parties is likely to result in a more fulfilling and satisfying set of experiences for future Deputy Secretaries, a more effective working relationship between the Secretary and Deputy Secretary, and accomplishment of the Department's agenda.

Rafael Borras
Under Secretary for Management
Department of Homeland Security

The Beginning

"I felt good coming into this position," recalls Rafael Borras, the fourth individual to hold the position of Under Secretary for Management at the Department of Homeland Security. While it is still a relatively new position, Borras says, "I did not feel constrained by the history of DHS. We are building on all the work that took place before I arrived. I talked to each person who previously held this position. There is now clarity in the Department about the position. I don't need to argue with anybody about turf."

"I joined the Department with a clear vision of what my priorities were," says Borras. "I felt we needed to focus on financial management, acquisition, and human capital. Those three items fit with my agenda, and it fits well with the Department's agenda, and it also fit my professional interests. These three priorities are also our major management responsibilities."

After he was confirmed, Borras says, "I found a great willingness to make improvements. Many of the staff here thought it was time to take on the major challenges. They wanted to show what they can do."

The Organization

The Department of Homeland Security (DHS) was created by the Homeland Security Act of 2002 and came into existence in January 2003. The Department brought together 22 organizations from across government.

DHS is now the third-largest Department in the federal government. It has a budget of nearly $60 billion and more than 240,000 employees. Among its best-known agencies are the Federal Emergency Management Agency (FEMA), the Transportation Security Administration (TSA), the United States Citizenship and Immigration Services (CIS), and the U.S. Coast Guard (USCG).

The Directorate for Management at DHS is relatively unique in government. Borras is one of two Under Secretaries for Management in government. The other Under Secretary for Management is at the Department of State, where Under Secretary Patrick Kennedy reports to Deputy Secretary for Management Thomas Nides (profiled on page 88). At DHS, the following members of the Department's C-Suite report to Borras:
- Chief Administrative Officer (CAO)
- Chief Financial Officer (CFO)

Rafael Borras

Tenure: Mr. Borras was nominated by President Obama to serve as Under Secretary for Management in January 2011, and confirmed by the U.S. Senate in April 2011. (Mr. Borras served as Under Secretary in a recess appointment lasting from March 2010 to his confirmation in April 2011.)

Private sector experience: Prior to being confirmed as Under Secretary, Mr. Borras served as Vice President of the Infrastructure and Environment Division, URS Corporation, from 2000 to 2010.

Federal government experience: From 1997 to 2000, Mr. Borras served in the General Services Administration as Regional Administrator, Mid-Atlantic region. From 1994 to 1997, he served as Deputy Assistant Secretary for Administration in the U.S. Department of Commerce.

Local government experience: From 1993 to 1994, Mr. Borras served as Deputy City Manager and Commissioner, Human Services in the City of New Rochelle, New York. He also served in the City of Hartford, Connecticut from 1991 to 1993 and the County of Miami-Dade, Florida from 1982 to 1985.

Non-profit experience: From 1985 to 1991, Mr. Borras served as Director of Communications for the International City/County Management Association.

Education: Mr. Borras received his undergraduate degree from Florida International University.

- Chief Human Capital Officer (CHCO)
- Chief Information Officer (CIO)
- Chief Procurement Officer (CPO)
- Chief Security Officer (CSO)

The Challenge

Since 2003, the "implementation and transformation" of DHS has been on the high-risk list published by the Government Accountability Office (GAO). In 2011, GAO wrote, "While DHS has taken action to implement and transform its management functions, this area remains high risk because DHS has not yet demonstrated sustainable progress in implementing corrective actions and addressing key challenges within its management functions, and in integrating those functions within and across the department and its components. DHS also needs to identify and acquire the resources needed to address those challenges." (GAOc)

In his confirmation hearings, Mr. Borras described the three major challenges facing him in his new role as Under Secretary (Department of Homeland Security):

- **Acquisition enhancement.** The challenge, said Borras, was to improve the current Department acquisition processes and procedures, including program management to minimize risk, fiscal responsibility, and improved end-to-end execution across the entire acquisition lifecycle.
- **Financial enhancement.** Borras's second challenge was to improve the Department's financial systems and capabilities in both the management directorate and the DHS agencies.
- **Human capital management enhancement.** The third challenge was to make sure that the Department has the right people in the right positions at the right time, with an appropriate balance between civil servants and contract employees.

Responding to the Challenge

The challenges were thus very clear to Borras when he started his job. Borras says, "My position is unique. I am very mindful of this. It is a great position. I am doing things which other Departments can't do. In the legislation creating the Department, Congress provided the appropriate authorities to give this position more clout. I have the authority I need. It is useful to have all the management lines of business reporting to me. Today, we do not have a problem with lack of coordination and integration between and among the management business chiefs."

While Borras concluded that he had the authority and structure in place to improve and transform management at DHS, he realized that he had to work to change the culture of his directorate and DHS. "There is the cultural part of my job which is less about policies. Culture and priorities interact with each other. We have many agencies (in DHS) which have their own history. We needed to get them to interact with each other and interact differently with each other. We want to change people's DNA, not just to change their minds."

In undertaking cultural change, Borras borrowed from his local government experience. "This is a lot like my experience in local government. There is an expression that you turn around a neighborhood block by block. As a result, I have been constantly focused on our priorities and our ability to execute. I needed to spend a lot of time on acquisition. This was our greatest vulnerability from a risk management point of view. We buy goods and services. If we can't come together

Vision and Core Missions
U.S. Department of Homeland Security

Vision

The vision of homeland security is to ensure a homeland that is safe, secure, and resilient against terrorism and other hazards where American interests, aspirations, and way of life can thrive.

Three key concepts form the foundation of our national homeland security strategy designed to achieve this vision:

- Security,
- Resilience, and
- Customs and Exchange.

The Core Missions

There are five homeland security missions:

- Prevent terrorism and enhancing security;
- Secure and manage our borders;
- Enforce and administer our immigration laws;
- Safeguard and secure cyberspace;
- Ensure resilience to disasters

around the need to improve our acquisition processes, something is wrong."

An important aspect to acquisition is that it always involves other administrative components of the Department. In describing this interrelationship, Borras says, "There is always an information technology piece, a security piece, a human resource piece, and a financial management component. Without giving our change initiative a special name, we used acquisition as leverage to get people to participate and actively engage. It wasn't just about tightening up our policy and procedures."

"By addressing all parts of the process, we are institutionalizing change in the Department," says Borras. "We are taking a long-term approach."

Borras is confident that the Department is making progress and improving. "We measure it one piece at a time. Our programs are constantly being evaluated. This is a mark of our success. If we find deficiencies, staff is willing to take their medicine. Employees come to our forums and are responding to our comments. We have slowly built momentum and gained buy-in from within the Department. We have all of our business line chiefs sitting in the same room. We are trying to raise the probability of success of our programatic investments and be good stewards of the taxpayer's money."

As noted, one of the major challenges facing Borras was enhancing the Department's reputation and evaluations with its oversight organizations. Borras says, "Our efforts have helped enhance our conversations with the Government Accountability Office and other oversight groups. We have now come back with a plan when we have a problem we are trying to solve and a way to measure our progress."

The efforts of Borras and DHS have been recognized by GAO. In a March 2012 report, GAO wrote, "The Department of Homeland Security (DHS) has updated and strengthened its strategy for how it plans to address GAO's high risk designation and resolve the department's management challenges … DHS has made progress … DHS realigned its acquisition management functions within a new office to address the health of major acquisitions and investments; conduct program and portfolio reviews of hundreds of information technology (IT) investments; and reduced the number of material weaknesses in internal controls." (GAOd)

Reflecting on DHS and Managing in Government

"It is the best job in government," says Borras. "I truly love this Department. We have a chance to improve the Department and make long-lasting changes."

"I have observed some political appointees who haven't been in government before get frustrated. I believe that you have to act like you are in charge. You set the agenda. I have seen some political appointees be too passive … I tell them that it is not about you or me. It is up to you to make [change] last with the career staff. My belief is that it is shame on both of us if change goes away during a change of administration."

William V. Corr
Deputy Secretary
Department of Health and Human Services

The Beginning

Bill Corr held several positions at the Department of Health and Human Services (HHS) during the Clinton Administration, including Chief of Staff, so he knew where he wanted to start his work as Deputy Secretary in the Obama Administration. "I knew the career staff at HHS would be outstanding. They are highly trained, talented, and deeply dedicated to the Department's mission of protecting and promoting the health of the American people and providing essential health services to those in greatest need. And I knew that my first and most important responsibility would be to identify and recruit an outstanding team of senior leaders."

Corr drew upon his prior experience in HHS to know how he needed to proceed. "The Secretary and I agreed that we wanted operating and staff division leaders who exemplified two key qualities—outstanding leadership and commitment to being a complete team player. We focused on these two qualities because we knew that to succeed in implementing President Obama's agenda for HHS, and to meet the ongoing responsibilities of our Department, we needed excellent coordination across our 10 operating agencies and we needed to work closely with other Departments on challenges we shared."

During the early days of the Administration, Corr worked closely with the White House Office of Presidential Personnel (OPP). In describing this experience, Corr says, "We worked closely with our colleagues at OPP to understand the experience and skills we needed in each senior level job. We valued the benefit of bringing in people from outside government to get private-sector experience, but we knew we needed leaders who could learn quickly how to operate within government because it is quite different in many respects."

In describing the beginning of his tenure as Deputy Secretary, Corr recalls, "You can be overwhelmed by all the issues and problems when you arrive, so you have to make time for hiring and personnel actions. It was the most important investment of time I made at the beginning."

The Organization

The Department of Health and Human Services (HHS) was created in 1953 as the Department of Health, Education, and Welfare. HHS was formed in 1979 when the separate Department of Education was created.

William V. (Bill) Corr

Tenure: Mr. Corr was nominated by President Obama to serve as Deputy Secretary of the Department of Health and Human Services in January 2009, and confirmed by the U.S. Senate in May 2009.

Private sector experience: Prior to being confirmed as Deputy Secretary, Mr. Corr served as Executive Director of the Campaign for Tobacco-Free Kids from 2000 to 2009. From 1974 to 1977, he directed four non-profit, community-run primary health care centers in the Appalachian Mountain area of Tennessee and Kentucky.

Federal government experience: Mr. Corr served as Chief Counsel and Policy Director for U.S. Senate Minority Leader Tom Daschle from 1998 to 2000. From 1993 to 1998, he served in a variety of positions at the Department of Health and Human Services, including service as Chief of Staff, Counselor, and Deputy Assistant Secretary for Health. From 1989 to 1993, he served as Chief Counsel and Staff Director for the Subcommittee on Antitrust, Monopolies and Business Rights, Senate Committee on the Judiciary. From 1977 to 1989, he served as Counsel to the Subcommittee on Health and the Environment, House Committee on Energy and Commerce.

Education: Mr. Corr received his B.A. in Economics from the University of Virginia and a J.D. from Vanderbilt University School of Law.

Today, the Department is one of the largest in government. It has a budget of over $900 billion and over 75,000 employees. The Department consists of 10 operating divisions, including such well-known agencies as the National Institutes of Health, the Food and Drug Administration, and the Centers for Medicare and Medicaid Services.

The Challenge

There were three major challenges facing Secretary Kathleen Sebelius and Deputy Secretary Corr at the beginning of the Obama Administration. The first challenge was a very ambitious agenda set forth by the Administration, including passage of health care reform. If the Administration succeeded in passing health care reform, it would become the responsibility of HHS to implement the new health care law.

Second, the Secretary and Deputy Secretary faced an enormous management challenge in running a Department as large as HHS with its diverse set of missions. The management challenge required coordination among the various components of HHS and a clear emphasis on implementation of the Department's strategic priorities

Third, the Department also faced the challenge of unexpected events. Corr says, "A major difference between my tenure in the Obama Administration and my time at HHS in the Clinton Administration is that the Department now has a critical emergency preparedness role. We now have emergency response capabilities for natural and man-made disasters that we did not have the first time I was here." As it turns out, the Department did have to confront a series of emergencies during its first term: the H1N1 swine flu crisis, the Haitian earthquake, the Japanese tsunami, and the oil spill in the Gulf of Mexico.

Responding to the Challenge

In response to the challenges facing the Department, Secretary Sebelius and Deputy Secretary Corr formed a clear understanding of the role of the Deputy Secretary. "The Secretary is a strong leader with executive experience as Governor of Kansas," and, Corr recalls, "from day one she expected that she, the Chief of Staff and I would operate as a team. We communicate daily, even when she is traveling, and we discuss a wide range of matters from the urgent to long-range planning."

"We had to hit the ground running as a team with the early, unexpected challenges we faced—particularly the worldwide H1N1 crisis and the Recovery Act implementation—as well as the early tasks of selecting personnel, policy priority-setting, the annual budget cycle, and other regular, annual challenges. My overriding job through all of this has been to ensure that we execute successfully."

A key component of the Department's success is to coordinate work across multiple agencies and with others outside HHS. In describing this role, Corr says, "The health and human service issues that HHS and other Departments face require us to engage in an unprecedented level of coordination across our agencies. When working with other Departments we try to identify the right people who are committed to the same issues and problems as our Department. For example, we work closely with the Department of Veterans Affairs and the Department of Housing and Urban Development on homeless issues and with the Department of Agriculture on nutrition issues. The passage of the Affordable Care Act," says Corr, "presented us with our greatest challenge in coordination. It impacted nearly every operating division of HHS and required us to work closely with the Departments of Treasury and Labor."

In describing his role as HHS Deputy Secretary, Corr emphasizes execution. "I have found that setting priorities and developing strategic plans are the easier set of tasks and that consistent implementation and execution are significantly

Mission Statement
U.S. Department of Health & Human Services

The mission of the Department of Health and Human Services (HHS) is to enhance the health and well-being of Americans by providing for effective health and human services and by fostering strong, sustained advances in the sciences, underlying medicine, public health, and social services.

At the Department, our number one priority will always be to protect the health of all Americans and provide essential human services, especially for those who are least able to help themselves.

more difficult. For example, designing a new approach or program to prevent HIV infection or reduce childhood obesity is easy compared to the challenges of implementing that approach or program over the several years needed to produce the desired improvements in health."

A key component of the Deputy Secretary's job is addressing problems by bringing people together to develop solutions and to ensure continuous momentum. Corr says, "One key aspect of my job is to get the right people in the room, determine the decisions that need to be made and ensure that we not lose our focus on our goals."

Another key component of the job, as described by Corr, is that of enabler. Corr says, "It is my responsibility to ensure that our leaders have what they need to do their job. I had a role in recruiting outstanding leaders to the Department who could work as a team. My job is to ensure they are empowered. We do this as a team. I am very proud of having identified people who can make a difference and bringing them into the Department. My job is to create a culture and then 'let people go'."

Finally, Corr has created an effective working relationship with the career civil servants in the Department. Corr says, "I can't say enough about how well the career staff in our Department have performed over the last three and one-half years. They have taken on an enormous, additional workload with the Affordable Care Act, the Recovery Act, the H1N1 pandemic and several other new challenges; and they have worked against extraordinarily tight deadlines. I hope they hear the Secretary's and my continued praise for their work." Corr recalls the advice from former HHS Secretary Donna Shalala. "She told me that our goal should be that career employees and political appointees work seamlessly so that by the end of an administration the career staff don't recognize any distinctions."

Reflections on Serving in Government

"Public service is challenging and rewarding," Corr says. "I consider myself incredibly fortunate to be able to participate in our nation's efforts to address major national issues. Working at HHS in my position is the chance of a lifetime to make an important difference in the lives of all Americans."

W. Scott Gould
Deputy Secretary
Department of Veterans Affairs

The Beginning

Scott Gould, like several other political executives profiled in this book, participated on President-elect Obama's transition team. "I had been appointed to co-chair the transition team for Veterans Affairs," recalls Gould. "We assembled about 20 people and we conducted 100 interviews and reviewed over 100 documents. We wrote a two-page memo to the President-elect and a 20-page white paper. We also briefed Secretary-designate Eric Shinseki on the Department. We analyzed the major operating units and support functions in the Department and provided the Secretary-designate with a starting point for action."

The Veterans Affairs transition team developed a three-part plan which included reorganizing the Office of the Secretary, improving the Department's management systems, and developing a plan to get the Department ready for implementation of the Post-9/11 GI bill, which provided improved education benefits for veterans serving on active duty on or after September 11, 2011. After the inauguration of the President, Gould helped prepare the Secretary-designate for his confirmation. "By the time I took this position, I had a good baseline knowledge about VA," says Gould. "My time on the transition gave me a sense of the issues and problems facing the Department. We all agreed that we needed to undertake an intensive transformation initiative at VA which would involve career employees."

In addition to his Presidential transition experience, Gould also had personal experience with VA. His father, a Navy veteran who served in both World War II and Korea, spent 11 years as an Alzheimer's patient at the VA Hospital in Bedford, Massachusetts. In 2010, Gould told a group of Veterans Health Administration staff members, "When I come to work each morning, I remind myself that today someone else is going through that experience. I'd like VA to be there for them too." Gould is a veteran himself, having served 26 years in the Navy as an active duty and reserve officer.

The Organization

The Department of Veterans Affairs (VA), elevated to Cabinet status in 1989, has a long history. Some date the nation's veterans programs back to 1636, when the Pilgrims of Plymouth Colony passed a law which stated that soldiers disabled during their war with the Pequot Indians would be supported by the colony. The Continental Congress of 1776 provided pensions for soldiers who were disabled in

W. Scott Gould

Tenure: Mr. Gould was nominated by President Obama to serve as Deputy Secretary of the Department of Veterans Affairs in March 2009, and confirmed by the U.S. Senate in April 2009.

Private sector experience: Prior to being confirmed as Deputy Secretary, Mr. Gould was Vice President for Public Sector Strategy at IBM Global Business Services. He also served as Chief Executive Officer of O'Gara Company and Chief Operating Officer of Exolve. Earlier in his career, he was a consultant at Theodore Barry and Associates.

Federal government experience: Mr. Gould served as Chief Financial Officer and Assistant Secretary for Administration at the Department of Commerce, and as Deputy Assistant Secretary for Finance and Management at the Department of the Treasury. In 1993, he served as a White House Fellow at the Export-Import Bank of the United States and in the Office of the White House Chief of Staff. Mr. Gould is a veteran of the United States Navy. As a Naval Intelligence reservist, Mr. Gould was recalled to active duty in 2001 to support the war in Afghanistan.

Local government experience: In 1991, Gould was appointed by the Governor of Massachusetts to conduct a financial and operational work-out of the city of Chelsea, the first municipality in the state to be placed in receivership by the general court.

Education: Gould attained a B.A. degree in Philosophy from Cornell University and a M.B.A. and Ed.D. from the University of Rochester.

the Revolutionary War. In 1811, the federal government established the first medical facility for veterans. Congress established a system of veteran benefits when the United States entered World War I in 1917. During the 1920s, veteran benefits were administered by three different federal agencies. The Veterans Administration was created in 1930 to consolidate and coordinate government programs for veterans.

Today, VA is the second largest federal government Department, with over 300,000 employees. It operates over 1200 medical facilities (152 VA hospitals, 278 VA Vet Centers, and nearly 800 VA community-based outpatient clients), 131 VA cemeteries, and 58 regional offices delivering veterans' benefits. VA's budget request for FY 2012 is over $132 billion, including nearly $70 billion in mandatory funding. VA saw over one million patients per week and issued 4.4 million benefit checks in each month in FY 2012.

The Challenge

The Department of Veterans Affairs faced numerous challenges when Gould arrived as Deputy Secretary in April 2009. "Secretary Shinseki and I immediately started working on our goals, staffing, and the FY 10 budget," says Gould. "We worked to develop an overall strategy and an approach to change management."

In recent years, VA has had many problems. These problems included the delivery of disability benefits and health care services, property management, and information technology. The most prominent has been the Department's struggle to reduce the disability backlog. In describing VA's placement on its high-risk list, the Government Accountability Office webpage "High Risk and Other Major Government Challenges: Department of Veterans Affairs" explains, "VA continues to face long-standing problems with large pending disability claims inventories, lengthy processing times, concerns about decision accuracy and consistency, and replacing an aging benefits processing system" (GAOa). GAO also identified VA problems in controlling its IT equipment and managing its IT resources, including data security issues.

Because of his career-long interest in human resources, Gould spent part of his first several months assessing the VA workforce. Gould found a workforce that needed strengthening. "I found a different style and culture in the Department than I had anticipated," recalls Gould. "We had to keep asking people, 'What do you think?' and 'How will this serve veterans?' They often had a hard time answering. The career team was not as willing to question assumptions as I had anticipated. We concluded that we had to build the analytical and core skills of the organization, as well as create a culture of advocacy where they feel confident to speak their minds."

Responding to the Challenge

Secretary Shinseki concluded that management improvement was a top priority for the Department. In reflecting on his previous experience working in government, Gould says, "Unlike previous Secretaries I had worked for who decided to focus on two to three priority issues, Secretary Shinseki decided to take on a broad array of issues simultaneously and exploit opportunities. We had a lot of things to do."

This management focus led to a clear division of responsibility between the Secretary, Deputy Secretary, and the Chief of Staff. "In many ways, I have the classic Chief Operating Officer job," says Gould. "I spend a lot of my time involved internally with our line and support units—health care, benefits, and cemetery, as well as information technology, procurement, financial management, human resources, and policy. I'm in charge of the operating plan to implement our vision, and working on budget issues. In general, I focus on working 'inside'

Mission, Vision, Core Values, and Core Characteristics
Department of Veterans Affairs

Mission
To fulfill President Lincoln's promise "To care for him who shall have borne the battle, and for his widow, and his orphan" by serving and honoring the men and women who are America's veterans.

Vision
To provide veterans the world-class benefits and services they have earned—and to do so by adhering to the highest standards of compassion, commitment, excellence, professionalism, integrity, accountability, and stewardship.

Core Values
- Integrity
- Commitment
- Advocacy
- Respect
- Excellence

Core Characteristics
- Trustworthy
- Accessible
- Quality
- Innovative
- Agile
- Integrated

issues, while the Secretary focuses on setting overall direction for the entire organization and managing 'outside' stakeholders."

Shinseki and Gould proceeded on their VA management transformation on two fronts: (1) working on the processes and the infrastructure of the Department, and (2) working on human resources. On the process and infrastructure side, some of the new systems implemented by the Department include:

- The Project Management Accountability System (PMAS), a disciplined approach to IT project development that ensures early identification and correction in under-performing IT programs
- Strategic Capital Investment Planning (SCIP), an initiative which identifies the full extent of VA infrastructure needs and develops solutions to address gaps
- VA's Linking Information Knowledge and Systems (LinKS), a system which collects outcome measurement data in areas such as acute, intensive, and outpatient care
- Veterans Relationship Management (VRM), a system to improve veterans' access to health care and benefits information

- Veterans Benefits Management System (VBMS), an initiative to improve case management and move to a paperless claims processing system for benefits.

Based on his assessment of the need for a stronger VA workforce, Gould moved out quickly on the people front. "We wanted to make the Department more people-centered," says Gould. One of the first major departmental HR initiatives was to rapidly increase the amount of training given to VA employees. "When we started our training initiative, people said it couldn't be done," says Gould. "We went all out to get it done. We worked with the private sector and the Office of Personnel Management to get as much done as we could. We wanted to train over 135,000 people per year in the Department—a goal we exceeded in FY 10 and are on track to accomplish in FY 11. We worked hard to get $200 million to invest in our people."

Coupled with the training initiative, the Secretary, Chief of Staff, and Gould focused on strengthening the Senior Executive Service. "We have over 400 SESers in the Department. I believe that working with the SES can make a real difference in the Department. We needed to work on the issue of performance ratings, as well as our allocation of SES members. This effort resulted in VA getting more SES slots. We are now working hard to get the right people into those jobs. We interview all SES candidates in the Office of the Secretary, which makes a significant impression on those interviewed. We have moved and removed some of our SES members."

Another human resource improvement led by Gould and the VA HR team is reducing the number of days it takes to hire people in the Department. "We are now getting the number of days to hire down from 108 to 76 and we want to go to 60," says Gould. "We are trying to develop ways to do hiring differently and we have been working closely with John Berry at OPM on this."

Reflecting on Serving in the Department of Veterans Affairs

"I consider myself lucky to be here. I like the mission and the people here; we are a team. I tell my colleagues that now is the time that we can make a difference," says Gould. "I've become especially interested in the problem of homeless veterans. Our goal is to reduce the number of homeless veterans to zero in five years. We are working on integrating our mental health programs, as well as reducing our claims backlog."

Gould concludes: "It's all been very challenging and rewarding—every minute of the day."

Innovation in Government:
Creating VA's Innovation Initiative*

By Paul R. Lawrence, Aloha McBride, and Mark A. Abramson

Organizations, both in the public and private sector, have come a long way since the employee suggestion box of the 20th century. For much of the last century, the suggestion box was the major vehicle for soliciting input from within organizations. Other than receiving mail and perhaps conducting focus groups, organizations were also limited in the ways that they received information and ideas from outside their organization.

Twenty-first-century organizations have a variety of powerful tools to obtain new ideas from both inside and outside their organizations. In the federal government today, the Department of Veterans Affairs has become a leader in implementing new ways to innovate. The VA Innovation Initiative (VAi2) was launched in 2010 as part of the Department-wide transformation effort led by Secretary Eric K. Shinseki, Deputy Secretary W. Scott Gould, and Chief of Staff John R. Gingrich.

"We launched the VA Innovation Initiative with the purpose of designing and managing a structured process for innovating at VA," says Deputy Secretary Gould, who also serves as chair of the Executive Selection Board of the Department of Veterans Affairs Innovation Initiative.

In describing the creation of the program, Jonah J. Czerwinski, Director of VAi2, recalls, "We had a venture capital mindset, but not exactly the venture capital toolset. We needed to use the tools that existed in government to bring about innovation, without making direct financial investments in companies."

In creating the program, Czerwinski and his team created a four-pronged approach:

Industry innovation competitions. "We launched with the Industry Innovation Competition in June 2010," recounts Czerwinski. "The goal of the program is to get the best thinking from the private sector to solve the Department's most pressing problems." As an outgrowth of a brainstorming session with VA colleagues, the VAi2 team determined that the Broad Agency Announcement (BAA) was the best tool to specify broad areas of high interest to the Department (such as redesigning the PTSD treatment experience or creating a mobile application for streamlined veterans benefits). While rarely used by VA, the BAA procurement vehicle was key for innovations because it permitted a more open engagement with industry and a more flexible process that included the ability to select more than one approach to a problem.

Since the creation of the program, over 600 ideas in 11 topic areas have been submitted to the Department. Based on the review of those ideas, a total of 37 pilot projects were selected for award and funding. So far, funding for the pilot projects range from a few hundred thousand dollars to $9 million. Pilot projects are designed to deliver results within 24 months. At the end of the project, the pilot is evaluated

---

* Originally published on the AOL Government website, April 11, 2012.

and a decision made as to whether a full and open competition will be pursued to implement the tested concept.

The competitions have been successful. Deputy Secretary Gould reports, "We have seen several promising innovations fielded. For example, one provides VA clinicians with secure mobile access to patient electronic health records and another puts EKGs on mobile devices, allowing cardiologists to review and respond to critical time-sensitive information from anywhere for the first time."

Employee competitions. "These competitions are similar to our industry competitions but are designed to draw on our own employees within VA to tap into their experience and expertise," says Czerwinski. "Employees submit ideas, which are subsequently crowdsourced to help us manage the inflow. We then select pilot projects which are implemented by VA employees."

Over 15,000 ideas from employees have been submitted to date. The VAi2 program invests in the internal pilot, such as software development to test an idea. No money is awarded directly to employees.

Prize contests. "We used the new authorities in the America COMPETES Reauthorization Act of 2010 to conduct prize competitions," recounts Czerwinski. VAi2 currently sponsors a challenge competition on the Challenge.gov website that seeks the development of an app that provides immediate access to resources that the homeless need. Volunteers and outreach workers would be able to use the winning app to look up the location and availability of shelters, free clinics, and other social services, and instantaneously be able to share this information with those in need. The challenge will award $10,000 to five finalists, with an additional $25,000 being awarded to the Grand Prize winner.

One of the outcomes of that effort led to rock star Jon Bon Jovi joining forces with the VA in an effort to challenge software developers to create mobile apps that can help homeless vets connect with services they need in real time and nearby.

Special projects. "When an emergent opportunity arises," says Czerwinski, "we may conduct a special project to generate rapid innovation." To date, VAi2 has managed two special projects: the Agent Orange Fast Track system and the Open Source Electronic Health Record project.

Innovation projects are supported on both the health side and benefits side of VA. Deputy Secretary Gould explains, "VA innovations cover more than health care. The first business incubator for veteran entrepreneurs was launched under VAi2 and now more than 200 veteran-owned ventures are thriving in the VETransfer pipeline less than a year since its launch."

A clear goal of the initiative has been to avoid becoming just another management fad to be tried and subsequently discarded. In order to institutionalize innovation at VA, the Department is in the process of transitioning VAi2 into a new Center for Innovation at VA. The Department of Veterans Affairs clearly offers a model for other Departments and agencies to follow in fostering innovation, both from within and outside their organizations.

Seth D. Harris
Deputy Secretary
Department of Labor

The Beginning

There were several beginnings for Seth Harris. In January 2007, Harris began working with the Obama campaign team. Starting in August 2008, he worked three days a week for the Obama Presidential transition planning team while continuing to teach law at New York Law School. In November 2008, he was appointed to oversee the transition teams for the Departments of Labor, Education, and Transportation and 12 other agencies. "I worked closely with Secretaries-designate Solis, Duncan, and LaHood," says Harris. "After the transition, I worked with Secretary-designate Solis and handed off all the materials we had collected during the transition. I then arrived at the Department in February 2009 as a Senior Advisor to the Secretary after the announcement of my selection as Deputy Secretary-designate. So I had the opportunity to re-learn the Department prior to becoming confirmed as Deputy Secretary in May. I also worked closely with the Acting Deputy Secretary during the February–May time period."

Harris was also very familiar with the Department of Labor because of his prior service in the Department during the Clinton Administration. Harris recalls, "I had worked six and a half years as a senior policy advisor at Labor. So I knew about the management structure of the Department and the role of the Deputy Secretary."

The Organization

The Department of Labor dates back to 1884 when it was created as the Bureau of Labor in the Department of the Interior. In 1888, the Bureau became independent as a Department of Labor without executive rank. The Bureau of Labor returned to Bureau status when the Department of Commerce and Labor was created in 1903. In 1913, all labor programs were transferred from the Department of Commerce and Labor to a new Department of Labor.

Today, the Department of Labor has a more than $12 billion discretionary budget, over 17,000 employees, and administers and enforces more than 180 federal laws. The Department's programs cover more than 125 million workers and 10 million employers. The Department has over 25 organizational units, including the Mine Safety and Health Administration (MSHA), the Occupational Safety and Health Administration (OSHA), the Employment & Training Administration (ETA), the Bureau of Labor Statistics (BLS), and the Employee Benefits Security Administration (EBSA).

Seth D. Harris

Tenure: Mr. Harris was nominated by President Obama to serve as Deputy Secretary of Labor in March 2009, and confirmed by the U.S. Senate in May 2009.

Academic experience: Prior to being confirmed as Deputy Secretary, Mr. Harris served as a Professor of Law at New York Law School and as Director of its Labor and Employment Law programs.

Federal government experience: Mr. Harris served for nearly seven years at the Department of Labor during the Clinton Administration. During that time, Mr. Harris served as Counselor to the Secretary of Labor and as Acting Assistant Secretary of Labor for Policy, among other policy-advising positions. Mr. Harris served as a law clerk to Judge William Canby of the U.S. Court of Appeals for the Ninth Circuit and Chief Judge Gene Carter of the U.S. District Court for the District of Maine.

Education: Mr. Harris is a graduate of the New York University School of Law, where he was Editor-in-Chief of the Review of Law and Social Change. He received his B.S. degree from the School of Industrial and Labor Relations at Cornell University.

In describing the Department, Harris says, "I'm still amazed at the complexity of these organizations. I have 13 line agencies, with each having many different product lines. Our customers range from non-English speaking migrant farmworkers to corporate chief executive officers. We have many market niches and each of our agencies faces a different set of political issues."

The Challenge

Harris found a different Department of Labor than the one he had left nearly a decade earlier. "Since my last time here, I found that we had some new programs," recalls Harris. "We were also faced with implementing the new Recovery Act. Due to retirements and other departures by senior career staff, I thought the Senior Executive Service corps had lost talent that we needed to succeed. Strengthening the SES corps was a critical management issue for the Department. I thought we had to start with our career managers and make changes there. We

Mission
Department of Labor

To foster, promote, and develop the welfare of the wage earners, job seekers, and retirees of the United States; improve working conditions; advance opportunities for profitable employment; and assure work-related benefits and rights.

had to strengthen the organization. I had to move people around to improve management in the Department. We also found a demoralized workforce."

Harris also faced the challenge of poor management processes and practices in some places. "We had to improve the business practices of the Department," asserts Harris. Harris concluded that the Department needed to launch a new strategic planning process. Harris also realized that, together with the strategic planning process, the Department needed new performance measures. "The Department was measuring the wrong things," says Harris. "The measures were typically internal and we were not measuring outcomes. The Department had focused on outputs and process measures previously. We realized that measuring outcomes is incredibly hard, but absolutely essential."

In addition to the management problems, Harris found a Department with too many levels. Harris recounts, "I wanted to make it simpler. None of the changes I proposed were large in budget terms, but we needed a new management structure. Early on, we decided to eliminate the Employment Standards Administration. That gave more authority to the agencies which had been below it and it gave those agencies the ability to work more effectively with the leadership team."

Responding to the Challenge

"How do you turn a giant ship?" asks Harris. This was the issue Harris had to answer for himself and the Department. He concluded that the Department had the right mission and a large staff which had much potential and a deep dedication to the Department's mission. "The raw material was there," comments Harris. "We needed to unleash the inner Labor."

"We concluded that we would use strategic planning as our tool for changing the Department," recalls Harris. "We articulated a vision for the Department— 'Good jobs for everyone.' That was a new goal we believed our staff would enthusiastically embrace. We wanted to articulate the vision clearly. We wanted to emphasize the lives of our customers. We asked our employees whether they were doing the Department's work to help people, and the answer was uniformly 'yes.' We wanted to get the organization to focus on [its] job of protecting workers. We wanted them to know that labor policy and labor still matter. We worked on a set of 13 outcomes which were a different set of measures than people had worked toward in the past. This turned out to be a very effective tool."

The Department of Labor's change management initiative thus consisted of four key components: a vision, a set of outcomes, performance goals and measures, and a strategic plan. "This has been a big change," says Harris, "both conceptually and intellectually for the Department. We also started agencies working on operating plans. I had been surprised by the lack of operating plans in almost half of our agencies. By using all these tools, we wanted to change the organization."

Harris also focused on Senior Executive Service members as potential change agents for the Department. "Improving management in the Department is a real challenge. We need to improve the SES and develop an ever-stronger corps of SES members. We needed to define what it means to be an elite manager in the SES and what skills they needed. We needed to do more skill development. I'm not just talking about training, I mean skill development. We also worked on individual performance measures and better SES evaluations. I recently participated in a nine-hour meeting of SES members. I stayed all day because I wanted to demonstrate my personal involvement. I emphasized their role as change agents."

Based on his previous experience in government, Harris says, "I realize how short the time you have in government really is when you're a political appointee. The challenge is whether you are going to leave 'footprints in concrete' or 'footprints in the snow.' There are so many things that can be undone after you leave or an administration changes. This time around, I came to a better understanding of how to succeed here. You have to change the processes and make it the new way of doing business. You need to implement repetitive processes. While it is difficult to do, you can do it. You can give people a new set of tools. You can start them using program evaluation and developing operating plans. I've learned that you need to engage the civil service to change the DNA of the organization. You can get the Department to start using new procedures which will be the way they do business in the future by building on and adapting existing procedures that they have used for years. Mixing the new with the old seemed to be a recipe for successful change. You have to get into the systems of government. You can change government, but it takes time."

Reflecting on Serving in the Department of Labor

"I was involved in the campaign, so I knew what the President wanted us to do," says Harris. "But governing has been harder than I thought. I had a good understanding of the issues, but it still has been hard."

"I really do care about the Department's mission. I want it to be successful. I want it to be efficient and effective. I wanted to make sure that we had a performance measurement and performance management system in place so that the Department could work."

David J. Hayes
Deputy Secretary
Department of the Interior

The Beginning

"My current time at the Department is much different than my first experience at Interior during the Clinton Administration," recalls David J. Hayes. "This time I came in at the beginning of the Administration with Secretary Ken Salazar. We had to build a new team, and at the same time we were addressing a backlog of issues that needed attention. During my previous experience, I joined former secretary Bruce Babbitt's excellent, well-established team, and I was able to focus on a more discrete agenda of key issues."

"I came back for a second tenure as Deputy Secretary because I love the Department's mission and I was inspired by the vision laid out by President Obama and Secretary Salazar," says Hayes. "I also wanted to expand the Deputy Secretary role beyond its traditional chief operating officer role. I view my job as lining up the management of the Department with the policies of the Department. The Department of the Interior has a broad jurisdiction, and I enjoy the organizational challenge it represents."

"I knew Secretary Salazar very well. I had been President-elect Obama's transition head for the Departments of Energy, Agriculture, and Interior; and for the Environmental Protection Agency. So Ken and I worked together on the transition. I knew that Ken wanted a strong Deputy Secretary."

The Organization

The Department of the Interior is one of the federal government's oldest Departments. Its origins date back to 1789 when portions of its activity were divided among the first three federal Departments (Foreign Affairs, Treasury, and War). Interior was formally created as a separate Department in 1849.

The Department has a budget of approximately $12 billion and over 70,000 employees. It contains nine major agencies, including such well-known organizations as the Bureau of Land Management, U.S. Geological Survey, the Fish and Wildlife Service, and the National Park Service. Lesser known but equally important bureaus include the Bureau of Reclamation, the Bureau of Indian Affairs, the Bureau of Ocean Energy Management, the Bureau of Safety and Environmental Enforcement, and the Office of Surface Mining.

Among its responsibilities, the Department of the Interior manages over one-fifth of the land area of the United States, plus the development rights to our

---

David J. Hayes

Tenure: Mr. Hayes was nominated by President Obama to serve as Deputy Secretary of the Interior in February 2009, and confirmed by the U.S. Senate in May 2009.

Private sector experience: Prior to being confirmed as Deputy Secretary, Mr. Hayes was Global Co-Chair of the Environment, Land and Resources department of the law firm Latham & Watkins.

Federal government experience: From 1997 to 2000, Mr. Hayes served as counselor to Secretary of the Interior Bruce Babbitt and later as his Deputy Secretary.

Academic/nonprofit experience: Mr. Hayes has served as a Consulting Professor at the Woods Institute of the Environment, Stanford University; as Chairman of the Board of Visitors for Stanford Law School; as a Senior Fellow at the World Wildlife Fund; and as Co-Chair of the Board of American Rivers.

Education: Mr. Hayes graduated *summa cum laude* from the University of Notre Dame and earned his J.D. from Stanford Law School, where he was an editor of the Stanford Law Review.

1.7-billion acre outer continental shelf. Interior provides water to over 30 million Americans, manages relations with each of the 565 federally recognized Indian tribes, and is home to the nation's premier earth sciences agency.

The Challenge

The Department of the Interior has a legacy of strong bureaus. Several of the bureaus have over 10,000 employees and report directly to one of the four Assistant Secretaries who oversee Interior agencies. The four Assistant Secretaries then report to the Secretary and Deputy Secretary.

A major challenge is bringing the various Interior components together. "The Office of the Secretary," says Hayes, "is the only place where everything comes together. Traditionally, the agencies have tended to work alone in Interior. Integration can only happen when the Secretary, Deputy Secretary, and Assistant Secretaries get involved."

Because of the many components that need to be linked, Hayes says, "The management function at Interior is very important. Secretary Salazar is more interested in management than many previous Secretaries have been. He and I— along with the Assistant Secretaries and bureau directors—are deeply involved in the formulation of the Department's budget."

Working together, Secretary Salazar and Deputy Secretary Hayes set five major priorities on which they wanted to focus the Department and its component agencies:

- Building a safe, secure energy future
- Protecting America's great outdoors
- Empowering Native American, Alaska Native, and Island communities
- Tackling America's water challenges
- Creating opportunities for America's youth in the outdoors

Responding to the Challenge

Hayes describes one of his various roles as that of convener. "I regularly broker meetings among our bureaus with stakeholders and with state and local governments. We have a major land, water, and wildlife management role throughout the United States, and our bureaus' missions and responsibilities can sometimes be in conflict."

Like the other Deputy Secretaries profiled in this chapter, Hayes has a second role in working closely with other federal Departments. "The President's Management Council is my link to the other Departments. For example, because the Department of the Interior manages energy development on one-third of the land mass of the United States and in our offshore waters, we are in the middle of the Administration's energy policy discussions. We routinely work closely with EPA and the Departments of Defense, Agriculture, and Energy on a broad range of energy-related issues," says Hayes. "Having strong lines of communication to my fellow Deputy Secretaries is an invaluable resource for me."

A third role played by Hayes as Deputy Secretary is crisis manager. "I was the operations lead for the Department on the Gulf Oil spill," Hayes says. "I spent every day—as did much of our team—from April 2010 to September 2010 on the oil spill." Joel Achenbach writes in *A Hole at the Bottom of the Sea* about the start of Hayes's involvement in the oil spill:

> David Hayes … arrived at his office that Wednesday morning, April 21, with no inkling that it would be anything other than a normal workday. He heard about the explosion within minutes of walking into Interior's massive building … by midmorning the scale of the disaster became more apparent, and Hayes's boss, Interior Secretary Ken Salazar, suggested that he jump on a plane and fly to New Orleans.

Mission
Department of the Interior

The Department of the Interior protects and manages the Nation's natural resources and cultural heritage; provides scientific and other information about those resources; and honors its trust responsibilities or special commitments to American Indians, Alaska Natives, and affiliated island communities.

Mission Areas
- Provide Natural and Cultural Resources Protections and Experiences
- Sustainably Manage Energy, Water, and Natural Resources
- Advance Government-to-Government Relationships with Indian Nations and Honor Commitments to Insular Areas
- Provide a Scientific Foundation for Decision-Making

Hayes would rather have stayed put; it was his daughter Molly's eighteenth birthday. He called his wife: "We may have a problem here."

… Hayes and press secretary Kendra Barkoff raced to Reagan National Airport—no luggage, not even toothbrushes—and talked their way onto a US Airways jet that had already closed its door and was about to taxi toward the runway. (Achenbach)

In looking back on the Gulf Oil spill, Hayes is proud of his Department's work. He says, "Our Department worked closely with the national labs, and our scientists at the USGS and elsewhere contributed invaluable research." Says Hayes, "We were also involved in the response, the cleanup phase. We negotiated with BP every step of the way. I am proud of what we did."

The Interior Department took the oil spill as a chance for reform, Hayes says. "The oil spill was an opportunity for us to address a number of long-standing institutional issues at the Department. We had to revamp our processes in response to the oil spill, and we did a major bureau reorganization based on the lessons we learned." In the midst of the crisis, Hayes says his team gained invaluable experience. "We increased our skills. It was a huge lift. We all spent long days during that period, but we kept the trains running."

Another role described by Hayes is that of facilitator. "There are now fewer things that I can do personally," he notes. "I have to delegate and act more as a facilitator. I do get personally involved when needed, but largely I try to let our team do their work." However, Hayes does recount a number of situations where his personal involvement has been important. "I have been involved in the California Bay Delta water situation, which is an historic effort by this Department to bring water delivery into the 21st century. I have also worked extensively on issues related to energy development in Alaska, which is a priority of this Administration."

Hayes played a major role in negotiating the final approval in the courts of the settlement of *Cobell v. Salazar*, a long-running and contentious American Indian trust class action. The court approval paved the way for payments to be made to as many as half a million American Indians who have individual money accounts in trust or restricted land managed by the Department.

"I worked with our Department's solicitor and a small team to wrap up the issue of Indian trust claims which had been in litigation for 15 years. My greatest satisfaction is seeing conflicts resolved and settlements reached, and this was a great example of that. There are always conflicting interests on every issue. The job of senior leadership is to balance those interests and point the ship forward again."

Following an earlier court ruling, Hayes scheduled consultation meetings with tribal leaders to begin discussions on the land consolidation component of the settlement. Hayes held six regional government-to-government tribal consultations to get input in developing an implementation strategy to benefit tribal communities and to help free up trust lands. "The Cobell settlement is the beginning of true trust reform," says Hayes. "Interior needs to be more transparent and customer-friendly, and we continue to move forward with important reforms in Indian trust management. I am proud of the work we have done so far, but we have more left to do."

Reflecting on Serving in the Department of the Interior

"I have spent most of my career in the field of conservation," says Hayes. "There is no place where you can do more to make a difference in conservation than at the Department of the Interior. We [have an] impact every day on a host of environmental issues. We have to be careful about managing our natural resources responsibly."

"I recommend public service. It is a wonderful opportunity to work on a host of important issues and explore personal growth. I tell people to jump in and try it. At the Department of the Interior, we came in at the start of the Administration with five major priorities, and we have worked as an entire Department to see them through. We have a shared mission, and that is working on behalf of the American people."

Dennis F. Hightower
Deputy Secretary
Department of Commerce

The Beginning

"I was sworn in at 9:00 a.m. and I was in my first budget meeting at 9:30 a.m.," recalls Dennis Hightower. "I quickly got the impression that running Commerce was like running a holding company—a collection of vastly different businesses, but with a common goal of helping U.S. businesses become more innovative and competitive. My first week there was *Commerce 101.* I did a lot of listening and learning. I did, however, already know much about Commerce. As a business executive, I had used many of the services of the Department over the years."

Hightower spent time during his first months at Commerce on the road. "I spent time out in the field where the work gets done," recalls Hightower. "I wanted to meet the Commerce employees, and observe firsthand how they performed their work. I used different forums to talk with employees. I would ask a lot of questions. I used this time to think strategically about the Department."

Based on this outreach, Hightower says, "I began to select three to five very specific objectives on which we could focus. I also was interested in getting more cross-fertilization in the Department. After about 60 days, my office started developing brief position papers describing both short-term things we could do (the low-hanging fruit) as well as longer-term, sustainable projects; and mobilizing members of the Office of the Secretary to support these efforts."

The Organization

Deputy Secretary Hightower got it right. The Department of Commerce is much like a holding company. The Department consists of 12 Bureaus and 10 staff organizations. Its Bureaus range from the Economics and Statistics Administration to the National Oceanic and Atmospheric Administration to the United States Patent and Trademark Office. The Department of Commerce was formed in 1903 when the Department of Commerce and Labor was split into two Cabinet Departments. The Obama Administration is now considering a major reorganization of the Department. In FY 11, the Department had a budget of over $17 billion and had nearly 55,000 employees.

Dennis F. Hightower

Tenure: Mr. Hightower was nominated by President Obama to serve as Deputy Secretary in July 2009, and confirmed by the U.S. Senate in August 2009.

Private sector experience: Prior to being confirmed as Deputy Secretary, Mr. Hightower served as Chief Executive Officer of Europe Online Networks S.A., a satellite-delivered, broadband Internet service provider based in Luxembourg. From 1987 to 1996, he was a senior executive of The Walt Disney Company, serving as President of Walt Disney Television and Telecommunications. During his career, he was a Managing Director at Russell Reynolds

Associates, a Vice President at Mattel, Vice President and General Manager of General Electric's lighting business in Mexico, Senior Associate at McKinsey & Company, and a manager at Xerox Research and Engineering Group.

Federal government experience: Mr. Hightower was a regular Army officer for eight years, rising to the rank of Major. He is a decorated Vietnam veteran. He also served as a member of the Department of Defense Business Board.

Academic experience: Mr. Hightower served as a Professor of Management at Harvard Business School.

Education: Mr. Hightower holds an M.B.A. degree from Harvard Business School and a B.S. degree from Howard University.

The Challenge

In addition to the challenge of overseeing Commerce's diverse portfolio of Bureaus and staff organizations, Hightower faced three unique challenges. The first was oversight of the 2010 Census. As discussed in the profile of Rebecca Blank on page 195, it was crucial that the Census fully succeed and that problems were kept to a minimum. As in past years, the Census received much attention from Congress. The second challenge was the implementation of the Department's Recovery Act initiatives, which provided nearly $4 billion to the National Telecommunications and Information Administration to expand access to broadband services in unserved and underserved areas in the United States. The broadband initiative was a high-visibility component of the Recovery Act and a major priority of the Administration. The third was to oversee the Department's role in reforming the U.S. Export Controls regulations that would help U.S. businesses become more competitive abroad.

Responding to the Challenge

During his time at Commerce, Hightower worked on many fronts. One major activity was oversight of several Administration priorities. "I worked on the 2010 Census, the broadband initiative of the Recovery Act, and the Export Control Reform Initiative," says Hightower. "In the broadband initiative, it was essential to accelerate the second and third phases to get the money out to the winning grantees to facilitate job creation. Successfully bringing NOAA's satellite program in-house was a major undertaking, involving close coordination with DoD, NASA, and the prime contractor."

Another activity of Hightower's was reaching out to the business community and working with Commerce agencies that deal directly with large, medium, and small businesses. "I saw the many opportunities that the Department has to reach out and touch businesses on all levels," says Hightower. "A new Department initiative, 'CommerceConnect' brought all of the capabilities of Commerce to one location (piloted in Detroit) to help small and medium size companies in depressed communities redeploy their products, services, and skill sets to new growth areas. We are involved in speeding up granting patents at the United States Patent and Trademark Office, assisting manufacturers at the National Institutes of Standards and Technology and the International Trade Administration (ITA), and assisting exporters at both ITA and the Bureau of Industry and Security. I wanted to explore how the Department and its components—that touch every phase of the business life cycle—could help businesses become more innovative and competitive at home and abroad."

Another front was the people side of the Department. Along with several of his fellow Deputy Secretaries, Hightower took a special interest in meeting and talking with employees. "I always believed in management by walking around," says Hightower. "You have to reinforce your strategy. You have to tell people what you are doing and why, and how they fit. I like to go to Commerce offices when I'm on the road. These visits increase the visibility of the Office of the Secretary and facilitate a dialogue. Also, you never know where the next good ideas will come from."

In focusing on the people side of the Department, Hightower had been influenced by the time he spent working with Jack Welch at General Electric. "Welch taught me that business wasn't about just making your numbers," recalls Hightower. "I learned it was also about values and creating the right environment. Welch spent a lot of time on succession planning, too. He used to say that numbers don't get the job done. It is people who get the job done."

A specific group in Commerce that caught Hightower's attention was the

Mission
Department of Commerce

The U.S. Department of Commerce promotes job creation, economic growth, sustainable development and improved standards of living for all Americans by working in partnership with businesses, universities, communities and our nation's workers. The Department touches the daily lives of the American people in many ways, with a wide range of responsibilities in the areas of trade, economic development, technology, entrepreneurship and business development, environmental stewardship, and statistical research and analysis.

Department's Senior Executive Service corps. Hightower says, "I think we clearly articulated a new approach for the Department among our SES members. We have made progress on performance measurement and we are moving on a balanced scorecard. We want to be sure that as a Department, we are working on the right things: things that move the needle in terms of outcomes—not just activities. We also detailed members of the SES to the Office of the Secretary to work on special initiatives. We wanted to increase the 'bandwidth' of our SES corps. We also wanted them to know how the fifth floor (the Office of the Secretary) works. We wanted to give people a firsthand look at the Department. We put high-powered teams together from across the Department—our best minds on our toughest problems. My direct involvement shows that we are serious about this. I've seen some extraordinarily talented people in the Department and I want to give them an opportunity to grow—some mini-succession planning in action. This has worked out well."

In describing his work with the Senior Executive Service, Hightower says, "We tried to leverage the skills and talents of the SES. We think this is the right thing to do. This is part of our strategic approach to making the Department a better place to work. We are always asking ourselves what we can do to motivate people. I have always said that 'management is getting people to do willingly what they otherwise might not want to do.'"

Hightower also oversaw the Department's budget process. "We are changing our approach to instill a rigorous prioritization approach to integrating budgets and performance [outcomes]," says Hightower. "We had a Bureau Chiefs and Deputies meeting to launch the budget season. In this meeting, each Bureau presented their plans and told us what their priorities were, and most important, how their plans aligned with the Department's key strategic thrusts. It was clear that we will need to make critical tradeoffs so we gave the Bureau heads the opportunity to tell us how they would reallocate resources, if needed. It was a great meeting. It was good for the Bureau heads to have their peers in the room talking about a common set of goals and objectives. We also wanted to foster an environment where the Bureaus could look at cross-cutting objectives. As a result, we uncovered many opportunities to piggyback and leverage resources across the Department. Now, the Bureaus are working together better than ever, and there is more positive communication and interaction between the fifth floor and the Bureaus."

Reflecting on Serving in the Department of Commerce

"This has been a very gratifying and exciting role for me at Commerce—facilitated in large measure by the Secretary's trust and confidence in my abilities to get things done as the chief operating officer," says Hightower. "It uses everything I've done in the past, particularly my work on strategy, change management, and fixing organizations. I've always believed that there are core leadership skills in both business and government that are interchangeable—personal integrity, people skills, competence, and an infectious passion for what you do."

Epilogue

Dennis F. Hightower is now Chairman of Hightower Associates, a strategic advisory firm that works with small and medium-sized companies to help them compete in the fast-changing and uncertain global economic arena.

Kathleen A. Merrigan
Deputy Secretary
Department of Agriculture

The Beginning

Kathleen Merrigan recalls her first days as Deputy Secretary in the Department of Agriculture: "Knowing that everybody would want to come in and make a case for priorities for the new Administration, I accepted all meeting requests for the first three months. This prevented a logjam of requests and allowed me to establish relationships with important constituent leaders."

The Organization

The Department of Agriculture is one of the oldest Departments in government, created in 1862. It has a budget of approximately $145 billion and over 110,000 employees, 90,000 of whom are based in state field offices and in 99 countries across the globe. The Department consists of 18 agencies and 15 staff offices. Agencies in the Department include the Forest Service, the Food and Nutrition Service, the Agricultural Research Service, the Animal and Plant Health Inspection Service, and the Food Safety and Inspection Service. The Department is responsible for a wide variety of activities, ranging from food safety to rural development to delivering food and nutrition programs.

The Challenge

A challenge faced by Merrigan, along with the other Deputy Secretaries profiled in this chapter, was the size and scope of the Department, including the tendency for each internal agency to view itself as somewhat independent of the Office of the Secretary. "Historically, the power in the bureaucracy has been in the hands of agency administrators," says Merrigan, once an agency administrator herself. "Administrators run their own budget, Congressional outreach, and public affairs offices."

Deputy Secretary Merrigan introduced outcomes-based budgeting, demanding that all proposals demonstrate their relative contributions to four priorities established by the Secretary and his team. "This required agency administrators and Under Secretaries to work together to articulate and achieve cross-cutting objectives and outcomes. Four years goes by very quickly. Focus and speed are essential."

Kathleen A. Merrigan

Tenure: Dr. Merrigan was nominated by President Obama to serve as Deputy Secretary of the U.S. Department of Agriculture in March 2009, and confirmed by the U.S. Senate in April 2009.

Academic experience: Prior to being confirmed as Deputy Secretary, Dr. Merrigan served eight years as Assistant Professor and Director of the Agriculture, Food and Environment graduate program at the Friedman School of Nutrition Science and Policy at Tufts University. She also served as an instructor at the Massachusetts Institute of Technology.

Federal government experience: Dr. Merrigan served as Administrator of the USDA Agricultural Marketing Service during the Clinton Administration. She served for six years as a senior science and technology advisor to the U.S. Senate Committee on Agriculture, Nutrition and Forestry.

State government experience: Dr. Merrigan served as a special assistant in the Texas Department of Agriculture where she worked on regulation and pesticide issues. She also served as Chief of Staff to a state senator in the Massachusetts State Senate.

Education: Dr. Merrigan holds a Ph.D. degree in Environmental Planning and Policy from the Massachusetts Institute of Technology, a Master of Public Affairs degree from the University of Texas, and a B.A. degree from Williams College.

While one set of initial challenges focused on the internal management of the Department, another set was external. The average age of farmers and ranchers in this country is 59, and more than 30% of farmers are over age 65. "We need a recruitment strategy to repopulate Rural America. With less than 1% of Americans directly connected to farming, the challenge is to remind policy makers and the American public why USDA and agriculture matter."

Responding to the Challenge

In responding to the challenges she faced, Merrigan had to divide her time between the internal management of the Department and the need for external outreach to the broad and growing number of groups interested in agriculture. Internally, the budget consumed much of Merrigan's time as the ongoing budget process and debt negotiations required major management initiatives to narrow priorities and find efficiencies.

In describing her experience implementing a new outcomes-based budget process, Merrigan says, "It was uncomfortable at first as people tried out this new way of doing things. But eventually people recognized the value of going forward in this way, particularly as budgets are being downsized and with a public that is increasingly skeptical of government investments. We also identified high priority performance goals. We chose performance goals that required agencies to work together. When OMB asked for a goal leader, I responded that each goal had multiple leaders. While that may make accountability more difficult in the short term, the lasting value is the synergistic energy and cross-fertilization that comes from multiple agency engagement." Merrigan also led an effort to rewrite the Department's strategic plan, the first draft of which she and the Secretary concluded was not ambitious enough. "We wanted stretch goals," says Merrigan. "There is too much at stake to play it safe."

In addition to managing the Department's budget process, Merrigan launched an extensive outreach program. Since becoming Deputy Secretary, Merrigan has visited more than 40 states. "I've lectured at dozens of college campuses, held producer round-tables in nearly every state, and conducted oversight visits of Recovery Act-funded projects. One of my primary goals as Deputy is to increase interest in the work of USDA and in American agriculture. I want people who have had mixed experience with USDA in the past—women and minorities and those involved in alternative production techniques—to hear from me directly that this is a different, more inclusive USDA."

Given the vast array of field offices, Merrigan has also made visits with field staff a priority. "I try and visit our field offices whenever I travel. Many employees in our county offices had never had people from Washington visit, not just in this Administration, but some tell me not in the 35 years that they have worked for USDA. Employees come to these meetings expecting a big speech, but after five minutes of remarks, I turn to questions and assure them that they can be frank and that everything is on the table."

During her tenure, Merrigan has played leadership roles in two major departmental initiatives: the Healthy Kids Initiative and the Know Your Farmer initiative (see *Innovation in Government: Creating The Know Your Farmer, Know Your Food Program* on page 79 for a further discussion on this initiative). Regarding the Healthy Kids Initiative, Merrigan says, "This was a USDA-driven and White House-orchestrated interdepartmental effort to improve the health of children by combating both obesity and hunger. The First Lady's Let's Move! campaign and passage of the Healthy Hunger-Free Kids Act in December 2010 are direct results of this early effort. Major reforms are now underway that will improve school meals and increase the availability of healthy food options in neighborhoods. We are all working with the First Lady to achieve the Administration's goal of ending childhood obesity in a generation."

Mission and Vision
Department of Agriculture

Mission Statement
USDA provides leadership on food, agriculture, natural resources, rural develop-ment, nutrition, and related issues based on sound public policy, the best available science, and efficient management.

Vision Statement
To expand economic opportunity through innovation, helping rural America to thrive; to promote agriculture production sustainability that better nourishes Americans while also helping feed others throughout the world; and to preserve and conserve our Nation's natural resources through restored forests, improved watersheds, and healthy private working lands.

The second of Merrigan's major initiatives was the Know Your Farmer, Know Your Food (KYF2) initiative, which highlights the critical connection between farmers and consumers. This initiative was aimed at carrying out the President's commitment to locally grown food by strengthening local and regional food sys-tems. "The initiative enabled us to reach out to different constituents and it has taken off like wildfire," says Merrigan. A unique feature of this initiative is that no budget or staff was dedicated to it. Instead of creating a new office, Merrigan organized the initiative through a cross-department task force, with every USDA agency rep-resented on it. Merrigan chaired the task force, which met every two weeks and is mostly made up of career mid-level managers who voluntarily add the KYF2 work to their regular work assignments. "The local and regional food systems effort will live beyond me and this particular Administration because we created cross-agency energy and engaged and empowered staff. People tell me that this management effort has been transformative and that they are enjoying their jobs now more than they have in years, even though in total, they are being asked to do more."

Reflecting on Serving in the Department of Agriculture

Merrigan reflects, "Even though I have worked in agriculture policy for the better part of my career, it still took me awhile to gain my footing. A bureaucracy this vast and complex is tough to manage. You have to know how to delegate, how to establish trust with your career managers, and then quickly decide where to leave your fingerprints. As a political appointee, time is not on my side and a critical skill is knowing when to say 'No.'"

Innovation in Government:
Creating The Know Your Farmer, Know Your Food Program*

By Paul R. Lawrence and Mark A. Abramson

Historically, a major criticism of government has been that it consists of individual government agencies (often called stovepipes or silos) which tend not to work very well with other agencies, even those within their own Department.

When she arrived at the Department of Agriculture (USDA), Deputy Secretary Kathleen Merrigan found some truth in this criticism of government. Many agencies within USDA viewed themselves as somewhat independent of the Office of the Secretary.

"Historically, the power in the bureaucracy has been in the hands of agency administrators," says Merrigan, once an agency administrator herself. "Administrators run their own budget, Congressional outreach, and public affairs offices."

A major stumbling block to innovation in government has been this tendency for each government unit to do "its own thing," independent of each other. Thus, while these units could achieve their individual missions, they often had difficulty in achieving cross-departmental goals or missions.

To achieve departmental missions, it is necessary to create new mechanisms which cut across agency boundaries. One such mechanism is cross-cutting departmental (or government-wide) initiatives to achieve a specific mission.

During the Obama Administration, the Department of Agriculture has been seen as a leader in developing and fostering such initiatives. At Agriculture, leading such initiatives became a significant component of the job of Deputy Secretary Merrigan. In addition to her ongoing budget and management responsibilities, Merrigan played leadership roles in two major departmental initiatives: the Healthy Kids Initiative and the Know Your Farmer initiative.

In describing the Healthy Kids Initiative, Merrigan says, "This was a USDA-driven and White House-orchestrated interdepartmental effort to improve the health of children by combating both obesity and hunger. The First Lady's Let's Move! campaign and passage of the Healthy Hunger-Free Kids Act in December 2010 are direct results of this early effort. Major reforms are now underway that will improve school meals and increase the availability of healthy food options in neighborhoods. We are all working with the First Lady to achieve the Administration's goal of ending childhood obesity in a generation."

The second of the Department's major initiatives is Know Your Farmer, Know Your Food (KYF2), which highlights the critical connection between farmers and consumers. Launched in September 2009, this department-wide initiative is aimed at carrying out the President's commitment to locally grown food by strengthening

---

* Originally published on the AOL Government website, March 28, 2012.

local and regional food systems. "The initiative enabled us to reach out to different constituents and it has taken off like wildfire," says Merrigan.

An innovative feature of this initiative is that it has no office, budget, or staff dedicated to it. The initiative was created to coordinate the Department's vast resources and expertise on local and regional food systems across its 17 agencies.

Instead of creating a new office, Merrigan organized the initiative through a cross-department task force, with every USDA agency represented on it. Merrigan chairs the task force, which meets every two weeks and is made up of career mid-level managers who voluntarily add the KYF2 work to their regular work assignments. The task force is charged with breaking down bureaucratic silos, developing common-sense solutions for communities and farmers, and fostering new partnerships inside USDA and across the nation.

"This initiative, fostering local and regional food systems, will live beyond me and this particular Administration because we created cross-agency energy and engaged and empowered staff. People tell me that this management effort has been transformative and that they are enjoying their jobs now more than they have in years, even though in total, they are being asked to do more."

Since its creation, the initiative has continued to expand. On February 29, 2012, Agriculture Secretary Tom Vilsack and Deputy Secretary Merrigan unveiled the Know Your Farmer, Know Your Food Compass. The KYF2 Compass is an interactive web-based tool which highlights departmental support for local and regional food projects and successful producer, business, and community case studies. The Compass includes an interactive U.S. map which shows local and regional food projects in all 50 states, with accompanying case studies, photos, and video content.

In launching the Compass, Deputy Secretary Merrigan said, "By encouraging all Americans to know their farmer, USDA is helping consumers learn more about agriculture and people producing your food. The KYF2 initiative helps farmers and ranchers tap into a vibrant, growing market opportunity. And it's also stimulating a broader national conversation about where our food comes from and how important agriculture is to our country."

As a follow-up to the February 29th launch of the Compass, Deputy Secretary Merrigan conducted a virtual town hall meeting on March 5 to further publicize the KYF2 initiative. The meeting was streamed live at www.whitehouse.gov, with questions coming from virtual participants via Twitter (#KYF2). Participants could also watch the town meeting on Facebook and submit comments.

As government continues to search for ways to innovate within the traditional bureaucracy, the use of cross-department or cross-government initiatives may increase in the years ahead. There is much to be learned from the Department of Agriculture about how to organize and foster such initiatives, without creating a new mini-bureaucracy to manage them.

Anthony W. Miller
Deputy Secretary
Department of Education

The Beginning

When invited to join Secretary Arne Duncan's team at the U.S. Department of Education, Anthony Miller did not anticipate becoming Deputy Secretary of the Department—the number two position. "I came with five other individuals and we worked as Special Assistants to the Secretary," recalls Miller. "We were all new and none of us had been here before. My first impression of the Department was pretty overwhelming. I didn't know where to sit, who else was here, or where I should park."

"I started working on strategic planning from day one. We had initially thought about my serving in the Department as Chief Operating Officer," states Miller. "As our staffing needs became clearer, the President decided to nominate me as Deputy Secretary. I was formally nominated in May 2009 and confirmed by the U.S. Senate in July."

The Organization

The Department of Education is the second "youngest" federal Cabinet Department (created in 1980) and is the smallest Department in terms of the number of federal employees (4,200). It has a budget of approximately $70 billion, making it the third largest source of discretionary funds in the federal government. In higher education, the Department provides about 45 percent of scholarship aid and about 75 percent of total financial aid. The federal government's contribution to elementary and secondary education is about 10 percent of total national spending, with the remaining 90 percent coming from state and local government funding. While it is a relatively new Cabinet Department, the federal role in education dates back to the 1860s when the federal government started to collect information on schools and teaching to help states establish school systems.

The Challenge

During the first year of the Obama Administration, Deputy Secretary Miller faced two major challenges:
* **Implementing the Recovery Act in the Department.** Congress passed the

Anthony (Tony) W. Miller

Tenure: Mr. Miller was nominated by President Obama to serve as Deputy Secretary of the Department of Education in May 2009, and confirmed by the U.S. Senate in July 2009.

Private sector experience: Prior to joining the Department in 2009, Mr. Miller was an operating partner with Silver Lake, a private equity firm. From 2003–2006, he was with LRN Corporation, where he was Executive Vice President of Operations. Prior to LRN, he worked for 10 years at McKinsey & Company, where he was a partner specializing in growth strategies, operating performance improvement, and restructuring for companies. Mr. Miller began his professional career with Delco Electronics, a subsidiary of GM Hughes Electronics, where he managed regional channel marketing.

Photo: Joshua Hoover, U.S. Department of Education

Local government experience: Mr. Miller advised the Los Angeles Unified School District from 1997–2000, developing student achievement goals and strategies, aligning budgets and operating plans, and designing metrics and processes for overseeing district-wide performance. He undertook similar work with the Santa Monica-Malibu Unified School District in 2001. He also served as an ex-officio member of the Los Angeles Unified School District Board of Education Budget and Finance Committee in 2002–2003.

Education: Mr. Miller is a graduate of Purdue University and holds an M.B.A. from the Stanford Graduate School of Business.

American Recovery and Reinvestment Act on February 13, 2009 and it was signed into law by President Obama on February 17. The Department received $97 billion in Recovery Act funds, an amount of money larger than its annual budget. The funds were intended to avert layoffs of school personnel and also to advance critical reforms in education.

- **Strengthening the Department's internal processes.** With the addition of Recovery Act funds, it became essential that the Department's management processes operate effectively and efficiently.

The challenge in years two and three shifted somewhat for Deputy Secretary Miller. "I learned about the cycles of government," states Miller. "During your first year here, you are doing the planning for the first time and learning the planning process. You are still working from the old budget. In year two, you really start implementing your agenda as well as identifying opportunities to improve processes. In year three, you can more systematically drive your policy agenda.

The reality is that this is a multi-year effort and you don't realize that at the beginning. In year three, we're now working to institutionalize changes to key planning and management processes and to implement a continuous improvement mindset as part of the Department's agenda."

Responding to the Challenge

The first order of business for Miller, in both his role as a Special Assistant and later Deputy Secretary, was getting the Recovery Act implemented. "We started working on the Recovery Act during our first days and that dominated our activities. Our first six months were devoted to getting the Recovery Act launched." In reflecting on this experience, Miller says, "If there was one thing we needed to do, it was the Recovery Act. We stood it up and got the money out. It's been a tremendous success in the education world, saving hundreds of thousands of educator jobs." Launching the program included developing guidance and providing technical assistance to recipients, including explaining the Act's unique requirements for how the funds could be used and the reports that needed to be submitted.

While the Department was successful in standing up the program and obligating the money to the states, it turned out that getting the money out was only part of the job. "After we got the money out, the states then had to work with local school districts to minimize the potential for waste, fraud, and abuse as funds were drawn down by districts to meet their most pressing needs," states Miller. "We encouraged them to spend the money early and wisely, but we didn't have any control over whether they kept part of the money to spend at a later date. We didn't want them to sit on the money. We wanted them to save jobs and advance reforms and do it as quickly as possible." Like many of the political executives in this book, Miller learned that there are many external factors outside the control of the Department that influence the ultimate impact of federal dollars.

The second order of business for Miller was strengthening the Department's administrative processes. During the early days of the Administration, it was essential to clarify the decision-making processes in the Department. "There are so many layers in government that you have to be clear about how and where decisions will be made," states Miller. "With the arrival of a new leadership team, you need to let people know how the decision-making process will operate."

While clarifying the decision-making process, Miller and Secretary Duncan's team also worked to set clear expectations and explicit goals for the Department. "We developed an operational plan and shared it with staff throughout the Department," says Miller. "It's important to let people know what is expected of their operating units. As leaders, we must be clearer and more transparent communicating performance expectations. This is basic management—setting forth your goals. We also started to link the planning process in the Department with

**Mission
Department of Education**

The mission of the Department of Education is to promote student achievement and preparation for global competitiveness by fostering educational excellence and ensuring equal access. It engages in four major types of activities:

- Establishes policies related to federal education funding, administers distribution of funds and monitors their use.
- Collects data and oversees research on America's schools.
- Identifies major issues in education and focuses national attention on them.
- Enforces federal laws prohibiting discrimination in programs that receive federal funds.

the budget process and get alignment. We have over 150 discretionary programs in the Department, which were not well aligned."

Like many Deputy Secretaries, Miller focuses on the people side of the Department. "We have a very talented organization, but we needed to get them aligned," says Miller. "We wanted to have the Senior Executive Service (SES) members in the Department assume more responsibility for organizational performance. So we based their performance plans on 80 percent individual performance and 20 percent on organizational performance. We wanted the SES members to know that they are expected to contribute to the larger organization. Once we laid it all out, it became clearer to people. Making things clearer is actually unleashing the energy of our SES members. I think they are thriving."

"You simply have to be relentless," says Miller. "You have to stay at it. It is easy to get distracted. There is simply so much going on. The environment is more chaotic and frenetic than I had anticipated. You have to identify what you want to accomplish. You have to focus on implementation and watch your priority list carefully. You need a planning system to track everything."

Miller also found that patience is required in government. "I was surprised at how many problems keep coming back to you," recalls Miller. "I can understand problems coming to you the first time and then the second time. But it starts getting frustrating when they come back the third time. So I've spent some time trying to find out the root cause of problems and how we can fix them once and for all."

Another surprise to Miller was the lack of strategic thinking in government. "I was surprised at not seeing more strategic planning or a strategic focus in government. Government doesn't seem to have much expertise in strategic planning.

We would also benefit from more consistent analytic rigor at the Department. I think you need a clear strategic direction that's grounded in factual analyses to manage most effectively."

Reflecting on Serving in the Department of Education

"This is an important moment in time to be here," says Miller. "Congress gave the Department the resources at the same time that there is a growing appreciation of the importance of education in our nation. We have the President's attention on education issues. We have a dynamic group of people working here, including an authentic leader in Arne Duncan. Everything came together in the first year—we got important legislation passed and we got resources. Secretary Duncan keeps reminding us that it is all about the kids. It isn't about us."

Innovation in Government:
Creating The Race To The Top Program
at the Department of Education[*]

By Paul R. Lawrence, Marc Andersen, and Mark A. Abramson

Undertaking innovation in government is a challenge. Government leaders must work with their existing tool kit, primarily grants and contracts, to bring about their desired results. It is rare that Congress gives government new authorities and a new portfolio of tools. (One exception is the creation of the Advanced Research Projects Agency-Energy in the Department of Energy). Thus, government must be creative in using the tools already on the books. (See the profile of Director Arun Majumdar on page 142.)

At the Department of Education, the Obama Administration used one of government's oldest tools—the 19th century grant-in-aid—to accomplish 21st century objectives. Under the leadership of Secretary Arne Duncan and Deputy Secretary Anthony Miller, the Department focused on one of its primary goals: dramatically improving educational performance in all 50 states.

Given the budget of the Department (it accounts for only 10% of total national spending on education, with the remaining 90% coming from state and local governments) and its limited leverage over state and local education institutions, the Department had to be creative in developing new approaches which would encourage movement toward reforming schools and improving educational performance across the nation.

The new approach was to create a nationwide competition among the states to receive new funding authorized by the American Recovery and Reinvestment Act of 2009. In order to compete for the funds, each state had to develop a plan which set forth its educational reform goals and targets.

Deputy Secretary Miller recalls, "The program invited and challenged states to approach education reform systematically. In the first two rounds, 46 states applied, which demonstrated the widespread interest and appetite to do things differently, and dramatically improve education."

Each state was required to develop a reform plan which includes activities in the following areas:
- Adopting standards and assessments that prepare students to succeed in college and the workplace and to compete in the global economy
- Building data systems that measure student growth and success, and inform teachers and principals about how they can improve instruction
- Recruiting, developing, rewarding, and retaining effective teachers and principals, especially where they are needed most
- Turning around the lowest-achieving schools

As of 2012, there have been 19 winners (two in Phase One, 10 in Phase Two, and seven in Phase Three). One innovative feature about the Race to the Top approach is that both "winners" and "non-winners" developed state plans which set forth their reform agenda. That is, through the competitions, 46 states began working on the reform agenda of the Department of Education.

---

[*]   Originally published on the AOL Government website, April 23, 2012.

"Many of these states—not just the winners—are pursuing at least pieces of their reform plans," Miller reports. So the Department's objective of educational reform is being achieved in both the states that received funding and those states that did not receive federal funds.

Secretary Duncan emphasizes this aspect of the program: "Each of the states (that applied) now has in place—win or lose—a blueprint of how they would like to move forward, statewide, on education reform."

A second innovative feature of the Race to the Top program is its emphasis on outcomes.

"Race to the Top continues the movement toward performance-based measures," says Timothy J. Conlan, Professor of Government and Politics at George Mason University. "In the past, grant requirements have focused on procedures and outputs. Race to the Top focuses on outcomes, not outputs."

The Race to the Top "competition" model is now being replicated. In 2011, nine states (from the 35 states that prepared plans) received Race to the Top-Early Learning Challenge awards to build statewide systems of high-quality early learning and development programs for low-income children from birth to age five (the Challenge is jointly administered by the Department of Education and the Department of Health and Human Services).

In 2012, the next five highest ranked states from the 2011 competition were invited to reapply to receive funding for early learning programs. In describing the model, Deputy Secretary Miller says, "Race to the Top is a good example of how our Department is working to transform from a bureaucratic agency to an engine of innovation, partnering with states to support their leaders in working together to produce real change that puts students first."

The 2013 Education budget contains plans to use the Race to the Top competition model to tackle the issue of college costs and quality by encouraging shared responsibility among states, families, and the federal government. Under the plan, the Education Department would invest $1 billion for a new Race to the Top focusing on college affordability and completion.

The goal of the new program is to drive reform, provide incentives to keep costs under control, and increase the number of work-study jobs. Plans are also underway to launch Race to the Top competitions at the school district level (in contrast to the previous state-level competitions). Other government Departments, including the Department of Transportation, are also considering using the Race to the Top approach for their programs.

In looking back on the success of the program, Deputy Secretary Miller reflects, "Race to the Top—a competitive program whose funding is less than half a percent of total K–12 spending—has done more to advance systemic education reform than any other program in the Department's history."

In addition, Race to the Top exemplifies a new approach to the way government does business. Historically, many grants programs have been allocated by formula across all 50 states. In contrast, Race to the Top created a competition in which the states with the highest ranked plans (based on a very detailed scoring process) received funding. Most importantly, states were required to state explicitly their goals and targeted outcomes.

Thomas R. Nides
Deputy Secretary for Management and Resources
Department of State

The Beginning

"I spent 10 years in the private sector before returning to government service at the State Department," says Tom Nides. "My return to government has exceeded my expectations, in part because of the people I am surrounded by every day. The State Department attracts an incredible cadre of people. I would put them up against people I've worked with in the private sector any day."

The Organization

The United States Department of State is the oldest federal agency, established in 1781 as the Department of Foreign Affairs. With over 270 missions in 190 countries, the Department of State is central to promoting America's economic prosperity and advancing our national security interests around the world.

The Department has two Deputy Secretaries who serve as principal advisers to the Secretary of State, assist the Secretary in the formulation and conduct of U.S. foreign policy, and provide general supervision and direction to all elements of the Department. The Deputy Secretary of State for Management and Resources serves as the Chief Operating Officer of the Department, overseeing the allocation of the Department's budget of over $50 billion.

Below the Deputy Secretaries, the Department is organized around six Under Secretaries:

- Under Secretary for Political Affairs
- Under Secretary for Management
- Under Secretary for Economic Growth, Energy, and the Environment
- Under Secretary for Civilian Security, Democracy, and Human Rights
- Under Secretary for Public Diplomacy and Public Affairs
- Under Secretary for Arms Control and International Security Affairs

The Challenge

Mr. Nides is the second person to serve as Deputy Secretary of State for Management and Resources. In addition to the challenges inherent in the conduct

Thomas R. Nides

Tenure: Mr. Nides was nominated by President Obama to serve as Deputy Secretary of State for Management and Resources in September 2010, and was confirmed by the U.S. Senate in December 2010.

Private sector experience: Prior to being confirmed as Deputy Secretary, Mr. Nides was Chief Operating Officer of Morgan Stanley, where he also served on the Management Committee and Operating Committee. He has served as Worldwide President and Chief Executive Officer of Burson-Marsteller and as Chief Administrative Officer for Credit Suisse First Boston.

Federal government experience: From 1986 to 1993, Mr. Nides served as an Assistant to the Majority Whip in the U.S. House of Representatives and Chief of Staff to the Speaker of the House. He also served as Chief of Staff to the United States Trade Representative.

Education: Mr. Nides received a Bachelor of Individual Studies from the University of Minnesota.

of U.S. foreign policy in an ever-changing world, Nides faced the challenge of further defining a newly formed and not well-understood role. Nides arrived in January 2011, after his predecessor, Jack Lew, moved to the White House. "I learned a lot from Jack Lew and he helped smooth the transition. But because this is still a new position, the role continues to require definition," says Nides. A strong working relationship with Deputy Secretary Bill Burns helped Nides define the position's roles and responsibilities. "I work very closely with Bill Burns. He understands the value and importance of this position for the Secretary and the Administration. He and I have a divide-and-conquer strategy in support of Secretary Clinton. We work closely together on managing the Department, as well as engaging other agencies and the White House. We work especially closely with the National Security Council and its director, Tom Donilon."

Secretary Clinton asked Nides to lead in five key areas:
- The Department's budget
- Economic statecraft
- The Quadrennial Diplomacy and Development Review
- The Iraq transition
- Afghanistan and Pakistan relations

Laying out clear goals within his areas of responsibility was important for Nides. He says, "I've learned you have to set goals. If you can't track it, no real progress can be made. My team keeps me informed as to what decisions I need to make and ensures that the President's and Secretary's priorities are reflected in the day-to-day work of the Department and our embassies and consulates abroad."

Responding to the Challenge

In describing his role, Nides says, "As Deputy Secretary of State, I could be focused on many issues and in many places. But few things are as important to me as fighting for the resources that our diplomats and development experts need to enhance our national security and economic security. Few things are more important than making the case for security, economic, and humanitarian assistance. And few things are more important than making sure that Washington appropriates funding in a rational way." (Department of State, 2011).

In managing the budget process for the Department, Nides says, "We work very closely with the Hill. We work closely with groups concerned about and interested in foreign assistance. We have to clearly communicate to the American public that the entire budget for the State Department and the U.S. Agency for International Development is a small fraction of the federal budget—less than one percent of the federal budget, not the 20 to 30 percent that most Americans believe is devoted to foreign assistance."

In a speech, Nides noted the challenge of working simultaneously to spend FY2011 funds, debate FY2012 funding, explain the just-released budget request for FY2013, and begin planning the budget for FY2014. "Managing these pipelines simultaneously is complicated," said Nides. "Unfortunately, it's the reality in which we live." (Clark).

Another major component of Nides' job is to advise the Secretary of State on economic policy. In this Administration, Secretary Clinton has put "economic statecraft" at the forefront of foreign policy. Economic statecraft is "how we harness the forces and use the tools of global economics to strengthen our diplomacy and presence abroad; and how we put that diplomacy and presence to work to strengthen our economy at home." Nides has championed this agenda during his two years on the job. Nides has said, "One reason I was so eager to work for Secretary Clinton is that I believe our foreign policy needs to be more engaged where business and diplomacy intersect."

Nides also has responsibility for leading the transition in Iraq from military-led to civilian-led operations. The transition was completed in December 2011. At the time, Nides said, "This is the largest military-to-civilian transition initiative since the Marshall Plan." Since then, Nides has led the Department's efforts to right-size its mission in Iraq, using a core set of principles to ensure that the United States has fulfilled its end of the Strategic Framework Agreement (the cornerstone

**Mission
U.S. Department of State**

Shape and sustain a peaceful, prosperous, just, and democratic world and foster conditions for stability and progress for the benefit of the American people and people everywhere.

of the U.S. and Iraq bilateral relationship), that both Iraqis and Americans expect effective programs that are mutually beneficial, and that the diplomatic presence should look like other U.S. missions across the globe. Nides said, "We'll continue to look … to make sure that our footprint is appropriate… we are going to look to ways to shift more of the cost structure locally… and continue evaluating (it) as this mission set is (…) being accomplished." (Department of State, 2012a)

Reflecting on Serving in the Department of State

"You can intellectually understand the job, but until you get here you don't understand the complexity of everything," reflects Nides. "In the business world, you have unexpected events, like the 2007–2008 economic crisis. In this job—just as the saying goes about change—crisis is the only constant." In a briefing on the FY 2013 budget, Nides said, "Since I presented last year's budget, there hasn't been a day when we weren't managing multiple crises at once."

As for other insights gathered during his time as Deputy Secretary, Nides says: "You have to be patient in government. You have to bring people along. You can't 'roll' them into doing things. You need to keep pushing your agenda and be disciplined in decision-making. It is a real intellectual challenge."

Daniel B. Poneman
Deputy Secretary
Department of Energy

The Beginning

"In many ways, this was a homecoming for me," says Daniel Poneman. "I had been here in 1989 when I was a White House Fellow. "

"My prior time in the Department helped me to understand how the Department operates. When you are young and working in the trenches, you can see what works well and what doesn't work well. My six years working at the National Security Council in the White House helped as well. You get a different view of the Cabinet from the White House. You can see the critical role the Cabinet agencies play in implementing the national agenda."

The Organization

The origins of the Department of Energy can be traced to the Manhattan Project and the race to develop the atomic bomb during World War II. In the 1970s, the Atomic Energy Commission—the Department of Energy's predecessor—was split into two separate agencies: the Nuclear Regulatory Commission, to regulate the nuclear power industry; and the Energy Research and Development Administration (ERDA), to manage the country's nuclear weapons arsenal and energy development programs and to pursue technology research and development.

In 1977, Congress created the Department of Energy by combining agencies including ERDA, the Federal Energy Administration, and the Atomic Energy Commission. Today, the Department has a budget of over $25 billion, approximately 15,000 employees, and more than 100,000 contractors. In describing the Department, Poneman says, "The Department is organized around three major program areas—energy, science, and nuclear security. In addition, we have launched the Advanced Research Projects Agency-Energy, or ARPA-E. Other important Department elements include the Energy Information Administration and Power Marketing Administrations."

The Challenge

Energy Secretary Steven Chu and Deputy Secretary Poneman faced serious challenges when they took office. One involved ensuring that the U.S. nuclear

Daniel B. Poneman

Tenure: Mr. Poneman was nominated by President Obama to be Deputy Secretary of Energy in April 2009, and confirmed by the U.S. Senate in May 2009.

Private sector experience: Prior to being confirmed as Deputy Secretary, Mr. Poneman served as a Principal of The Scowcroft Group, providing strategic advice to corporations on a wide variety of international projects and transactions. He practiced law for nine years in Washington, D.C., first as an Associate at Covington & Burling, later as a Partner at Hogan & Hartson.

Federal government experience: Mr. Poneman served as a White House Fellow in the Department of Energy in 1989. After serving as a White House Fellow, he joined the National Security Council staff as Director of Defense Policy and Arms Control. From 1993 to 1996, he worked as Special Assistant to the President and Senior Director for Nonproliferation and Export Controls at the National Security Council.

Education: Mr. Poneman received A.B. and J.D. degrees with honors from Harvard University and an M.Litt. in Politics from Oxford University.

deterrent remained safe, secure, and effective, while reducing nuclear proliferation threats and cleaning up the environmental legacy of weapons materials produced during the Cold War. In addition to these challenges, Chu and Poneman were tasked by the new Administration to implement an ambitious energy agenda. Poneman recalls, "When I got here, the Secretary had developed three areas on which he wanted us to focus: driving the nation's transformation to a clean energy economy, including more jobs and increased productivity; enhancing nuclear security; and promoting scientific and technological leadership, which helps drive innovation and competitiveness."

Responding to the Challenge

A major activity during Poneman's first year was reaching out and engaging the Department's employees. "The Department is all about its people. It's a great organization which depends on a good esprit de corps. The people I work with are glad to be here. They have engaging work. Our employees are working on the major issues facing the nation—climate, energy, and national security. These are

Mission, Goals, and Management Principles
Department of Energy

Mission

The mission of the Department of Energy is to ensure America's security and prosperity by addressing its energy, environmental, and nuclear challenges through transformative science and technology solutions.

Goals

- **Transform our Energy Systems**—Catalyze the timely, material, and efficient transformation of the nation's energy system and secure U.S. leadership in clean energy technologies.
- **The Science and Engineering Enterprise**—Maintain a vibrant U.S. effort in science and engineering as a cornerstone of our economic prosperity, with clear leadership in strategic areas.
- **Secure Our Nation**—Enhance nuclear security through defense, nonproliferation, and environmental efforts.
- **Management and Operational Excellence**—Establish an operational and adaptable framework that combines the best wisdom of all Department stakeholders to maximize mission success.

Management Principles

- Our mission is vital and urgent.
- Science and technology lie at the heart of our mission.
- We will treat our people as our greatest asset.
- We will pursue our mission in a manner that is safe, secure, legally and ethically sound, and fiscally responsible.
- We will manage risk in fulfilling our mission.
- We will apply validated standards and rigorous peer review.
- We will succeed only through teamwork and continuous improvement.

great challenges for the nation and reflect the President's and the Secretary's top priorities." Poneman concluded that the Department needed to develop a set of guiding management principles. "The purpose was to support our programmatic objectives," says Poneman. "They were all about how we will operate and manage the Department. You won't be surprised that as more people participated in developing these principles, the inclination was always to add more of them, more details and caveats. But the goal was to establish simple yet clear guidelines for how we do business at the Department that would apply equally to both our federal and our contractor employees. So we took and studied all the comments, but then boiled it all down to seven principles. The key is to incorporate them into our daily actions, so they don't become just empty rhetoric."

During his first year, Poneman also prioritized the Department's management efforts into the following areas: human capital, project management, transparency, and roles and responsibilities. Poneman says, "We wanted to emphasize management excellence, which we see as critical to achieving the Department's mission. It affects everything we do at DOE." Because of the major management challenges facing the Department, Poneman says, "I've spent more time on management issues than I thought I would. Everything is a balance, so sometimes that meant I had less time to devote to interagency meetings or policy issues. But getting management right is essential to succeeding as a Department."

One specific management initiative which consumed a great deal of Poneman's time during his tenure at Energy was project management. Poneman says, "I think we have made real, significant progress in project management. Especially within our nuclear security and environmental cleanup portfolios, we have a number of large, complex projects to manage. These projects typically involve a range of technical, cost, and schedule issues that have to be addressed as we move forward, so managing them effectively is critical." He added, "Secretary Chu and I have both been personally engaged on these issues. That senior-level focus has been important, because it makes clear to everyone throughout the Department that excellence in project management matters."

Poneman found the "deep dive" approach to project management to be very effective. The deep dives replaced the standing 90-minute quarterly meetings in which major projects were discussed briefly. "I learned a lot from Dan Lehman, the director of our Office of Project Assessment," says Poneman. "We have used a deep-dive management approach as a key tool. Instead of covering many projects in a meeting, we devote an entire meeting to one major project and discuss it for an hour and a half. When you dive deep into the details of a project, you find a lot of information that you can't get when you just look at it from the top. You have to drill down and by thinking through the answers to these tough questions as a group, we are able to develop new solutions that hadn't been thought of before. As Dan Lehman says, 'The key is to manage, manage, and manage.'"

Throughout his tenure as Deputy Secretary, Poneman has continued to devote a significant amount of time to people issues facing the Department. "I've worked on ensuring that we have a process for getting good people into the Department and then retaining them once they are hired and are here," says Poneman. Poneman told *Government Executive* that he viewed hiring as only one part of the personnel challenge. Poneman says, "[Hiring] is just the front edge. Our mission is evolving, and we need to continue to provide career paths that are exciting so we not only attract but retain talent" (Peters).

Reflecting on Serving in the Department of Energy

"I am grateful to have the opportunity to wake up every day and come to work on crucial national issues," comments Poneman. "The Department has an important agenda and a chance to make a difference for tomorrow. We are trying to transform the way the nation produces and uses energy. It's an ambitious goal, but one that I'm confident we can achieve."

Chapter Six

The Producers

Understanding the Job of the Producer

This chapter is not about the recent Broadway show *The Producers.* Instead it focuses on five political executives who run production type organizations in the federal government. These executives are driven by numbers and producing the results expected of them.

While the factory floor is not an image commonly associated with government organizations, there is an element of manufacturing in these organizations. Bill Taggart, former Chief Operating Officer, FSA, tells us, "We needed to think like a manufacturing plant. You have to get down on the floor, wander around, see folks, and engage them. During my first couple of weeks on the job, I visited FSA regional offices. I was the first COO that many of the regional office staff had ever seen. Headquarters had become isolated from the field."

Key Role: Process Improvement

While the image of the factory floor offered by Bill Taggart conjures up memories of Frederic Winslow Taylor and scientific management, the comparison is very apt for a select number of government organizations. Factory managers, like the producers in government, worry about inputs, accuracy and errors, cycle time, and outputs. Managers of factories aim to achieve routine and constant flow,

---

The Producers

Allison A. Hickey, page 104

Under Secretary for Benefits, Veterans Benefits Administration Department of Veterans Affairs

David J. Kappos, page 110

Under Secretary of Commerce for Intellectual Property and Director, United States Patent and Trademark Office (USPTO), Department of Commerce

John S. Pistole, page 116

Administrator, Transportation Security Administration, Department of Homeland Security

David H. Stevens, page 121

Assistant Secretary for Housing and Commissioner, Federal Housing Administration (FHA), Department of Housing and Urban Development

William J. Taggart, page 125

Chief Operating Officer, Office of Federal Student Aid (FSA), Department of Education

---

and they pride themselves on reducing variation and increasing factory efficiency.

David Kappos, Director, USPTO, tells us, "We understand our inputs and outputs at USPTO." A major initiative led by Director Kappos was to examine and reengineer the number of reviews of a patent submission. "We have good numerical data on this," says Kappos. "We want to reduce the number of reviews on a submission. We want to reduce the rewriting. We are at three reviews and we have gotten it down to between 2.3 to 2.4. The goal would be 2.0. That would be a major reduction." The PTO Patent Dashboard presented on page 113 provides information on three of the 14 indicators that PTO tracks on a monthly basis.

The five individuals profiled in this chapter all had experience on the "factory floor." David Stevens spent the early part of his career as a loan officer. David Kappos spent his career working closely with USPTO and the intellectual property community to improve the patent application process. Bill Taggart's career in the banking industry served him well in working with the student loan "ecosystem," which includes the lending industry in a key role. Retired Brig. General Hickey had spent 27 years in the military and had firsthand experience with the Department of Veteran Affairs as a retired military officer. John Pistole had firsthand experience in airline safety as Assistant Special Agent in Charge, Boston. While in that position, he helped lead the investigation and recovery efforts for the Egypt Air Flight 990 crash off the coast of Rhode Island. So when it came to understanding the production tasks for their organization, all had firsthand experience on the front line and understood frontline production issues.

Selecting Producers

When politicians talk about "running government like a business," they have a point when they are discussing the government agencies which are run by people whom we have labeled the producers. These agencies benefit greatly from having an individual with business experience. All five of the producers profiled in this chapter brought significant backgrounds to their government positions. Most important, they served in leadership positions directing activities similar to those they would in government.

David Kappos spent his career in intellectual property at IBM. David Stevens, Commissioner, FHA, came from a real estate and banking background, including working at Freddie Mac. Bill Taggart came to FSA from the banking industry. Their prior private-sector careers had prepared them well for their government positions. In reflecting on his selection, David Stevens says, "I understood the business. I had lots of experience in the business. Some of the previous incumbents had not really understood the industry. I was one of the few Commissioners in this position who had practical industry experience."

Historically, many previous appointees selected to run production-type agencies came to their positions with strong policy backgrounds. Their experience in the private sector was often limited or non-existent. While there were business leaders who were selected as Cabinet Secretaries over the years, the sub-cabinet has been largely dominated by "policy types." The shift from the hiring of "policy types" to "managerial types" began to pick up momentum in Washington during the 1990s with a growing recognition that managerial experience is often exactly the type of experience needed to run many government organizations.

The shift to managerial types was clearly seen in 1997, when the Clinton Administration actively sought to recruit a business person to run the Internal Revenue Service (IRS). Historically, the head of IRS had been a tax lawyer. While the tax lawyers knew the complexity of tax laws, many did not have any prior experience managing large organizations. In describing his recruitment to serve as Commissioner of IRS, Charles Rossotti writes:

> [I]n February 1997, I found a pink phone slip with a message from an executive search firm about its assignment to find a business executive to be IRS commissioner ... Putting a businessperson in charge of the IRS seemed to me like a sensible idea ...
>
> [The executive recruiter] convinced me that it would ... be helpful for the Treasury Department to hear my insights on how to recruit a businessperson for the job.
>
> [Deputy Secretary Summers] launched into an explanation of why the Administration needed a person with strong management experience to run the IRS. It was the largest civilian operation in the federal government and needed astute management, especially of its troubled computer program, he said ...
>
> The following Sunday night, I was surprised to get a call from Treasury Secretary Robert Rubin. He got right to the point—he would like to talk to me seriously about taking the IRS job. The job was "the most important management job in the civilian government," he said, adding that my background in the information systems industry might make me the right person to fill it (Rossotti).

Rossotti ultimately agreed to accept the position and served a five-year term as IRS Commissioner from 1997 to 2002.

Since the appointment of Rossotti, the trend toward selecting individuals with management and private-sector experience as IRS Commissioner has continued. Mark Everson succeeded Rossotti in 2002 and brought extensive private-sector experience as a manager to the position, as well as his previous government experience. Everson's private-sector experience included his tenure as Group Vice President of Finance for SC International Services and his 10 years in senior financial positions with the Pechiney Group. The current Commissioner, Douglas Shulman, brings both public and private-sector experience to the position and continues the trend of non-tax lawyers selected to the position.

Working Style of Producers

There is a unique profile for the selection of political executives to run production agencies. In addition to their managerial or business experience, there is also a working style which serves producers well in these types of agencies. This working style can be characterized as:

- Hard-charging and high energy
- Disciplined and focused on delivering the outputs of the organization
- Data-oriented
- Engagement-oriented, reflected in their outreach to employees as seen in the holding of town hall meetings, visiting regional offices, and regularly communicating with employees via blogs or newsletters.

Just as there is a desired professional background and working style for the ideal producer, there are also working styles which might *not* be conducive to leading production organizations. Such working styles might include:

- A tendency to like working on and looking at only big issues
- Low to moderate interest in the nitty-gritty details of the operations of the organization
- Low to moderate interest in reaching out to meet with or communicate with frontline workers in the organization
- Preference to work primarily in their offices with personal and headquarters staff

While the above are clearly generalizations, they are presented to serve as guidelines for appointing officials as they place the right person in the right job. The concepts of a "policy person" and a "managerial person" are archetypes which can be used in sorting candidates for the right job. A "policy person" is clearly appropriate for the position of Assistant Secretary for Planning and Evaluation (ASPE) in the Department of Health and Human Services.

Based on observations over the years and research conducted for this book, a "managerial person" faces a high probability of being frustrated by the "lack of action" and "all that talking and debating" when placed in a policy job. Producers find greater satisfaction in agencies in which there are clear objectives and performance data. As Bill Taggart tells us, "There are two separate sets of skills—the implementers are not the policy folks and the policy-makers are not implementers."

Other Production Agencies

In addition to the five agencies profiled in this chapter, there are other organizations throughout government which we categorize as production agencies. While not comprehensive, the list and descriptions of each agency have been prepared to assist the Office of Presidential Personnel and Cabinet Secretaries in better understanding the unique nature of the factories of government.

Other Federal Government Agencies Categorized as Production Agencies

Department of Health and Human Services
Centers for Medicare and Medicaid Services

The Centers for Medicare & Medicaid Services (CMS) was created in 1965. CMS's role is to provide the nation with an affordable health care system and informed consumers. CMS oversees the nation's three largest health care programs, serving a total of over 105 million citizens:

- Medicare
- Medicaid
- CHIP (Children's Health Insurance Program)

Medicare provides financial assistance to over 50 million elderly and disabled individuals needing health care while Medicaid provides health care funds for 57 million low-income, aged, blind, and disabled citizens. CHIP provides assistance for over 7 million children from low-income families that don't qualify for Medicaid.

CMS has a workforce of over 5,000 employees. In 2009, the Medicare hotline received nearly 26 million calls, and its website had nearly 410 million views.

Department of Homeland Security
U.S. Citizenship and Immigration Services

The U.S. Citizenship and Immigration Services (USCIS) is responsible for overseeing all of the country's legal immigration. The agency issues green cards, grants citizenship, and is involved in processes like overseas adoption and humanitarian programs for refugees.

USCIS became part of the Department of Homeland Security in 2003 when it split off from the former Bureau of Immigration and Naturalization, which had existed under different names and structures since its creation in 1891.

The USCIS has 18,000 employees working in 263 offices globally and receives approximately six million immigration applications and petitions each year as well as over 65,000 H-1B (temporary visa) petitions. USCIS runs over 5.3 million E-Verify queries annually. In 2009, USCIS naturalized 743,715 citizens, taking 5–24 months to process each one, depending on where and when the application was filed. USCIS issues approximately 620,000 green cards annually. USCIS receives over $2.5 billion annually in application fees.

Department of Transportation
Federal Aviation Administration

The Federal Aviation Administration (FAA) was created as the Federal Aviation Agency in 1958 and assumed its current name when it was integrated into the Department of Transportation in 1966. The FAA is responsible for regulating all U.S. air travel, implementing flight inspection standards, issuing pilot certificates, operating an air traffic control system, and carrying out programs to reduce damage to the environment due to aviation. FAA oversees about 50,000 flights every day, directed by 123 air traffic control towers. The FAA has over 48,000 employees.

Department of the Treasury
Bureau of Engraving & Printing

The Bureau of Engraving & Printing (BEP), founded in 1862, focuses on developing, printing, and regulating all U.S. currency notes, as well as producing portions of U.S. passports, military identification cards, naturalization documents, and White House invitations.

In 2010, nearly 2,000 employees at the three BEP facilities printed and distributed 6.4 billion currency notes to the 12 Federal Reserve Banks, and planned on producing a total of 7.6 billion currency notes in 2011. The BEP collects, destroys, and replaces mutilated currency notes. BEP is also responsible for developing new anti-counterfeiting technologies.

Internal Revenue Service

The Internal Revenue Service (IRS) was created in 1862 by President Abraham Lincoln in an effort to generate revenue to fund the Union Army during the Civil War. The IRS remains the nation's tax administration service, responsible for helping taxpayers understand and meet their tax obligations. The IRS sends out 200 million notices and letters annually.

In 2010, over 95,000 IRS employees processed 230 million tax returns, 116 million of which were filed electronically, and collected $2,345 billion in revenue. Nearly 84 percent of all taxes were filed voluntarily, correctly, and on time, and refunds are received by the taxpayer 3–8 weeks after they are filed. The IRS website had nearly 305 million visits in 2010.

U.S. Mint

The U.S. Mint was founded in 1792. Its primary mission is to produce circulating coinage for the United States. The Mint generates revenue by producing and selling proof, uncirculated, and commemorative coins and medals. The U.S. Mint distributes coins to the Federal Reserve banks, maintains physical custody of the nation's $100 billion silver and gold assets in the Fort Knox Bullion Depository, and oversees four coin production facilities in Philadelphia, Denver, San Francisco, and West Point. The Philadelphia and Denver facilities produce coins for circulation, the San Francisco facility specializes in producing proof and commemorative coins, and the West Point facility produces uncirculated bullion and commemorative coins. The Mint produced 6.4 billion circulating coins in 2010. The U.S. Mint has 1,800 employees.

Social Security Administration

The Social Security Administration (SSA) was created in 1935 when President Roosevelt signed the Social Security Act to provide financial support for retired and disabled workers, as well as their families after their death. The SSA functions as an independent federal agency with over 67,000 employees, administering monthly benefits to retired and disabled workers from a fund made up of mandatory contributions to those covered by the SSA.

In 2010, 57 million Social Security beneficiaries received a total of $740 billion in the form of monthly checks, with services distributed with 99.8 percent accuracy through a network of 1,500 offices. SSA received over 3 million disability claims in 2010 and completed 737,616 hearing requests for those whose claims were denied.

Allison A. Hickey
Under Secretary for Benefits, Veterans Benefits Administration
Department of Veterans Affairs

The Beginning

"I was obviously not a stranger [to] government," recalls Allison Hickey. "I knew the government, its culture, and rules. I had spent 27 years in the military and 17 years in the Pentagon. Part of my first day felt very normal, but there were differences. I came in without knowing anybody—not a single soul. This is different from the military where you know a lot of people."

"I had to learn a new set of languages and meet new people. I had a staff meeting quickly, so people could size me up. I was the brand-new person. I wanted them to know who I was. I wanted them to see me."

One of the first questions posed by Hickey to her new colleagues was whether the Veterans Benefits Administration (VBA) had a strategic plan. While the Department of Veterans Affairs had a department-wide plan, Hickey was surprised to find that there was no VBA strategic plan. After reviewing the VA strategic plan, Hickey set out to create a 45-day plan which had been requested by Senator Patty Murray during her confirmation hearings. Hickey recounts, "This became our transformation plan. We needed to change and better align ourselves to our business."

While Hickey was new to the civilian side of government, she was not new to transformation challenges. She had been involved in Air Force strategic planning during the 1990s and then was chosen to implement the strategic plan and lead the Air Force transformation in the mid-2000s. Based on that experience, Hickey says, "I thought I fit the VBA position description pretty well. They wanted somebody to lead a major historical transformation initiative. I had heard Secretary Eric Shinseki describe this challenge at a conference and immediately felt called to serve this vital mission. I must admit, this is a journey of faith for me. I view this job as a calling."

Her early days consisted of visits to employees in VBA regional offices. "I wanted to learn the VBA business and understand the process. I wanted to see what they were doing and experience firsthand our claims processes and challenges. I did this for all lines of business. I wanted to understand our businesses."

The Organization

The Veterans Benefits Administration (VBA) is one of the three major components of the Department of Veterans Affairs: the Veterans Health Administration,

Allison A. Hickey

Tenure: Retired Brig. General Hickey was nominated by President Obama to serve as Under Secretary for Benefits of the Department of Veterans Affairs in January 2011, and confirmed by the U.S. Senate in May 2011.

Private sector experience: Prior to being confirmed as Under Secretary, Brig. General Hickey served as a leader of Human Capital Management at Accenture.

Federal government experience: Brig. General Hickey served for 27 years in the U.S. Air Force, having served on active duty in the Active Air Force, Air National Guard, and Air Force Reserve. Her positions in the Air Force included  serving as Director of the Air Force's Future Total Force Integration office at the Pentagon where she handled strategic planning, mission development, and resource implementation for more than 140 new Air Force units. Prior to holding that position, she served as Assistant Deputy Director of Strategic Planning for the Air Force and Chief of the Air Force Future Concepts and Transformation Division. As a pilot and aircraft commander, she accumulated more than 1,500 hours of flight time in KC-10A, KC-135A, T-38, and T-37 aircraft.

Education: Brig. General Hickey graduated from the U.S. Air Force Academy in 1980.

the National Cemetery Administration, and VBA. VBA provided compensation and pension benefits to an estimated 4.3 million veterans and survivors in FY 2012, 10% of whom were 100-percent disabled. With a workforce of over 20,000 civil servants, VBA manages the following benefit programs:

- The Compensation and Pension Service is responsible for disability compensation and pension claims.
- The Education Service administers a wide variety of education programs, including the Post-9/11 GI Bill for more than one million students.
- The Insurance Service provides the full range of national life insurance programs, including Servicemembers Group Life Insurance (SGLI), Veterans' Group Life Insurance (VGLI), and Servicemembers' Group Life Insurance Traumatic Injury Protection (TSGLI).
- The Loan Guaranty Service is responsible for housing loans and related activities.

- The Vocational Rehabilitation and Employment Service provides counseling, training, and related activities to service-connected disabled veterans.
- Transition services are provided for departing service members.

The Challenge

There was no shortage of challenges upon taking over as Under Secretary. "I starting asking questions," recalls Hickey, "and I identified the following major challenges:
- No integrated plan,
- No metrics for success,
- No common message, and
- Hardworking employees with their chins down."

Hickey started by looking at VBA's claims and benefit process. She was quick to conclude, "We needed to change our processes. I knew about process improvements." Hickey also knew about technology. "I was surprised," says Hickey, "by how far behind we were on using technology. We were still very paper-bound, touching over one billion pieces of paper manually in a year. That is equal to 200 Empire State Buildings stacked end to end. The Veterans Health Administration was ahead of us, having turned their paper medical records into a paperless environment a decade ago. We have all these paper files in VBA. I decided to take this on. We needed to reduce the paperwork."

A key component of making change at VBA, concluded Hickey, was its employees. "I found diligent people who were working hard. They needed help. The staff at VBA was eager to change and I found a willingness to change. The agency had a bad reputation on the street, but that is not what I saw when I went out. I wanted to get our chins up. Our employees had been down. This was helped by developing our 45-day plan which began to tell our story."

Like the other producers profiled in this chapter, Hickey faced an inventory and a backlog. On top of the existing inventory and backlog of regular claims, there were new Agent Orange claims to settle which required reallocating staff from processing other claims to complete the Agent Orange backlog. Over the last two years, VA received 260,000 claims from three new Agent Orange conditions which required a surge of over 37 percent of VBA's workforce to work on adjudicating these claims.

The Veterans Benefits Administration has completed over one million claims each of the last two years, reflecting an unprecedented growth in claims. In the summer of 2012, VBA had 870,000 claims in its inventory. The claims backlog is defined as those claims that have been pending longer than the goal of 125 days. Approximately 558,000 claims were in backlog in summer 2012. VBA's backlog reduction goal is 60 percent in contrast to the current 66 percent in backlog.

Responding to the Challenge

Hickey found that in responding to one challenge, another became even more perplexing. "We are doing very well on increasing access," reports Hickey. "But it is a double-edged sword. We have done such a good job on access, we are now getting a historical demand for services never seen before. It was easy to open up access, now we have to work through this new demand."

Veterans today are filing more claims than their counterparts did in the past. Hickey reports, "This has resulted in an increase in complexity and workload. We are hitting a pressure point. Demand is growing through the roof. There is also an ongoing exodus of service members which will drive up demand and claims. Historically, veteran file rates have been 20 percent. We are now at 45 percent and we expect it to go up to as much as 90 percent as a result of the new mandatory Transition Assistance Program."

It was clear to Hickey that the agency needed to dramatically change the way it was doing business. Hickey found it very helpful to use the "People, Process, and Technology" framework in leading the VBA transformation initiative.

People. VBA has created "express lanes" for certain claims. "We are able to push these less complicated claims through at a faster pace," describes Hickey. "If we can do this, there will be less work on the front end. We can get less complicated claims through which will then allow us to spend more time on tougher, more complicated claims. We are trying to manage our throughputs." These segmented lanes increase claims processing speed through handling of similar claims, placing a veteran's claim in one of three lanes: Express (30 percent), Core (60 percent), or Special Operations (10 percent) based on specific criteria. Another step was providing additional training to VBA employees through the Challenge Training Program, which both increased quality and reduced errors at an earlier point in the process.

Additional people transformation initiatives include quality review teams, intake processing centers, and cross-functional teams.

Process. One key process improvement was releasing a simplified notification letter, which has enabled VBA to increase productivity by 15 percent and resulted in a 14-day reduction in average processing time. The simplified letters consolidated the previous two separate documents into one clear and concise letter containing the VBA decision and the reasons for the decision. Hickey notes that with one million claims annually, a 15 percent improvement is significant.

Additional process transformation initiatives include rater decision support tools, fully developed claims, and disability benefits questionnaires.

Technology. In the area of technology, the creation of the e-Benefits portal was a major step. Hickey says, "Right now, we are in the season of technology. All the parts are coming together now. We are happy with our e-Benefits website which has helped us increase access. We now have nearly two million users and there is increasing utilization by veterans. We are now preparing veterans to come

Mission, Vision, Core Values, and Core Characteristics
Department of Veterans Affairs

Mission
To fulfill President Lincoln's promise "To care for him who shall have borne the battle, and for his widow, and his orphan" by serving and honoring the men and women who are America's veterans.

Vision
To provide veterans the world-class benefits and services they have earned—and to do so by adhering to the highest standards of compassion, commitment, excellence, professionalism, integrity, accountability, and stewardship.

Core Values	Core Characteristics
• Integrity	• Trustworthy
• Commitment	• Accessible
• Advocacy	• Quality
• Respect	• Innovative
• Excellence	• Agile
	• Integrated

into the system differently than they have in the past. In very short order, veterans will file their claims online through e-Benefits like they do their taxes at IRS."

The movement to electronic records has been a challenge. The original deadline of July 2012 was not met. "Instead," says Hickey, "we are now working on 'fix and deploy.' We are focusing on fixing and have spent time on that this summer. We have the system released, but not deployed. We will have 16 offices that will be using the system by the end of the year. We wanted to do this right. In the mid-1990s, VBA deployed a system too early and we didn't want to do that again."

In addition, the Stakeholder Enterprise Portal for VSOs and Physicians now facilitates stakeholder roles in a secure environment with identity access tools to submit and track claims and evidence online.

Reflecting on the Relationship between the Department of Veterans Affairs and the Department of Defense

"We still have to work on the DoD-VA handoff," asserts Hickey. "There is a cultural transformation starting at DoD and there is great interest there in improving the handoff. Historically, DoD has viewed the new veteran as somebody else's problem. DoD lets go and then VA takes on. I didn't realize how quick the drop was after folks leave the military. There are still too many cases where VA doesn't own the case yet. All the key information we need to do our job comes from DoD. But we are getting there and Secretary Shinseki and Secretary Panetta are committed to improving the handoff."

David J. Kappos
Under Secretary of Commerce for Intellectual Property and Director, United States Patent and Trademark Office Department of Commerce

The Beginning

The process of confirmation and transition into government is both exciting and challenging. David Kappos found that out. "The whole confirmation process places heavy demands on political appointees," recalls Kappos. "I was confirmed at 11:00 a.m. on a Friday and I was supposed to start work on the following Monday. I had to leave my family on short notice. There was no time to plan on where to stay. But I managed to get to D.C., find a hotel, and start on that Tuesday."

"At 11 a.m. on Tuesday, I conducted my first staff meeting," says Kappos. "Everybody was a bit nervous about the new guy on board. I knew the issues facing the USPTO, so I wanted to get off to a fast start. I know you only have a certain period of time in these jobs so I didn't want to waste a single day. I wanted to get a running start and hit the ground running, but I didn't want to jump out of the chopper shooting."

The Organization

Like several of the organizations described in this book, the responsibilities of the United States Patent and Trademark Office (USPTO) are set forth in the Constitution of the United States. Article I states that the federal government will "promote the progress of science and useful arts, by securing for limited times to authors and inventors the exclusive rights to their respective writing and discoveries." The USPTO organization was created by an act of Congress in 1952 and placed in the Department of Commerce. The Patent Office within the USPTO (headed by the Commissioner for Patents) reviews newly filed applications, publishes pending applications, and issues patents to successful applicants. The Trademark Office (headed by the Commissioner for Trademarks) examines and approves applications for trademark registration.

Over the years, there have been key legislative modifications related to the operations of the USPTO. In 1991, the USPTO became fully supported by user fees to fund its operations as a result of the Omnibus Budget Reconciliation Act of 1990. In 1999, the American Inventors Protection Act designated USPTO as a Performance-Based Organization (PBO), much like the Office of Federal Student Aid. In the case of USPTO, the policy making role on intellectual property (the

David J. Kappos

Tenure: Mr. Kappos was nominated by President Obama to serve as Under Secretary of Commerce for Intellectual Property and Director of the United States Patent and Trademark Office in June 2009, and confirmed by the U.S. Senate in August 2009.

Private sector experience: Prior to being confirmed, Mr. Kappos was Vice President and Assistant General Counsel for Intellectual Property Law at IBM. During his career at IBM, he served in a variety of positions as an intellectual property law attorney and as Assistant General Counsel for IBM Asia Pacific. In addition to his position at IBM, he served on the Board of Directors of the American Intellectual Property Law Association, the Intellectual Property Owners Association, and the International Intellectual Property Society.

Education: Mr. Kappos received his B.S. degree in Electrical and Computer Engineering from the University of California, Davis in 1983, and his law degree from the University of California, Berkeley in 1990.

Under Secretary of Commerce for Intellectual Property) and the operational role (the Director of USPTO) have been held by the same individual. The PBO designation granted the USPTO certain managerial flexibilities.

The Challenge

There was no shortage of items on the Kappos agenda when he arrived. "I was well aware of several key issues based on my prior experience and impressions of the agency. I had been working on intellectual property issues my whole career, so I came into the job with a sense that I knew the agency and the challenges it was facing," says Kappos, "And, of course, I had a lot to learn about its inner workings as well." In addition to intellectual property issues, there were also a host of issues facing USPTO as an organization. "I knew we had to improve the application process and workload issues, including the backlog problem," says Kappos. "I also knew we had to improve the IT infrastructure, as well as improve the agency's workforce and work processes. The agency manual for its patent attorneys had not been updated for the 21st century."

Responding to the Challenge

As described earlier, a major activity of the USPTO is to review newly filed patents and move the application patent from receipt to final disposition—either issuing a patent or declining the patent. A key indicator of USPTO is the number of patent applications awaiting the "First Office Action." As Director of USPTO, Kappos has led the effort to reduce the backlog and speed up the review process. The task is made even more challenging by the continued increase in number of patent applications, now over 500,000 annually.

"The USPTO has a critical role to play in our economic recovery," says Kappos. "And that's why people really care about the backlog, which hinders innovation and economic growth. In response, we set specific targets. Our goal is to get the backlog under 700,000. We haven't been under that figure for many years. The goal is to get it down to a backlog of 325,000. That would be about 70 dockets per examiner, which is about right. We have a production inventory system. We are aiming to reach the 325,000 goal by 2015. We couldn't just give people the goal of 325,000 for 2015. That goal was too far away. So we set 699,000 for FY 2011. Getting under 700,000 would be a major accomplishment."

In response to these myriad challenges, Kappos launched an aggressive campaign on many fronts. As described by Kappos, "The job of leadership is to work on all the challenges. You need to do it all. There is no one single thing that you have to do; you have to do a hundred things. Change is the sum of a lot of little things. I don't believe there is a magic bullet or a single fix. I believe it is about making day-by-day changes and continuously working toward improvement. I believe philosophically that you are never done. Change goes on forever."

In addition to the usual challenges of budget uncertainty and budget reductions that faced all the political executives profiled in this book, Kappos and the USPTO faced a unique set of budget challenges. With the 1990 legislative changes, USPTO became a 100-percent fee-funded operation. Under the existing funding system, however, USPTO only has access to the portion of its collections provided in the annual appropriations bills. Thus, when actual fee collections exceed the level of spending authorized by Congress, the additional funds collected by USPTO remain unavailable for spending. Legislative changes were sought to replace the current funding system. Changes in the funding system, according to Kappos, would reduce the patent backlog and enable the completion of a high-quality patent examination in a shorter amount of time.

Patent reform legislation, the Leahy-Smith America Invents Act (AIA), was passed by Congress in September 2011 and represented the first major reform to the patent system since 1952. The new legislation, however, did not include the creation of a public enterprise revolving fund which would have ensured that all fees collected by USPTO supported processing efforts of the agency without fiscal year limitations. That change had been included in the Senate passed legislation.

Kappos faced another set of challenges when the FY 11 budget was enacted

Figure 6.1: USPTO Patent Dashboard* Selected Indicators

Unexamined Patent Application Backlog

August 2012

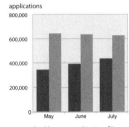

Backlog vs. application filings

● Applications filings   ● Application backlog

The unexamined patent application backlog is the number of new utility, plant, and reissue (UPR) patent applications in the pipeline at any given time which are awaiting a First Office Action by the patent examiner. Continuation, continuation-in-part, and divisional applications are included in the total.

First Office Action Pendency (months)

August 2012

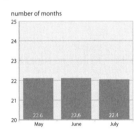

Last three months, FY 2012

First Office Action pendency is the average number of months from the patent application filing date to the date a First Office Action is mailed by the USPTO. Our goal is to reduce first action pendency to an average of 10 months by 2015. The term "pendency" refers to the fact that the application is pending or awaiting a decision.

Traditional Total Pendency (months)

August 2012

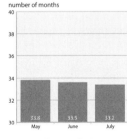

Last three months, FY 2012

This is the measure of total pendency, as traditionally measured. Historically, pendency has been measured as the average number of months from the patent application filing date to the date the application has reached final disposition (e.g., issued as a patent or abandoned) which is called a "disposal". Our goal is to reduce Traditional Total Pendency to an average of 20 months by 2015. This pendency includes the time periods awaiting action by the USPTO, as well as any time awaiting reply from an applicant.

* From USPTO website, http://www.uspto.gov/dashboards/patents/main.dashxml

United States Patent and Trademark Office
An Agency of the Department of Commerce

Vision and Mission
United States Patent and Trademark Office

Vision
Leading the World in Intellectual Property Protection and Policy

Mission
To foster innovation and competitiveness by:
- Providing high quality and timely examination of patent and trademark applications, guiding domestic and international intellectual property policy, and delivering intellectual property information and education worldwide.

in April 2011, limiting USPTO total spending to $2.09 billion. Thus, USPTO could not spend money which it had already taken in. Based on the reduced level of authorized spending, USPTO made a series of significant reductions for the remainder of FY 11 (ending in September 2011) which required:
- Delays in the start of the Three-Track program which would have expedited patent examinations
- Postponement of the opening of a satellite office in Detroit
- Freezing of hiring—both new positions and backfills
- Scaling back IT projects
- Suspension of overtime
- Reduction in employee training

Based on his experience, Kappos says, "I've learned that your success depends on resources. If you don't have the resources, you can't do what you need to do. This is very clear to me."

The backlog continued to rise in April 2011 to over 706,000, but then went down in May 2011 to just over 703,000. In June 2011, the number of patents pending fell below 700,000 for the first time—to 695,086. In the following 14 months (through August 2012), the number continued below 700,000. In August 2012, the number fell to its all time low—623,168.

Reflecting on Running PTO

"It's been an enjoyable experience," says Kappos. "But the final results are not yet in. We have made progress and are still working on many items on our agenda. If I leave and haven't achieved our goals, then I would have failed. Fulfillment in this job is all about accomplishing our mission and improving our organization."

John S. Pistole
Administrator, Transportation Security Administration
Department of Homeland Security

The Beginning

"I was impressed with the quality of the people here," recalls John Pistole, "especially the senior staff. We had a top-notch Deputy who had been Acting Administrator for 18 months. The agency was only eight years old at that point. The staff had a combination of different experiences and disciplines which impressed me."

"My second observation was the enormity of the task. Our job is to get people from point to point safely, with a 100-percent customer satisfaction as well. We literally have hands-on contact with the American public."

"Secretary Napolitano asked me to come and do this. There was great work being done here. I thought I could make a difference."

The Organization

The Transportation Security Administration (TSA) was created by legislation in November 2001 in the aftermath of the 9/11 attacks. The agency began operations in 2002. In 2003, TSA was moved from the Department of Transportation to the Department of Homeland Security (DHS) after the creation of DHS. TSA is responsible for:
- Security screening of passengers and baggage at over 450 airports
- Vetting more than 14 million passenger reservations and over 13 million transportation workers against the terrorist watch list each week
- Conducting security regulation compliance inspections and enforcement activities at airports and for cargo screening operations

Today, TSA has over 51,000 employees and a budget of over $8 billion. Included among its employees are:
- Over 45,000 transportation security officers (TSOs) who screen more than 1.8 million passengers each day
- Nearly 3,000 behavior detection officers at airports across the nation
- Thousands of federal air marshals who are deployed daily on domestic and international flights

John S. Pistole

Tenure: Mr. Pistole was nominated by President Obama as Administrator of the Transportation Security Administration in May 2010, and confirmed by the U.S. Senate in June 2010.

Federal government experience: Prior to being confirmed as Administrator, Mr. Pistole served for 26 years with the FBI. Mr. Pistole served as Deputy Director of the FBI from 2004 to 2010, and was heavily involved in the formation of terrorism policies. He also served as Deputy Director of the FBI and Executive Assistant Director for Counterterrorism and Counterintelligence. He was the second longest-serving Deputy Director of the FBI. Pistole be-

Photo: Brigitte Dittberner

gan his career as a Special Agent in 1983, serving in the Minneapolis and New York divisions before serving as Supervisor in the Organized Crime Section at FBI headquarters in Washington, D.C. During his career, he led or was involved in several high-profile investigations, including the Christmas Day 2009 attempted attack on Northwest Flight 253 and the 2010 Times Square bombing attempt.

Education: Mr. Pistole received his undergraduate degree from Anderson University in Indiana and his law degree from the Indiana University School of Law-Indianapolis.

The Challenge

As noted by Pistole, TSA has daily hands-on contact with the American public. Thus, it is one of the most visible federal agencies. There is no shortage of high-visibility incidents to occur between transportation security officers and citizens. Pistole says, "We are involved in incidents which get media attention. Often, the initial reports in the press may not be exactly what happened."

In addition to public security, the agency has continued to receive intense scrutiny from Congress and has become one of the most highly controversial government agencies. There continue to be frequent calls for the privatization of TSA and the hiring of private transportation security officers.

Responding to the Challenge

Like the other producers in this chapter, Pistole quickly came to the conclusion

Transportation Security Administration

Mission, Vision and Core Values
Transportation Security Administration

Mission
The Transportation Security Administration protects the Nation's transportation systems to ensure freedom of movement for people and commerce.

Vision
As a high performing counterterrorism organization, the Transportation Security Administration will provide the most effective security in the most efficient way.

Core Values
To enhance mission performance and achieve our shared goals, we are committed to promoting a culture founded on these values:

Integrity:
- We are a people of integrity who respect and care for others and protect the information we handle.
- We are a people who conduct ourselves in an honest, trustworthy and ethical manner at all times.
- We are a people who gain strength from the diversity in our cultures.

Innovation:
- We are a people who embrace and stand ready for change.
- We are a people who are courageous and willing to take on new challenges.
- We are a people with an enterprising spirit, striving for innovations who accept the risk-taking that comes with it.

Team Spirit:
- We are a people who are open, respectful and dedicated to making others better.
- We are a people who have a passion for challenge, success and being on a winning team.
- We are a people who will build teams around our strengths.

that his agency needed to change the way it was operating. "We had been using a one-size-fits-all approach," says Pistole. "But I knew it didn't have to be this way. As an FBI agent, I would get on a plane with special treatment. So I knew we were already treating people differently. I knew that there were many possibilities of doing things differently."

As TSA approached its 10th anniversary as an organization, Pistole engaged in a reexamination of the agency. Pistole says that the agency had an enormous mission in its early years and had not yet had time to step back and review everything it does. "I believe we are not about avoidance," states Pistole, "but instead about risk management … We need to focus on the unknown. We have to be sure that we spend our resources on the right things. We want to expand the TSA Pre✓™, which we are now testing at 15 airports." By the end of 2012, TSA Pre✓™ will be in 35 airports.

In describing TSA Pre✓™, Pistole says that it is dedicated lanes for individuals who have already been vetted. Pistole recalls, "We needed to change our mindset. In Fall 2010, we added World War II veterans who were coming to Washington, D.C. on charter flights. I had seen some gracious pat-downs but I thought we could go further. I had to find out whether I had the authority to change protocols. I did not see our current protocols as sustainable long-term. We want to keep traveling safe, but we can redefine mission. It will take common sense. We need to look at things from a risk-based approach."

In October 2011, TSA began the TSA Pre✓™ program with Delta Air Lines and American Airlines in which selected individuals could receive expedited screening. The TSA Pre✓™ program is part of TSA's movement toward a strategy for enhanced use of intelligence and other information to implement a risk-based security (RBS) approach in all facets of transportation, including passenger screening, air cargo, and surface transportation. In testimony before the House Committee on Homeland Security, Pistole said, "Our objective is to mitigate risk in a way that effectively balances security measures with privacy, civil rights, and civil liberties concerns while both promoting the safe movement of people and commerce and guarding against a deliberate attack on our transportation systems. RBS in the passenger-screening context allows our dedicated TSOs to focus more attention on those travelers we believe are more likely to pose a risk to our transportation network while providing expedited screening to those we consider pose less risk." (Pistole)

Pistole says, "TSA Pre✓™ is important to us. We are expanding the populations eligible to participate. We want to expand so that different populations can participate." Since the start of the program, TSA has expanded TSA Pre✓™ benefits to military active-duty members traveling through Reagan Washington National Airport and Seattle-Tacoma International Airport. TSA has also implemented other risk-based security measures, including modified screening procedures for passengers 12 and younger and 75 and older. Flight attendants and pilots are now receiving the expedited screening.

The RBS approach is driving major changes at TSA and new ways of doing business with the public. To successfully implement these changes, Pistole needed the support of the organization. He recalls, "I asked our senior staff in D.C. how they felt about making these changes. It turned out that there was widespread support at headquarters, not total support but significant support. I then had a two-day conference with our 120 security directors and regional staff to get their feedback. Everybody seemed supportive. I needed people fully on board and needed my top managers to lead their people. I wanted the entire organization to have buy-in. If senior staff did not feel comfortable with all this, that was okay with me and I told them that we can make other arrangements for them. Several people ended up moving."

Pistole's long career at the Federal Bureau of Investigation influenced several of his key actions at TSA. One was the creation of a new Office of Professional Responsibility. In describing the new office, Pistole recalls, "It is interesting to be in a very young agency. When I got here, I felt a need to improve our handling of in-house ethics issues or disciplinary actions. So we created the new office, similar to the one at the FBI."

Another key action influenced by his time at the FBI was the movement to increased training at TSA. "While we don't quite have a TSA Academy, we did get space in Georgia," says Pistole. "We have 4,800 supervisors who we want to put through a two-week leadership training program. Previously, everybody was trained locally. Our goal is to make TSA into a good counterterrorism agency."

Reflecting on his Tenure at TSA

"I knew there would be criticism in this job, but I saw challenges and opportunities in nearly every situation," says Pistole.

"I have found that change is not easy. Risk-based security is a paradigm shift. We have to manage expectations. Since 2002, we have screened seven billion people. We need them all to arrive safely while we provide the most effective security in the most efficient way."

David H. Stevens
Assistant Secretary for Housing
and Commissioner, Federal Housing Administration
Department of Housing and Urban Development

The Beginning

The process of being nominated and confirmed to a federal position is slow. With the exception of the Cabinet and selected other positions which usually are confirmed between the end of January and mid-February at the start of a new administration, the remaining appointees arrive slowly throughout the year. Most of the individuals profiled in this book, with several exceptions, arrived in the summer of 2009—five to six months after the inauguration of the new President. David Stevens arrived in July 2009 after being nominated in April. "I started talking to Secretary Donovan about this position in February," recalls Stevens. "The appointments process was slow. It's never quick. You have the White House review, the FBI review, and the financial review. It's a long process."

Since nominees are not allowed in federal office buildings prior to their confirmation (unless they receive another type of appointment in the interim), Stevens did his homework for the new position on weekends while still working at his prior position. "I would spend weekends with binders to learn more about the Department. I would also make phone calls on weekends to talk with people about the position. These phone calls were very helpful to me. You need to use your pre-confirmation time wisely. You should talk to previous incumbents and find out about their experience. I used the time to become as knowledgeable on issues as possible and find as many resources—both people and written materials—as I could."

The Organization

The Federal Housing Administration (FHA) was created in 1934 as a key component of New Deal legislation. In 1965, it was incorporated into the newly created Department of Housing and Urban Development. The FHA provides mortgage insurance on loans made by FHA-approved lenders throughout the United States. The FHA does not directly issue loans itself. Since its creation, the FHA has insured over 39 million home mortgages and over 52,000 multi-family project mortgages. It currently has a portfolio of $1 trillion in insured mortgages. FHA currently has 3,000 employees.

The FHA mortgage insurance provides lenders with protection against losses as a result of homeowners defaulting on mortgage loans. Similar to the United States Patent and Trademark Office, FHA's operating expenses are funded by self-

---

David H. Stevens

Tenure: Mr. Stevens was nominated by President Obama to serve as Assistant Secretary for Housing at the United States Department of Housing and Urban Development (HUD) and Commissioner of the Federal Housing Administration (FHA) in April 2009, and confirmed by the U.S. Senate in July 2009.

Private sector experience: Prior to being confirmed as Assistant Secretary, Mr. Stevens served as President and Chief Operating Officer of Long & Foster Companies, which includes Long & Foster Real Estate and its affiliated businesses, including mortgage, title insurance, and home service connections.

Mr. Stevens served as Senior Vice President of Single Family Business at Freddie Mac and Executive Vice President, National Wholesale Manager at Wells Fargo. He also worked 16 years in a variety of positions at the World Savings Bank, including Senior Vice President running its national lending practice.

Education: Mr. Stevens earned a B.A. from the University of Colorado at Boulder in 1983.

---

generated income. The proceeds from mortgage insurance paid by homeowners are put into a special account that is used to operate the FHA program.

The Challenge

In the latter part of the first decade of the 21st century, problems in the housing industry were well-known and front-page news. As a consequence of the economic crisis of 2007–2009, housing prices had fallen for 30 straight months by the start of 2009 and home equity had dropped precipitously. As a result, there was a dramatic increase in the number of home mortgages in default. The financial health and stability of FHA itself was in question. As a consequence of the collapse of the subprime mortgage industry, which increased the demand for FHA-insured loans, FHA insured about 30 percent of new mortgages in 2009 as compared with four percent in 2006. In looking back, Stevens says, "We faced the equivalent of a private-sector bankruptcy."

Responding to the Challenge

"I spent my first days at FHA assessing the organization," recalls Stevens. "I would go out into the field and talk with our staff. We held large staff meetings and an off-site planning retreat. I wanted to better understand the major issues facing the Department. I focused on what I thought I could accomplish and would make a real difference."

During his initial assessment, Stevens says, "It became obvious to me that we needed to better manage risk. We needed a risk office and a chief risk officer. I felt FHA needed to go outside of the organization to recruit some top-notch deputy assistant secretaries. We needed to recruit people with experience in credit risk, credit policy, and lending."

Unlike several of the executives profiled in this book, Stevens concluded during his assessment of the organization that a full-scale reorganization was not needed. "I decided," recalls Stevens, "that I didn't want to reorganize. So I put my efforts into assessing the talent already in the organization. At Freddie Mac, I had spent too much time on reorganization rather than on dealing with other crucial issues. My time at Freddie Mac was very valuable to me. I worked on multiple issues there which turned out to be excellent training for this position."

While Stevens did not launch a major reorganization, the creation of a new Office of Risk Management and the new position of a Deputy Assistant Secretary for Risk Management (the chief risk officer) demonstrated the need to fill in gaps in the organization's capability. Stevens sought Congressional approval to formally establish the position and create a permanent risk management office. "This will be a permanent change," says Stevens, "and last beyond any single administration." Stevens told Congress that the creation of this office would expand FHA's capacity to assess financial and operational risk, perform more sophisticated data analysis, and respond to market developments.

While the creation of new capability was an important step in increasing the effectiveness of FHA, Stevens concluded that there remained major skill gaps in the agency. "The staff here hasn't received much management training over the years. We set a requirement that everybody receives at least 20 hours of training. This was never done before." On related fronts, Stevens worked to improve the hiring process and to bring on additional staff to FHA to respond to the increased workload. "One of our big initiatives was improving the hiring process. We got it down to 76 days from 180 days. This is now a model across the government. It was simply taking too long. We did a flow chart to lay out the process, which the Office of Personnel Management has used. We now think that we can shave off even more days from the process. In addition, we hired about 100 new people."

The major challenge to which Stevens had to respond was strengthening the financial stability of the organization. "We had to sort out the reserve fund and get it above the two percent requirement," says Stevens. "It was below the required two percent when I arrived. This was a major concern at the White House and the National Economic Policy Council. We needed to get a bunch of new policies

---

Mission
Office of Housing
Department of Housing and Urban Development

- Contribute to building and preserving healthy neighborhoods and communities;
- Maintain and expand homeownership, rental housing and healthcare opportunities;
- Stabilize credit markets in times of economic disruption;
- Operate with a high degree of public and fiscal accountability; and
- Recognize and value its customers, staff, constituents and partners.

---

so the agency won't face financial problems in the future. We also had to change the entire system. We worked with lenders on many issues." Stevens also worked closely with the Administration in raising insurance premium rates, which put FHA on a much sounder financial footing for the years ahead.

Because of the crisis situation confronting Stevens when he arrived at FHA, he adopted a management strategy to focus on just a few major issues. "I've learned to just focus on two or three issues and give those my full attention," says Stevens. "That meant I gave other issues much less attention. On the other issues, I just needed to know enough to give people my go-ahead to keep them going. You really have a short time here and you have so much to get done, you have to focus on just a few things. I had to focus on a couple of things and dig in to get them done."

Reflecting on Running FHA

"The job ended up being bigger than I thought," reflects Stevens. "I came here in the middle of the storm. We were really fighting a housing crisis. In the past, the job had really not had much visibility. The agency is important again and nobody would think of appointing somebody not fully qualified for this job. We were able to accomplish much of what we have done because of the crisis. FHA is now a major player in Washington. We have become the voice of housing in government. The White House, the National Economic Policy Council, and the Department of Treasury all now call upon us when there is a housing issue facing the Administration."

Epilogue

David H. Stevens is now President and Chief Executive Officer of the Mortgage Bankers Association (MBA), the national association representing the real estate finance industry.

William J. Taggart
Chief Operating Officer, Office of Federal Student Aid
Department of Education

The Beginning

Bill Taggart performed extensive due diligence prior to accepting the position of Chief Operating Officer (COO) at Federal Student Aid (FSA). "As a former management consultant," says Taggart, "I knew how to assess organizations. Therefore, I had a good idea of the situation I was walking into. I began discussions with the Department in February 2009. By late February, I had a meeting with Tony Miller, who was then a special assistant to Secretary Arne Duncan. We reviewed the challenges and expectations of FSA and the COO role. Secondly, all the previous FSA annual reports and strategic plans were available on the Internet. Those documents gave me a lot of insight about the organization. Lastly, I read about the pending legislation which would substantially change the way FSA operated. All of these sources of information helped me to obtain a clear view on the current state of affairs at FSA. After careful consideration, I determined that I was well suited for this type of leadership challenge. As a former recipient of federal financial aid, I felt honored to be appointed the COO of FSA."

The Organization

Federal Student Aid was the first performance-based organization (PBO) in government. It was created by the 1998 Reauthorization of the Higher Education Act. The legislation creating FSA designated that the office would be led by a Chief Operating Officer with a strong background in technology and management who would have a performance-based contract and report directly to the Secretary of Education. The agency also received flexibilities in procurement and personnel management. Since the designation of FSA as a PBO, only two additional federal government organizations—the Air Traffic Organization in the Federal Aviation Administration and the United States Patent and Trademark Office in the Department of Commerce—have been designated PBOs. The key concept of the PBO is to separate the operations of a government activity (in this case, the delivery of student financial aid) from the development of policy on financial aid (which is the responsibility of the Secretary of Education and the Assistant Secretary for Postsecondary Education).

Federal Student Aid provides over $130 billion in financial aid to nearly 14 million college students annually. FSA administers both the Department's education grant programs (about $30 billion) and loan programs (about $100 billion). In

William J. (Bill) Taggart

Tenure: Mr. Taggart was appointed in June 2009 by U.S. Secretary of Education Arne Duncan as the third Chief Operating Officer for the Office of Federal Student Aid.

Private sector experience: Before joining the Department of Education, Mr. Taggart was President and Chief Executive Officer of Veritas One Consulting, LLC. Prior to Veritas One, he served in a number of leadership positions at Wachovia Corporation, including Chief Operating Officer of Corporate and Investment Banking, Head of Client Services, President of Info-One, and Chief Administrative Officer for Wachovia Insurance. Mr. Taggart also worked for First Union Corporation as Managing Director of Strategic Support Services for the automation and operations division, and for IBM in technology, consulting, and marketing roles.

Education: Mr. Taggart received a Master's degree from Harvard University's Graduate School of Business Administration and a Bachelor's degree in Business Administration from Howard University.

March 2010, Congress passed the Health Care and Education Reconciliation Act of 2010 which assigned additional responsibilities to FSA to ensure that student aid was operating efficiently and effectively. The Act ended the provision of subsidies to private banks to give out federally insured loans. Instead, loans are now administered directly by the Department of Education. At the end of May 2011, FSA was managing a loan portfolio of over $800 billion. In addition, FSA processes more than 16 million FAFSA (Free Application for Federal Student Aid) applications. There are now more than 32 million individual borrowers who have 100 million student loan accounts.

The Challenge

After arriving at FSA in June 2009, Taggart spent his initial days assessing the state of FSA. "The organization had a very experienced staff with a great passion for students. However, employee morale was down," recalls Taggart. "The previous several years had been difficult ones for the organization and it had a big impact on employees. I found there were many unhappy employees. I also found

Mission, Vision, and Core Values
Office of Federal Student Aid

Mission
Funding America's Future, One Student at a Time

Vision
To be the most trusted and reliable source of student financial aid, information, and services in the nation

Core Values
- **Integrity.** Do the right thing above other interests and hold everyone accountable.
- **Customer Service.** Know what our customers (students and borrowers) want and ensure we meet their expectations.
- **Excellence.** Strive to be the very best in all we do by embracing a culture of continuous improvement.
- **Respect.** Value individuals by acknowledging the diversity of their contributions, ideas, and beliefs.
- **Stewardship.** Uphold the sacred trust of taxpayers as we work to support the goals of Congress and the Administration.
- **Teamwork.** Work in collaboration with our colleagues and partners to produce the best possible results.
- **Programs.** Work in collaboration with our colleagues and partners to produce the best possible results.

that the working relationship between FSA and the rest of the Department of Education needed improvement. I assessed that the organization was very good at crisis management and could respond to unplanned events quite well. In addition, FSA was a leader in working with private-sector firms through its public-private partnership framework. That said, the organization did not have a current strategic plan and was not fully prepared for the passage of new legislation if and when it was enacted."

Responding to the Challenge

One top priority for Taggart was employee engagement at FSA. "Human capital challenges were significant," recalls Taggart. "Many of the staff worked at FSA an average of 18 years but did not feel valued by senior management. Nearly 20 percent of them will be eligible to retire in the next five years. We had only 975 people, with headcount falling, while our workloads were up 200 percent in some cases. It was clear that we needed to hire more staff to perform tasks that were deemed as 'inherently governmental.' We needed to hire the right people, with the right competencies, who knew how to work in a team-based environment. I held several town hall meetings to get the employees' unfiltered feedback. They had a lot on their minds and were very vocal. That meant to me that they cared about the organization. It would have been much worse if I had been met with silence. It was essential for me to help the employees to feel better about the organization. I decided to get them involved in developing a new vision, mission, and core values for the organization. Over 200 employees participated in the process and helped to develop a new working relationship between the FSA employees and the COO."

Like many large operational organizations, FSA has a clear sense of purpose which Taggart capitalized on. "The good news was that I found that FSA employees have great passion for students," he recalls. "Many told me about how they had received student loans when they were in college. I realized that I could use the 'natural energy' for postsecondary students to rally the employee base and move the organization forward. They all believe in federal financial aid for postsecondary students and are proud that FSA provides assistance to students. We decided to become a more customer-driven organization which meant placing more of our focus on students. In this tough economy, students are more dependent on federal aid than ever before. We wanted to make sure we were able to meet their needs."

In addition to the commitment of his organization to its mission, Taggart had a transformational event to bring about significant change in the organization. "On March 30, 2010, new legislation was passed making FSA the sole originator of federal student loans," he says. "The team started planning for this change well before I arrived in June 2009. We needed a plan in place just in case the legislation passed. We wanted to show the American people that we could accomplish this task. I kept telling the organization that we were moving into a more visible role in government similar to a new play opening on Broadway. There were a lot of people looking at us. The new law gave us something to rally around. The entire organization could participate in moving FSA into the future. Everybody felt part of the process. Our organization jelled at this moment. We were all in the same boat together."

FSA worked very closely with private-sector firms to ensure that their operating platform was scalable and could handle the increased business volumes. "We expect to see increased annual volumes for FAFSAs, and loan servicing and Pell Grants to increase significantly. Therefore, we used public-private partnerships to ensure we were ready. In fact, 85 percent of the FSA administrative budget goes to private-sector firms. This gave us flexibility to grow rapidly when conditions warranted."

During the long road to passage of the new legislation, the role of FSA as the operational arm of student aid was very clear. "We worked well with the

Figure 6.2: Participants in federal student aid ecosystem

CONGRESS	THE PRESIDENT, DEPT OF ED, AND OTHERS IN EXECUTIVE BRANCH	PRIVATE LENDERS
Sets statutory standards on student aid funding and appropriate budgets	Set regulatory standards and policy on student aid funding	Service outstanding FFELP loans to students

POSTSECONDARY INSTITUTIONS	STUDENTS	GUARANTY AGENCIES
Determine students' aid packages and disburse funds	Receive and repay student aid to finance postsecondary education	Insure FFELP loans and service part of defaulted loan portfolio

OTHER FSA CONTRACTORS	FSA-CONTRACTED SERVICERS	FSA-CONTRACTED PRIVATE COLLECTION AGENCIES
Provide systems and services to support FSA's core operations (e.g. applications, disbursement)	Service Direct Loan portfolio and portions of FFELP portfolio	Recover funds from defaulted loans

Source: *Adapted from* Federal Student Aid Strategic Plan FY 2011–2015, *U.S. Department of Education, Federal Student Aid, 2010.*

Department on the new legislation," says Taggart. "The Office of Postsecondary Education is responsible for policy development and FSA serves as the implementation arm. We respond to questions about the impacts of pending legislation. It is not our job to opine on policy. We give advice on how best to implement pending legislation in the most effective and efficient way possible. I was struck by these two synergistic skill sets: the implementers and the policy makers must work well together. At the beginning each group talked a somewhat different language, but over time we began to understand each other better and our knowledge began to overlap, making the team highly effective."

In addition to increasing the morale of the organization and implementing the new legislation, Taggart also set about to reevaluate and reengineer, where necessary, the entire ecosystem that goes along with FSA. "The FSA organization is the core of student financial aid," he says. "After understanding FSA, you then have to learn about the entire ecosystem that goes with it. The ecosystem includes our 10,000 contractors, over 2,500 lenders, 34 GAs and the 6,200 colleges and universities we serve. The COO at FSA is not just running FSA, he or she provides oversight to the entire ecosystem. Your job is to influence how the entire system works. You have to know how to give the right amount of guidance. You can't just focus on the interworkings of FSA."

Reflecting on Running FSA

"You can look at projects like this (e.g., 100% Direct Lending) from a risk/ reward perspective," Taggart told *Inside Higher Education*. "If someone looked at this project purely on risk, they probably would have run the other way ... But how many times in your career do you get an opportunity to lead an effort of this size and magnitude for the benefit of American students and their families and the taxpayers?" (Lederman).

Epilogue

William J. Taggart is now the President and CEO of Atlanta Life Financial Group (ALFG), the only African-American owned and privately held company in the country, with a financial services platform that includes asset management, investment banking/brokerage and insurance.

Chapter Seven

The Infrastructors

Understanding the Job of the Infrastructor

During our interviews for this project, we invited a group of political executives to participate who appeared at first to be only loosely connected: Jonathan Adelstein at RUS, Arun Majumdar at ARPA-E, Victor Mendez at FHWA, and Joseph Szabo at FRA. By the time the project was completed, we realized that they had much in common. All facilitate the development and enhancement of the nation's economic infrastructure. All are seeking cheaper and better ways to provide energy, highways, broadband, and railroads. Their efforts directly enable our nation's economic growth. We discovered that in different ways, each is focused on developing a crucial aspect of the nation's infrastructure.

During the period in which we interviewed them, all four were involved in the implementation of the American Recovery and Reinvestment Act. In two agencies, RUS and FRA, Recovery Act activities substantially transformed the organizations into faster, more flexible

The Infrastructors

Jonathan S. Adelstein, page 137
Administrator, Rural Utilities Service (RUS), Department of Agriculture

Arun Majumdar, page 142
Director, Advanced Research Projects Agency-Energy (ARPA-E), Department of Energy

Victor M. Mendez, page 147
Administrator, Federal Highway Administration (FHWA), Department of Transportation

Joseph C. Szabo, page 153
Administrator, Federal Railroad Administration (FRA), Department of Transportation

agencies. In the case of ARPA-E, a new agency was built from the ground up to support and develop transformative energy approaches and technologies. For FHWA, the Recovery Act provided increased funding for highway infrastructure projects. All faced the challenge of publishing notices of funding, receiving and reviewing applications, and making awards—all in a very short timespan under increased scrutiny and transparency. In the case of three of the agencies—FRA, RUS, and FHWA—the Recovery Act dramatically increased their workload. "Getting the broadband money out was really a major accomplishment for us," recalls Adelstein. "You have to understand that our workload increased 20 times over our previous workload."

Key Roles

The infrastructors uniquely blend several key characteristics of the other groups discussed in this book:
*   Collaborators/Instructors
*   Producers
*   Scientists/Engineers/Technical Experts

Serving as a Collaborator/Instructor

All four political executives profiled in this chapter had substantial outreach and "educational/instructor" responsibilities in their positions. They all had to collaborate with their stakeholder groups, as well as educate them on the government's funding availability for infrastructure. All viewed information sharing with stakeholders as part of their jobs. Because of their educational role and their role in infrastructure development, we labeled this group as the infrastructors.

While we were familiar with the traditional government grant-making process, we found that all four individuals profiled in this section played a teaching/instructor role to state governments, their respective industries, applicants for funding, and the recipients of their funding. Building the nation's infrastructure is not a "hands-off" activity. At RUS, staff was active in reaching out to organizations that had not applied in the first round of applications. Adelstein recalls, "We got people to apply in the second round who had not applied in the first round. We developed an interactive process in which we communicated more effectively with potential grantees. This process led to the outcomes we desired. We got some good applications. We wanted to encourage the right people to apply." In addition to reaching out to new applicants, RUS sent selected first-round submissions (which had not been accepted) back to applicants to be revised and resubmitted in the second round. These efforts, believes Adelstein, resulted in improved applications in the second round.

A significant stakeholder for both Victor Mendez and Joseph Szabo is state government. Because of his background as Director of the Arizona Department of Transportation, Mendez brought the perspective of a state transportation official to DOT headquarters in Washington. A major priority for Mendez was to find new ways for FHWA to engage with the states. One new vehicle for FHWA was the Every Day Counts (EDC) program. As part of that program, FHWA partnered with the Association of State Highway Transportation Officials (ASHTO) to host 10 Regional Innovation Summits. The summits are a vehicle for FHWA to disseminate EDC strategies and technologies. The EDC program also enabled Mendez to engage the transportation industry to find innovative ways to reduce the time it takes to complete highway construction projects (see *Innovation In Government: Creating The Every Day Counts Program* on page 151 for a further discussion on this initiative).

In the case of Joseph Szabo and FRA, the agency had to take an aggressive role in reaching out to the states to assist them in completing the Stakeholder

Agreements with rail owners or rail operators who would operate the proposed projects—a key requirement to receiving Recovery Act funding. Szabo recalls, "We thought the states and the private sector would be able to negotiate the agreements, but that wasn't happening. We had to help them on their service agreements. We helped get them to where they needed to be." This involvement followed an aggressive outreach program at the start of the program. FRA held listening sessions with key stakeholders at which they explained the high speed rail initiative and received feedback on the program.

Outreach was also high on the agenda of ARPA-E Director Majumdar during his first year. A major part of an infrastructor's job is reaching out to the community in two-way conversations—both to learn what the community is doing and to inform the community of federal government funding opportunities. Majumdar recalls, "I reached out to universities. I set up informal meetings to just chat with experts to find out their issues and thoughts. I wanted to know what people were already doing."

The teaching role is also seen in working with Congress. Majumdar says, "I tell them (Congress) what we do. I like to explain our agency in layman terms. I try to make it easy for them to understand and talk to them in terms of impacts and savings, which gives them the big picture."

Serving as a Producer

All four political executives had to aggressively manage their organizations to produce the results expected of their organizations. In all four cases, the expectation was to "get the money out" quickly in response to the Recovery Act. At FRA, Szabo had to borrow staff from other parts of the Department of Transportation to handle the increased workload. Szabo, like Adelstein, had to work with his agency to "speed it up" and make it more flexible. Just like the producers discussed in Chapter Six, the four individuals profiled in this chapter had to closely manage their organizations' "inputs and outputs" and make sure all the organizational tasks associated with the Recovery Act were completed in a timely, efficient, and transparent manner.

Serving as a Scientist/Engineer/Technical Expert

All four jobs required substantial expertise. In the case of Mendez and Majumdar, they had the engineering backgrounds necessary in their respective positions. In launching ARPA-E, Majumdar confronted many of the same challenges faced by the scientists profiled in Chapter Nine: serving as the interface between his organization and political leaders in Congress and in government, contributing to the national debate about new approaches to energy, and strengthening (or in this case, building) the institution. Majumdar devoted a substantial amount of his time and energy to recruiting talent to join the newly created ARPA-E. In reflecting on his tenure at ARPA-E, Majumdar says that one of his proudest accomplishments is recruiting a first-rate technical team at ARPA-E.

In the case of Adelstein, his service as a Congressional staff member and Commissioner at the Federal Trade Commission gave him expert knowledge of the issues associated with broadband. Joseph Szabo's firsthand experience working in the rail industry assisted him in understanding the technical aspects of rail.

Selecting an Infrastructor

In Chapter One, we discuss how important it is for the Office of Presidential Personnel to identify the right set of experiences for political executives. This is especially crucial in the selection of infrastructors. OPP must determine the right mix of experience for these positions. Should they emphasize the technical/engineering aspects of these jobs, or the collaborative nature of the positions? There will also be times in an agency's history when an individual with a strong production background will be needed.

Regardless of the mix of experience selected, we believe that the ability (and experience) to effectively collaborate should become a requirement for infrastructor positions. In building the nation's infrastructure, the federal government has become a funder to other organizations (state and local governments, the private sector, non-profit organizations) that actually build or create the infrastructure required. Thus, ability to work with and to share information with the "builders" has now become crucial.

Other Infrastructor Agencies

In addition to the four agencies profiled in this chapter, there are other organizations throughout government that we categorize as infrastructor agencies. While not comprehensive, the list and descriptions of each agency have been prepared to assist the Office of Presidential Personnel and Cabinet Secretaries in better understanding the unique nature of these agencies, which play a key role in building the nation's infrastructure.

Other Federal Government Agencies Categorized as Infrastructor Agencies

Department of Commerce
National Telecommunications and Information Administration

The National Telecommunications and Information Administration (NTIA), created in 1978, serves as the Executive Branch agency principally responsible for advising the President on telecommunications and information policies. NTIA also manages the federal use of spectrum, performs cutting-edge telecommunications research and engineering, and administers infrastructure and public telecommunications facilities grants. As part of the Recovery Act, NTIA was given responsibility to administer the $4.7 billion Broadband Technology Opportunities Program (BTOP). The program made awards in three project categories: comprehensive community infrastructure projects to deploy new or improved broad Internet facilities; public computer center projects to establish new public computer facilities or upgrade existing ones to provide broadband access to the general public; and sustainable broadband adoption projects, which focused on increasing broadband Internet usage and adoption. In FY 11, NTIA had a budget of nearly $41 million and had over 300 employees.

Department of Energy
The Office of Energy Efficiency and Renewable Energy

The Office of Energy Efficiency and Renewable Energy (EERE) invests in clean energy technologies with the goal of strengthening the economy, protecting the environment, and reducing dependence on oil. The Office aims to achieve its mission through:
- Enhancing energy efficiency and productivity
- Bringing clean, reliable, and affordable energy technologies to the marketplace

EERE was charged with distributing over $16.8 billion in Recovery Act funding for energy efficiency and renewable energy projects. Examples of EERE Recovery Act funding included weatherization of low-income homes; awards to states and territories to support energy efficiency projects; and awards to cities to support deployment of community-based renewable energy projects, such as biomass, wind, and solar installations.

Department of Transportation
Federal Transit Administration

The Federal Transit Administration (FTA), created in 1968, makes both formula and discretionary awards to support a variety of locally planned, constructed, and operated public transportation systems throughout the United States. Such transportation systems include buses, subways, light rail, commuter rail, streetcars, monorail, passenger ferry boats, inclined railways, or people movers. FTA awarded over 1,000 grants for a total of $8.78 billion in Recovery Act funds for transit capital assistance and fixed guideway infrastructure investment (which modernizes or improves existing fixed guideway systems, including the purchase or rehabilitation of rolling stock, track, equipment, or facilities). In FY 11, the FTA had a budget of over $10 billion and more than 550 employees.

Jonathan S. Adelstein
Administrator, Rural Utilities Service
Department of Agriculture

The Beginning

"When I got here," recalls Jonathan Adelstein, "I quickly found that we had a crisis in management regarding the information technology system we were using to accept applications for broadband projects. The process was in meltdown due to the unprecedented number of applications for loans and grants. RUS was working with another agency on application intake and it just wasn't working."

"It was a pretty stressful situation in the beginning. On top of the technology problems with incoming applications, there were issues arising with the way the rules had been set up. We had to quickly dig out of a hole on the broadband program. The rules for the first funding round had been put together before I arrived and the program was not working in the way that those who put it together had anticipated. The agency also had not had a boss for awhile prior to my arrival. So there was also a lot of unfinished business to complete."

"I had known about the telecommunications part of the agency from my days at the Federal Communications Commission," recalls Adelstein. "So I knew those programs relatively well. I was also involved in helping to write the 2002 Farm Bill, which gave the agency direct authority to finance broadband services. When it comes to digging out, it's good to have come from a family in the construction business. My Dad taught me to always be shovel-ready."

The Organization

The Rural Utilities Service traces its roots back to the Rural Electrification Administration (REA), a New Deal agency created in 1936 with the primary goal of promoting rural electrification. In 1994, REA was reorganized into the Rural Utilities Services (RUS). "RUS has a different history from other parts of the Department of Agriculture," says Adelstein. "We were put together with other rural development agencies."

Today, RUS is one of three agencies that make up the Department of Agriculture's Rural Development mission area, which is headed by the USDA Under Secretary for Rural Development. The other agencies reporting to the Under Secretary include the Rural Housing Service and the Rural Business and Cooperative Service. In FY 11, RUS had a budget of over $9 billion and over 700 staff working to deliver the electric, telecommunications, water, and environmental programs of the agency.

Jonathan S. Adelstein

Tenure: Mr. Adelstein was nominated by President Obama to serve as the Administrator of the Department of Agriculture's Rural Utilities Service in April 2009, and confirmed by the U.S. Senate in July 2009.

Federal government experience: Prior to being confirmed as Administrator, Mr. Adelstein served as Commissioner of the Federal Communications Commission from 2002 to 2009. Previously, Mr. Adelstein worked for 15 years as a staff member in the United States Senate. During that time, he served as a senior legislative aide to Senate Majority Leader Tom Daschle, as a professional staff member on the Senate Special Committee on Aging, and as a legislative assistant to Senator Donald W. Riegle, Jr.

Academic experience: Mr. Adelstein was a Teaching Fellow in the Department of History, Harvard University. Mr. Adelstein was also a Teaching Assistant in the Department of History, Stanford University.

Education: Mr. Adelstein received a B.A. in Political Science and an M.A. in History from Stanford University

The Challenge

The challenge was clear. The American Recovery and Reinvestment Act provided $7.2 billion to the Department of Commerce's National Telecommunications and Information Administration (NTIA) and the Department of Agriculture's Rural Utilities Service to expand access to broadband services in the United States. The funding was administered through the Broadband Technology Opportunities Program (BTOP) at NTIA and the Broadband Initiatives Program (BIP) administered by RUS. BIP provided over $3.5 billion in funding for loans, grants, and loan/grant combinations to assist in rapidly expanding the access and quality of broadband services across rural America. The challenge was both to get the money out and to do so without any waste or abuse. The goal of the program was to provide access to over seven million residents and 350,000 businesses in rural America.

In addition to implementing the Recovery Act's rural broadband initiative, Adelstein also had to continue to manage the other programs within RUS which included:

- The electric program which provides loans for improving electric service in rural areas, including construction of generation plants and transmission and distribution lines
- The water and waste program, which offers grants and direct and guaranteed loans; it also distributed over $3 billion in stimulus funding
- The loan programs that provide low interest financing for rural telecommunications, broadband and electric systems; various grant programs for distance learning, telemedicine, rural public television equipment, All Hazards Warning Radio (NOAA Weather Radio) transmitters and assistance to communities with extremely high electricity costs as well as a loan and grant program to finance water, sewer, and solid waste projects in rural areas.

Responding to the Challenge

"I had always thought of the Rural Utilities Service as a scrappy little agency in a big behemoth of a Department, with an independent streak," recalls Adelstein. Mr. Adelstein had the opportunity to test RUS to see how scrappy it really was.

"By the time I was confirmed by the Senate in the summer, much of the work on setting up the Recovery Act's Broadband Initiatives Program had been completed with oversight from the Secretary's office and the White House," remembers Adelstein. "So I didn't have a role in the design of the first round of the program. I had to work with what I found. I gave a speech to the agency within a week of my arrival. I gave them my vision for the agency and I tried to let the staff know that I supported their mission."

The next step for Adelstein was to set his agenda and decide on its implementation. "I had to focus on the execution of the broadband program," states Adelstein. "I had to defend its progress on the Hill, and that meant moving the ball forward so I had a better case to make. This became my key role. So there was a fairly set agenda when I arrived which I couldn't change until we launched the second round of funding. The policy decisions of the first round had already been made. As we entered into the second phase of the broadband initiative, we were able to draw on the lessons of the first round." In the second round of applications, Adelstein made significant changes. "First," recalls Adelstein, "we had another agency managing the intake contract and we worked hard to better manage that process. It worked much more smoothly thereafter."

"Second, the Vice President encouraged us to become more flexible in implementing the program. His support of flexibility was very important, as I used it as a mantra during the policy development process. We got more flexibility and a better balance between grants and loans, creating a new 75 percent grant/25 percent loan combination which contained incentives for higher loan components. Obtaining this flexibility was essential in reaching the most underserved areas. We worked closely with the White House on it. In round two, we were driving the

Mission and Vision
Department of Agriculture

Mission Statement: Rural Development in the Department of Agriculture

USDA Rural Development is committed to the future of rural communities. Our role is to increase rural residents' economic opportunities and improve their quality of life. Rural Development forges partnerships with rural communities, funding projects that bring housing, community facilities, utilities and other services. We also provide technical assistance and financial backing for rural businesses and cooperatives to create quality jobs in rural areas. Rural Development promotes the President's National Energy Policy and ultimately the nation's energy security by engaging the entrepreneurial spirit of rural America in the development of renewable energy and energy efficiency improvements. Rural Development works with low-income individuals, State, local and Indian tribal governments, as well as private and nonprofit organizations and user-owned cooperatives.

Vision Statement: Rural Utilities Service Broadband Initiatives Program

Rural Utilities Service will support the expansion of broadband service in rural areas through financing and grants to projects that provide access to high speed service and facilitate economic development in locations without sufficient access to such service.

process which made it easier for us to determine what changes needed to be made. These new flexibilities created a different mindset within RUS. We now wanted to get the money out in a different and more focused way. This created a different culture in the agency." RUS also gained the flexibility to add priority points for projects that provide significant assistance to essential community facilities, promote rural economic development, and support chronically underserved areas.

Using the new flexibilities to implement the broadband program, Adelstein worked with his career civil service to execute the program. "I worked closely with the career staff here to make revisions in the second funding round," recounts Adelstein. "I wanted their buy-in and inspiration. I wanted to know their ideas. We shared ideas and got different opinions on various options for round two. I believe in listening to staff. We had a very collegial relationship; it was not top-down. We had an ongoing dialogue."

In defining his job, Adelstein says, "My job was to let the staff see the goal and keep the political pressures off them. We didn't let politics interfere with our awards process. I was aware of the politics of it all but I didn't let it interfere with the agency. We made our decisions on merit. That took some time. I couldn't micromanage it, but I tried to stay focused on our job and we exceeded expectations. It was a collaborative process. I think this will have a long-term impact on how the agency operates. We knew the goals we wanted to accomplish."

In looking back on the completion of the second round, Adelstein says, "We got the money out to areas that could benefit the most. We worked closely with the White House in revising the program. We had the agency's reputation on the line. I'm proud that our agency could do this. The Broadband Initiatives Program was a new program for us which we had to create. We met our September 30th deadline on September 23. There wasn't much margin of error. Nobody took any vacation during the summer of 2010."

"You have to understand that our workload increased 20 times over our previous workload," emphasizes Adelstein. "This was a massive increase in funding which had to be distributed in a small amount of time. Our staff really did step up to get this done. We proved the naysayers wrong. We showed that we are more flexible than people thought we were. We pushed the organization to become more flexible and to move faster. Everybody worked together. The agency became less balkanized. We changed how the agency was operating. The agency had been around for 75 years and they had never done anything like this. We worked as a team. We pulled it off."

Reflecting on the Future of RUS

"I've had a long interest in rural broadband development," says Adelstein. "I've been working on this for a long time. Rural broadband is a good investment and very cost-efficient. Its benefits spill over into health care, education, the environment, energy uses, and many other applications. It is an indispensable part of rural development. Rural areas need these projects or they may turn into ghost towns. It is like the impact in the past of rail lines or highways. Rural Americans need broadband for job development and to stimulate businesses in these areas. I'm convinced that it will save money if we do it right and not on the cheap. Rural areas have special needs. We want to get it done right."

Arun Majumdar
Director, Advanced Research Projects Agency-Energy (ARPA-E)
Department of Energy

The Beginning

"I had a very good and fulfilling academic career in California," recounts Arun Majumdar. "I would have been happy to stay in academia, but the ARPA-E opportunity came up. I thought the time was ripe to look at energy and the environment. It was an opportunity to shape a new program in an important area."

"My first day was October 26, 2009, when I met with Secretary Chu, who was in California on that day to announce the first set of ARPA-E awards. I then took the red-eye flight to Washington that night, so I could arrive and start the job the next morning. I found a team that was already here and very hard at work to get the program up and running."

The Organization

ARPA-E was created by the America COMPETES Act which was signed into law in August 2007. The creation of ARPA-E had been recommended by the National Academies in a 2006 report. While ARPA-E was authorized in 2007, it did not have an initial budget until April 2009 when the American Recovery and Reinvestment Act provided $400 million in funding. The first Funding Opportunity Announcement was made in May 2009, with the first awards being made in October. In response to this Announcement, ARPA-E received 3,700 concept papers. From the 3,700 concept papers ARPA-E requested 334 full proposals and selected 37 projects for funding.

In December 2009, ARPA-E launched the second round of funding opportunities. In April 2010, Vice President Biden announced a second round of awards. ARPA-E was appropriated $180 million for FY 11. A fourth round of funding opportunities was announced in April 2011.

As of spring 2012, ARPA-E has invested in 180 projects in 12 program areas totaling over $500 million in funding. Awards, negotiated as cooperative agreements by the government and the awardee, range in size from $400,000 to $9 million, with an average award value of $3 million. During its first year, six projects that received a total of $23.6 million from ARPA-E have generated more than $100 million in outside capital investment. In the ARPA-E *2010 Annual Report,* Majumdar writes, "Leveraging private capital has enabled ARPA-E projects to accelerate technical development, aggressively create jobs, acquire capital equipment, and expand facilities."

Arun Majumdar

Tenure: Dr. Majumdar was nominated by President Obama to serve as the first Director of the Advanced Research Projects Agency-Energy (ARPA-E) in September 2009, and confirmed by the U.S. Senate in October 2009.

Academic experience: Prior to being confirmed as Director, Dr. Majumdar was the Associate Laboratory Director for Energy and Environment at Lawrence Berkeley National Laboratory and Professor of Mechanical Engineering and Materials Science and Engineering at the University of California, Berkeley. He served as head of the Berkeley National Laboratory's Environmental Energy Technology Division from 2007 to 2009. He has also been a faculty member at the University of California, Santa Barbara and at Arizona State University.

Education: Dr. Majumdar received his bachelor's degree in Mechanical Engineering at the Indian Institute of Technology, Bombay in 1985 and his Ph.D. from the University of California, Berkeley in 1989.

The Challenge

The challenge was clear: to launch a new organization, develop program areas, make awards, provide technical oversight to awardees, and demonstrate results in the creation of transformational energy technologies. The unique mandate to ARPA-E is to support energy technologies that would fundamentally transform how the nation uses energy. The agency was created to make revolutionary improvements in energy, not evolutionary improvements.

ARPA-E invests in and develops technologies that are too risky for private-sector investments, but if successful have the potential to enhance the national, economic, and environmental security of our nation. In short, ARPA-E aims to fund projects which identify disruptive energy technologies that can make current technologies obsolete. The goal of ARPA-E as described by Majumdar in the agency's *2010 Annual Report* is to "make clean energy technologies cheaper than traditional approaches so that they can scale without subsidies and enable sustainable businesses to grow."

Responding to the Challenge

Majumdar faced three distinct tasks during his first two years at ARPA-E. The first task was to focus externally to form new relationships crucial to the success of ARPA-E. The second task was to focus internally on creating a new government organization. The third task was to launch the right projects and start demonstrating results.

In undertaking his external outreach activities, Majumdar recalls, "During my first days, I reached out to key people in the Department of Energy. It was a new agency and I needed to reach out. I put together an advisory committee of notable individuals in the field to get their feedback. I wanted to know if we were doing the right things. I also spent time reaching out to the Office of Management and Budget during my first months on the job. I found that understanding Congress was really crucial. I was learning on the job."

The outreach activities were crucial in launching the organization. "I reached out to other relevant government agencies to see if there is synergy with what we do. I reached out to universities. I set up informal meetings to just chat with experts to find out their issues and thoughts. I wanted to know what people were already doing. We decided to have a big meeting in Washington, D.C., in which we would bring together all of our stakeholders. We held the meeting just two months after we decided to undertake it. It was quite an impressive event. People were engaged. We want to be a catalyst for change." Based on his outreach activities, Majumdar concludes, "There is no substitute for retailing. You have to go see people one on one and get to meet them. You also have to meet the right people."

One external group that received special attention from Majumdar is Congress, both members and their staff. "I tell them what I do," says Majumdar. "I like to explain our agency in layman terms. I try to make it easy for them to understand and talk to them in terms of impact and savings, while giving them the big picture. It's been a pleasant and enjoyable experience to work so closely with Congress. I'm from California and have never worked with Congress before. You need to spend time with them. They need to trust you. That takes time and you have to devote ongoing meetings to them."

Majumdar's efforts with Congress paid off. After he announced his resignation, U.S. Senator Chris Coons (D-Del.), a member of the Senate Energy and Natural Resources Committee, issued a statement which read, "It is a true shame that we're losing someone as innovative and talented as Arun Majumdar. In just three years, Dr. Majumdar has stood up a new agency, helped move Recovery Act funds into job-creating programs, and served as a reliable troubleshooter and trusted secretarial advisor. As the director of ARPA-E, Dr. Majumdar has been an extraordinary ambassador for the ecosystem of innovation that will power the next generation of energy production in this country, and is certainly one of the most inspiring people I've met in my time here in the Senate. Dr. Majumdar's research experience at UC Berkeley and investment experience with startups helped him seamlessly bridge the worlds of government, laboratory, and finance." (Coons)

Advanced Research Projects Agency • ENERGY

Mission and Values
ARPA-E

Mission
ARPA-E's mission is to fund projects that will develop transformational technologies that:
- Reduce America's dependence on foreign energy imports;
- Reduce U.S. energy related emissions (including greenhouse gasses);
- Improve energy efficiency across all sectors of the U.S. economy, and
- Ensure that the U.S. maintains its leadership in developing and deploying advanced energy technologies

Values
ARPA-E's core values are the essential standards by which it operates and executes its mission. The distinctive culture the values create gives us our unique character. ARPA-E is:
- Visionary
- Agile and Fast
- Dedicated to Excellence
- High-Impact

Equally challenging was the internal task of creating a new organization. Majumdar says, "I started recruiting people. I wanted to get the right people. Putting together your team is critical. As a new agency with special hiring authorities, we had the flexibility to recruit outside of the civil service system. People didn't have to wait for six months. We have proven that good people will come here. We were able to get nearly all the people we wanted."

Majumdar is very aware of the opportunities inherent in creating a totally new organization. "We came in with a clean slate," says Majumdar. "There was no 30-year history to overcome. I think it is difficult to change existing organizations. The pace of change in older organizations is much slower. The pace here is really fast. We have a 'let's get it done' attitude. We have a sense of urgency. We are, in fact, building the plane while we are flying it."

According to Majumdar, the next step after hiring the right people is to create the right culture in which they can flourish. "I want innovation to be the DNA of ARPA-E. It is part of our core strategy. Once you get people here, you have to give them the freedom to solve problems. We want people who like being challenged. You have to create an atmosphere to allow them to have a real impact. You need to create a culture of openness and discussion. You don't want a top-down environment. What I have done is to create a culture which empowers people at ARPA-E, while also holding them accountable. I want people to succeed and want to create an environment for success. So the key elements to creating a culture are getting talent, creating an open dialogue, and allowing people to realize their potential."

The final internal task facing Majumdar was to create the operating style of ARPA-E in developing program areas and selecting projects. "Our model," says Majumdar, "is to give people 'white space' and let them pitch an idea. We have good exchanges when we bring people together. We discuss ideas and exchange opinions. We are looking for big changes, not incremental changes. This process might take six to eight months until a program manager has put together a project. It all begins with a program idea. We then hold a technical deep dive or a workshop. Our program managers are key. There is the concept paper review and full proposal review prior to project selection. After project selection, they become part of the team of the people we support. The program managers provide technical advice and visit the projects twice a year and sit down with awardees to provide technical guidance. We want to make sure the idea succeeds."

In undertaking the third key task of picking the right set of projects, Majumdar says, "I think we are looking at the right kinds of technology. We are imagining new ways to approach energy. I think we have done very well. We are doing some neat stuff. We have the private sector fully engaged. We are telling people about our early successes." One set of projects that ARPA-E is watching closely are renewable power projects that focus on innovative technologies in several sustainable energy areas such as extremely efficient photovoltaic solar collectors, wind turbines, and geothermal energy. Another promising area is the development of batteries for transportation, which would make electric cars cheaper and with longer range than those based on gasoline technology.

Reflecting on Serving at ARPA-E

"This is my way of paying back to the nation," says Majumdar. "I'm an immigrant, so this is a real opportunity for me to serve my country. It's the best job I've ever had."

"My goal is to leave behind an organization with a set of core values and a talent pool that will position ARPA-E for the future. I want to build the organization which has a high level of technical excellence, which requires getting the right people."

Epilogue

Arun Majumdar resigned his position at the Department of Energy in June 2012 to return to California.

Victor M. Mendez
Administrator, Federal Highway Administration
Department of Transportation

The Beginning

"I was anxious to get started," recalls Victor Mendez. "The confirmation process had taken longer than I had anticipated. I was nominated in April 2009 and confirmed in July."

"I had experience with the Federal Highway Administration (FHWA) during my time as Director of the Arizona Department of Transportation. I had a good sense of the career leadership at FHWA. I thought they were very solid. And I thought that FHWA was well positioned to make a difference."

The Organization

The Federal Highway Administration has a long history. A predecessor agency, the Office of Road Inquiry, was founded in 1893. In 1905, the name of that organization was changed to the Office of Public Roads and it was placed in the Department of Agriculture. The name was changed in 1915 (to the Bureau of Public Roads) and in 1939 (to the Public Roads Administration). The Public Roads Administration was abolished in 1949 and was then reestablished as the Bureau of Public Roads and placed in the Department of Commerce. The Federal Highway Administration was created as part of the Department of Transportation legislation in 1966 and began operations in DOT in 1967.

In FY 11, FHWA had a budget of $42 billion and a staff of nearly 3,000 civil servants. The FY 12 budget requested a major increase in FHWA's funding ($70 billion) to rebuild the nation's infrastructure of highways and bridges.

The Challenge

The challenge became quickly apparent to Mendez upon his arrival. "We decided on several priorities," recalls Mendez. "First was the Recovery Act, on which we had a major role. Second was the reauthorization act. Third was innovation, because I felt that transportation projects were taking too long to complete. We need to cut delivery time. Finally, there were environmental issues. We wanted more green options for FHWA. We had to reduce our carbon footprint."

Victor M. Mendez

Tenure: Mr. Mendez was nominated by President Obama to serve as Administrator of the Federal Highway Administration in April 2009, and confirmed by the U.S. Senate in July 2009.

State government experience: Prior to being confirmed as Administrator, Mr. Mendez served as Director of the Arizona Department of Transportation (ADOT) from 2001 to 2009. During his career at ADOT, he also served as Deputy Director and as a transportation engineer.

Federal government experience: Mr. Mendez worked as a civil engineer for the U.S. Forest Service in Oregon.

Education: Mr. Mendez earned a B.S. degree in Civil Engineering from the University of Texas at El Paso and an M.B.A. from Arizona State University.

Responding to the Challenge

"I spent time on the Recovery Act from day one," says Mendez. "My top priority was to focus on what we should be doing to implement the Act. We had to ensure that funds to the states got allocated and that they received their funding in time. We didn't want any state to lose funding by not getting their funding requests to us on time. We wanted to put people to work. Nearly all the states did a good job in getting their funding requests to us. Secretary LaHood and the Vice President did, however, have to make some phone calls to the states. I think we had to call 10 or 12 states to speed up their request for funding."

"We got all of the funds out by February 27, 2010," says Mendez. "Our deadline had been March 1. Meeting the deadline took a tremendous effort by our staff and I'm very proud of them. Then on Monday, March 2, we had to start to furlough our staff due to the Congressional standoff on unemployment benefits. People often talk about how government should be run like a business. In this case, I don't think business would treat its people this way. Furloughing people is not treating them very well. This is not a way to run any type of business. We want high energy and high performance from our employees and then something like this happens. We did the best we could in this situation and tried to limit the impact of the furlough."

Essential to the successful implementation of the Recovery Act was enlisting the support of FHWA workers and stakeholders. Mendez comments, "I learned a lot from working with Janet Napolitano when she was Governor of Arizona. She knew about the importance of working with stakeholders and employees. I've learned you have to work with different groups of people and it is best to be open with them."

His desire for openness with employees prompted Mendez to use a variety of outreach tools to communicate with employees. "When I first got here, I drafted a message to employees," says Mendez. "We have done webinars and teleconferences to employees. We also have two annual meetings with all of our divisional managers and office managers. It is important for me to communicate with people and get out and mingle. I also follow up with employees via e-mail." The emphasis on communication was crucial to Mendez. "It may not be a great insight," says Mendez, "but I found communication to be very important. You need to repeat information to people and tell them what you are doing. You have to keep employees informed on the importance of issues and you have to work to develop your message to them."

In addition to communicating with his employees, Mendez also wanted to improve communication and the relationship between Washington and state transportation officials. "There is a real gap," reflects Mendez, "between people in Washington, D.C. and people out in the states who are actually delivering. I've been on the receiving end at the state level, so I understand the types of engagement you can have with the federal government. I found that people in D.C. often don't have a lot of 'on-the-ground' experience. I've tried to create new ways for FHWA to engage with the states. My only disappointment is that I would have liked to have spent more time with states. I came here to work with the states and then my attention quickly shifted to the Recovery Act."

One initiative to improve engagement with all stakeholders, including states and FHWA employees, was the Every Day Counts program launched by Mendez. "I talked to employees and stakeholders about this. We are trying to reduce project time for our construction projects by 50 percent, as well as to increase efficiency. We wanted ideas to improve operations. We didn't want to do a lot of studies, we wanted to implement new ideas."

The Every Day Counts program became a major vehicle for Mendez to work with the transportation industry. "I was concerned about the way the industry conducts business," comments Mendez. "Our construction projects take too long. It often takes 13 years to finish a project. I wanted to raise this as an issue and see if we could make progress in reducing the time it takes for major projects. I wanted to put more focus on innovation in the industry and demonstrate that shorter projects could be undertaken. People said that we could cut the time by 10 percent, but I said 'Why not cut it by 50 percent?' I wanted to find out whether we could use technology to be more innovative and could implement projects faster." In his previous position as Director of the Arizona Department of Transportation, Mendez received much praise for overseeing the building of the Regional Freeway System in the Phoenix area six years ahead of schedule.

Vision, Mission & Core Values
Federal Highway Administration (FHWA)

FHWA Vision
Our agency and our transportation system are the best in the world.

FHWA Mission
To improve mobility on our Nation's highways through national leadership, innovation, and program delivery.

Core Values
These are our core values that help us define our purpose and our mission:
• Public Service
• Integrity
• Respect
• Personal Development
• Collaboration
• Family

In describing his experience launching and supporting the Every Day Counts initiative, Mendez says, "I think it has made a difference. It is bigger than I thought it would be. The entire industry is now talking about speeding up project delivery. We at FHWA saw this as a big issue and we raised people's attention to it and we now have industry working on this across the United States." Examples of the 15 Every Day Counts initiatives include a toolkit on specific strategies shortening project delivery time and projects using new technologies, including prefabricated bridge elements and the use of geosynthetic reinforced soil for bridge systems. The 15 projects resulted from a long vetting process which evaluated hundreds of ideas.

Reflecting on Running FHWA

"I like what I do all day long," says Mendez. "The job is a challenge but I enjoy it. We have a good leadership team and they are good to work with. If we see an issue, we deal with it. Everybody contributed to implementing the Recovery Act. We got that done."

Innovation In Government:
Creating The Every Day Counts Program[*]

By Paul R. Lawrence and Mark A. Abramson

After being confirmed as Administrator of the Federal Highway Administration in July 2009, Victor Mendez quickly assessed the major challenges facing the agency.

"We decided on several priorities," recalls Mendez. "First was the Recovery Act, on which we had a major role. Second was the (transportation) reauthorization act. Third was innovation, because I felt that transportation projects were taking too long to complete. We need to cut delivery time. Finally, there were environmental issues. We wanted more green options for FHWA. We had to reduce our carbon footprint." The innovation initiative was named Every Day Counts (EDC).

"I talked to employees and stakeholders about this. We are trying to reduce project time for our construction projects by 50 percent, as well as to increase efficiency. We wanted ideas to improve operations. We didn't want to do a lot of studies, we wanted to implement new ideas ... I chose the name Every Day Counts to express the sense of urgency I feel about doing this. We really have no time to waste in building our 21st century transportation system and saving our planet."

The Every Day Counts program became a major vehicle for Mendez to work with the transportation industry. "I was concerned about the way the industry conducts business," comments Mendez. "Our construction projects take too long. It often takes 13 years to finish a project. I wanted to raise this as an issue and see if we could make progress in reducing the time it takes for major projects. I wanted to put more focus on innovation in the industry and demonstrate that shorter projects could be undertaken. People said that we could cut the time by 10 percent, but I said 'Why not cut it by 50 percent?' I wanted to find out whether we could use technology to be more innovative and could implement projects faster."

In his previous position as Director of the Arizona Department of Transportation, Mendez received praise for overseeing the building of the Regional Freeway System in the Phoenix area six years ahead of schedule.

EDC initiatives were developed to identify and deploy innovation aimed at shortening project delivery, enhancing the safety of highways, and protecting the environment. EDC was organized around three pillars:

- Reducing the carbon footprint of FHWA
- Accelerating technology and innovation deployment
- Shorter project delivery

Examples of Every Day Counts projects include a toolkit on specific strategies shortening project delivery time. One component of the shortening project delivery time pillar was the "Planning and Environment Linkages" module focused on reducing duplication and making more informed project level-decisions.

Another EDC component focused on using new technologies to accelerate project delivery, including prefabricated bridge elements and the use of geosynthetic reinforced soil for bridge systems. EDC projects resulted from a long vetting process which evaluated hundreds of ideas.

---

[*] Originally published on the AOL Government website, March 20, 2012.

In addition to the above projects, EDC has an active website which includes a Communities of Practice landing page where those involved in transportation can join their peers, partners, and national subject matter experts to ask questions and participate in discussion on EDC initiatives. The site also includes an EDC Innovation box that allows the public to make suggestions to FHWA on how it can shorten project delivery and accelerate technology and innovation deployment. There is also an active EDC Forum and an Innovation Corner to which key FHWA staff members contribute.

In describing his experience launching and supporting the Every Day Counts initiative, Mendez says, "I think it has made a difference. It is bigger than I thought it would be. The entire industry is now talking about speeding up project delivery. We at FHWA saw this as a big issue and we raised people's attention to it and we now have industry working on this across the United States."

Joseph C. Szabo
Administrator, Federal Railroad Administration
Department of Transportation

The Beginning

"With a strong background in railroad safety and operations, I was thrilled for the opportunity to join the Federal Railroad Administration," recalls Joseph Szabo. "Through the Recovery Act, we were providing a boost to local economies across America by investing in rail infrastructure. As a result, the high-speed rail program was being built from the ground up and we had to ensure it was done in an expedited and efficient manner. Since my first day at FRA, we were squarely focused on launching the high-speed rail program. It was a time of change and growth for the agency and the FRA team was up for the challenge."

The Organization

The Federal Railroad Administration was created as part of the Department of Transportation Act in 1966. It inherited the railroad safety functions previously performed by the Interstate Commerce Commission (which was abolished by Congress in 1995). The Federal Railroad Safety Act of 1970 and subsequent legislation granted FRA plenary authority in regulating railroad safety in areas such as the inspection, testing, and maintenance of track, signals, and mechanical equipment; as well as railroad operating practices, hazardous materials, and other areas. The Passenger Rail Investment and Improvement Act of 2008 (PRIIA) authorized the funding of several new discretionary grant programs for passenger rail under FRA.

FRA also has a research and development program, and has responsibility for several small grant programs for specific purposes such as rail line relocation or disaster assistance. In addition, FRA provides operating grants to Amtrak, and was historically the pass-through agency for funds provided by Congress to the railroad. In FY 11, FRA had a budget of over $4 billion and over 900 employees.

The signing of the American Recovery and Reinvestment Act of 2009 on February 17, 2009, expanded the mission and reach of FRA. Together with PRIIA, the Recovery Act gave FRA responsibility to assist states, localities, other federal agencies, and industry and transportation sector stakeholders to ensure the appropriate coordination among all parties in managing Recovery Act rail investments. FRA was tasked to administer $8 billion in high-speed rail grants, something unimaginable in the past. In announcing FRA's high-speed intercity passenger rail

Joseph C. Szabo

Tenure: Mr. Szabo was nominated by President Obama to serve as Administrator of the Federal Railroad Administration in March 2009, and confirmed by the U.S. Senate in April 2009.

Private sector experience: Prior to being confirmed as Administrator, Mr. Szabo served as State Legislative Director of the United Transportation Union (UTU) and Vice President of the Illinois State Federation of the American Federation of Labor and Congress of Industrial Organizations (AFL-CIO). He started his railroad career in 1976 with the Illinois Central Railroad and worked in numerous positions, including as a yard switcher, road trainman, and a commuter passenger conductor.

State and local government experience: Mr. Szabo served as Mayor of Riverdale, Illinois, a member of the South Suburban Mayors Transportation Committee, and Vice Chairman of the Chicago Area Transportation Study's Executive Committee. In 2002, he chaired the Governor's Freight Rail Sub-Committee.

Education: Mr. Szabo holds a B.A. degree in Labor Relations from Governors State University.

---

grant awards in January 2010, President Obama said, "Through the Recovery Act, we are making the largest investment infrastructure since the Interstate Highway System was created, putting Americans to work … That investment is how we can break ground across the country, putting people to work building high-speed rail lines, because there's no reason why Europe or China should have the fastest trains when we can build them right here in America."

The Challenge

The enormity of the challenge was clear to Szabo when he arrived. While his interest had long been in railroad safety and operations, Szabo found that implementation of the Obama Administration's high-speed rail program would take much of his time and energy. He faced the challenge of leading FRA during a significant transformation as it evolved from being primarily a railroad safety regulatory agency to one also responsible for grant management of a sizeable new program that happened to be a top DOT priority. In addition to administering a high volume of grant dollars, Szabo had the responsibility to ensure that quality projects were selected through a merit-driven process, and that the funds were spent in a prudent and transparent manner.

The challenge of overseeing a Presidential and departmental priority initiative should not be underestimated. Szabo reflects, "We clearly had the attention of the Secretary and Deputy Secretary. We were coordinating numerous activities simultaneously and providing daily progress reports. We were operating under immense scrutiny while facilitating change, and we had to get the job done right. If not, our missteps would have been magnified. However, it is extremely rewarding to work on a Presidential spotlight initiative and know we're transforming the way Americans will travel now and in the future."

Responding to the Challenge

Instead of focusing solely on railroad safety, Szabo faced a challenge similar to that faced by Jonathan Adelstein at the Rural Utilities Service (RUS): transforming an old-line agency to undertake an entirely new set of activities under a very tight time schedule. That is, FRA had to establish a major grant program from the ground up, distributing $8 billion to states through the Recovery Act. In reflecting on his experience at FRA, Szabo says, "We really did transform the agency. Almost overnight, it went from being a relatively small safety agency to one that was also a grant-making organization supporting both Amtrak and other passenger rail investment programs. We were required to strategically ramp up our efforts due to the wildly enthusiastic response of applicants seeking grant funds under a program that didn't yet exist."

Szabo also had to balance the agency's traditional deliberative and risk-averse approach with a new need for speed. "We had to determine," recalls Szabo, "how much information we needed about each of our grant applicants. We could not take a cumbersome approach as we might have done in the past. We created an expedited program, working closely with states to help fast-track money for these critical projects. " A related change is that the agency, again much like RUS, had to become more agile. "A major accomplishment," says Szabo, "is that we became more proactive in getting out our rules and regulations on high-speed rail to ensure a fair and equitable application evaluation and review process. We took great pains to look at things from our stakeholders' point of view and anticipate their needs."

Another challenge facing Szabo was that the organization was not adequately staffed to manage an $8 billion program that had to meet a Congressionally mandated deadline of September 30, 2012, for the distribution of high-speed rail dollars. "We had to identify what barriers needed to be overcome and what our staffing needs would be to do that. This required borrowing employees with specific expertise from

Purpose and Vision
Federal Railroad Administration (FRA)

Purpose
The purpose of FRA is to:
- Promulgate and enforce rail safety regulations
- Administer railroad financial assistance programs
- Design and manage an unprecedented investment in the creation of a nationwide passenger rail network.
- Conduct research and development in support of improved railroad safety and national rail transportation policy
- Provide for the rehabilitation of Northeast Corridor rail passenger service
- Consolidate government support of rail transportation activities

Vision for High-Speed Rail in America
To transform the nation's transportation system, by rebuilding existing rail infrastructure while launching new high-speed passenger rail services in 100–600 mile corridors that connect U.S. cities and mega regions. Similar to how interstate highways and U.S. aviation system were developed in 20th century: partnership between public sector and private industry, including strong Federal leadership that provided a national vision.

other agencies within DOT," recounts Szabo. "The Secretary and DOT leadership pledged to provide additional staff support to assist us in establishing and expediting implementation of the program. On a parallel track, our Deputy Administrator, Karen Rae, led efforts to engage the states in the process to assess their strengths and needs. We hosted listening sessions with key stakeholders about the high-speed rail initiative to educate them and obtain buy-in. We began extensive national rail planning efforts to reflect these conversations and highlight key principles that created a roadmap being used to build high-speed rail in key corridors across America. Specifically, we issued a strategic rail visioning document, just 58 days after the passage of ARRA [Recovery Act]. From that point on, we met or exceeded every deadline that was set forth by Congress and the Administration, including solicitations for grant applications, the selection of recipients, and the obligation of the funding," Szabo says.

In describing his relationship with the states, Szabo says, "The relationship between FRA and the states has evolved considerably. We had to adopt an aggressive approach to support our state partners if they were to successfully negotiate stakeholder agreements where needed. These so-called service outcome agreements (SOA) required states to secure the cooperation of freight railroads and/or entities that would ultimately operate the new and expanded intercity passenger rail services."

"Our goal was to get these stakeholder agreements right the first time around," recalls Szabo. "It was a daunting challenge, requiring the parties to enter uncharted waters, but we did not want to encounter any unforeseen hurdles in distributing the high-speed rail dollars so that work could begin."

Working closely with the states required FRA to change the way it had customarily done business. Szabo recalls, "It meant we needed to fully understand the legitimate concerns and fears of stakeholders as they developed mutually beneficial agreements. It was a critical point in the process, and it proved that by bargaining in good faith, win-win outcomes could be reached."

In implementing its piece of the Recovery Act, FRA assumed a new role that it had not played before: that of technical advisor to the states. "It was a major undertaking to harness and leverage the necessary resources to provide such assistance," states Szabo. "For some states, we had to walk them through the complex, competitive application process and how to initiate and complete the stakeholder agreements. Many state departments of transportation had no dedicated railroad staff or divisions. Some had only one or two folks working on rail issues. Only a handful had a dozen or more working on rail issues. Assessing and addressing our own needs would prove to be critical in helping states define their own. It was an invaluable learning experience for our agency as we determined the most effective tools and resources needed to provide that assistance."

Reflecting on Serving in the FRA

"This has been a fascinating time to be at FRA," says Szabo. "We have awarded more than $8 billion in two years. I believe that most of my predecessors would agree that this has probably been one of the most challenging undertakings ever for FRA: one that fundamentally expanded the mission and scope of the agency forever."

"We not only had to enhance our own capacity, but that of other partners so we could build the momentum which will ultimately change America's transportation landscape for the centuries to come. We were already good custodians of the taxpayers' investment, but the high-speed program made protecting these investments more important than ever. We are building the equivalent of the interstate highway system and that took over 40 years to complete."

"I'm really proud of all the employees at FRA. They responded to the challenge and have done an excellent job as we make history building a world-class rail network for future generations. "

Chapter Eight

The Regulators

Understanding the Job of the Regulator

Government regulators are modern tightrope walkers who perform a constant balancing act between what some might call too much regulation and others might call not enough regulation. The stakes are high for government's regulators. Their decisions impact the well-being of the nation's citizens (in some cases, their life and death) and the nation's economic well-being. When asked what is most fulfilling about his job, Joe Main, Assistant Secretary of Labor for Mine Safety and Health, says, "It is the daily update on mining incidents. It is a good day when we don't have any incidents. The number of incidents has been declining. I am satisfied when miners go to work in the morning and then go home safely each night."

The regulators profiled in this chapter are constantly balancing the cost implications of their regulations with the agency's desired result (such as reductions in deaths on the nation's highways, in the nation's mines, or due to faulty consumer products). David Strickland, Administrator of NHTSA, describes his balancing act:

The Regulators

Michael R. Bromwich, page 167

Director, Bureau of Ocean Energy Management, Regulation and Enforcement (BOEMRE), Department of the Interior

Joseph A. Main, page 173

Assistant Secretary of Labor for Mine Safety and Health (MSHA), Department of Labor

David L. Strickland, page 178

Administrator, National Highway Traffic Safety Administration (NHTSA), Department of Transportation

Inez Moore Tenenbaum, page 182

Chairman, Consumer Product Safety Commission (CPSC)

"We understand the relationship between safety and costs and we want to work with manufacturers on safety. We want cars to be very safe but we are aware that we don't want them to be too costly for people to buy them."

There is no agreement on the number of regulatory agencies in government. Figures range between 25 and 50, depending on which agencies are counted. Some of the financial regulatory agencies are well-known—the Securities and Exchange Commission, the Commodity Futures Trading Commission, and the Federal Deposit Insurance Corporation. Another group of regulatory agencies are well-known for their oversight responsibilities in the area of food and drug safety—the Food and Drug Administration in the Department of Health and Human Services, and the Food Safety and Inspection Service in the Department of Agriculture. In addition, many government agencies have some regulatory responsibilities in their portfolio of activities.

There are two governance models for regulatory agencies. The first, common in the financial regulatory agencies, is the Commission model, in which there is one Chair and four Commission Members. In the case of a five-person Commission, the laws creating regulatory agencies usually stipulate that no more than three of the Commissioners should be affiliated with the same political party. The party that holds the White House names the person to serve as Chair. The second model is to have a single Administrator for the organization. In the profiles presented in this chapter, three of the agencies profiled have single Administrators (NHTSA, MSHA, and BOEMRE) and one has a Chair and four Commissioners (CPSC).

Key Challenges

Serving as a government regulator involves many challenges. In our interviews with the five political executives profiled in this chapter, each describes facing one or more of the challenges discussed below. The four challenges are:

- Operating in a politically contentious environment
- Getting the rules out *and* running an organization
- Responding to unexpected events while keeping the organization running
- Constantly engaging with and responding to stakeholder concerns

Operating in a Politically Contentious Environment

While all the positions described in this book are to some degree politically contentious, the job of the regulator is highly contentious. Public and Congressional attitudes toward regulation are highly volatile and subject to wide swings in support depending on the current political environment. Inez Tenenbaum, Chair of the CPSC, tells us, "It has been a roller coaster. We have so many contentious issues. Many of our rule-making initiatives were mandated by Congress ... I was expecting a more positive environment. I wasn't expecting so much conflict."

Coupled with a politically contentious environment is the high visibility that comes with being a regulator. Tenenbaum says, "I've been surprised at the high visibility and high profile of the agency. Many of our issues—cribs, baby bumpers, window coverings—have received much attention." Michael Bromwich, former Director of BOEMRE, was surprised "at the great press attention and political intensity that surrounded our issuing of permits. Things are somewhat quieter right now in summer 2011, but not much."

Getting the Rules Out *and* Running an Organization

Due to the unique nature of the job, the regulators have both policy and management responsibilities. In a five-member Commission, the Chairman becomes the individual responsible for managing the organization in addition to his or her responsibilities as a voting member of the Commission. At the CPSC, Tenenbaum's responsibilities include running the organization, managing the rule-making process, and voting on the rules that the Commission will issue. At NHTSA, David Strickland is charged with getting the rules out and serving as the leader of the organization.

A major initial activity of both Tenenbaum's and Strickland's was to speed up their agency's process for getting its new rules out. Chairman Tenenbaum describes one of her initial actions at the agency, "I told our staff and the Office of General Counsel to pick up the pace. Everything was simply taking too long. The delays were burdensome on industry. Industry needed to know what we were going to do, so they could be ready to respond." David Strickland expresses a similar frustration, "It was taking six months to elicit comments on some of our rules. We didn't have that long. We had to speed it up." The job of managing the rule-making process falls to the agency Administrator or the Chair. In the Chair model, individual commission members have little or no responsibility for oversight of the speed and management of the rule-making process.

Responding to Unexpected Events While Keeping the Organization Running

Two of the political executives profiled in this chapter—Joe Main at MSHA and Michael Bromwich at BOEMRE—faced a major national crisis during their tenures. Joe Main confronted the challenge of investigating and responding to the Upper Big Branch mine explosion which occurred in April 2010, seven months after his confirmation in October 2009. Michael Bromwich arrived at BOEMRE in June 2010, two months after the Deepwater Horizon explosion and subsequent environmental crisis, with a charge to serve both as a crisis manager and a turn-around manager for the organization.

David Strickland and Inez Tenenbaum also faced crisis, albeit somewhat less dramatic. Strickland arrived at NHTSA in January 2010 in the middle of the Toyota recall crisis. When Tenenbaum arrived at CPSC in 2009, the organization was still responding to the aftermath of the 2007 recall of Chinese-made toys contaminated with lead paint.

While all five political executives were prepared to deal with the crisis at hand (or in the case of Tenenbaum, the aftermath of a previous crisis), they also had to continue to run their organizations while dealing with the crisis. In effect, their workload doubled and they acted in the roles of both crisis manager and chief executive officer concurrently. Joe Main recounts, "I'm very proud that I was able to keep the agency running in spite of Upper Big Branch. We had a successful strategy in place and we kept it going. We kept doing our work ...." In reflecting on his experience at BOEMRE, Bromwich recalls that he not only had to deal with the immediate aftermath of the Deepwater Horizon crisis, but also faced the challenge of reorganizing the agency, getting the permits issuance process running again, and getting the organization's employees back on track.

Constantly Engaging with and Responding to Stakeholder Concerns

Each regulatory agency has its own distinct set of stakeholders, all of whom make their views well-known. It is possible to map each regulatory organization's stakeholders, which range from citizens/consumers to corporations to foreign governments. While most regulatory agencies interact with regulated industries, there is a group of regulatory agencies that deals directly with citizens. These agencies include NHTSA and the CPSC. In the case of NHTSA, David Strickland recounts meeting with families of individuals who have died in car crashes. "They come to meet with me," says Strickland. "It gives me a sense of the importance of my job."

In the case of NHTSA, the passage of the Cameron Gulbransen Kids Transportation Safety Act mandated that the agency prepare new safety regulations to avoid accidents such as the one in which a minivan backed over Cameron because he was not visible from within the automobile. Cameron's father worked with Congress to pass the law mandating new regulations. In the case of CPSC, a major activity of Inez Tenenbaum's was to implement the requirements of the Virginia Graeme Baker Pool & Spa Safety Act which was enacted by Congress in 2007. Virginia Graeme Baker, granddaughter of former Secretary of State James Baker, drowned when the powerful suction from a hot tub drain trapped her underwater. In 2010, CPSC launched *Pool Safety: Simple Steps Save Lives,* a national public education campaign to raise public awareness about drowning and entrapment prevention. Tenenbaum went on the road to several cities to launch the campaign.

Tenenbaum also works directly with corporations. "I have been reaching out to stakeholders, instead of waiting for them to come to me," Tenenbaum recounts. "I want to work with companies on voluntary standards. Voluntary standards are the first step. We let industries regulate themselves, unless their regulations are ineffective. Sometimes voluntary standards are too little and too late. We want the stakeholders to come talk to me and the other Commissioners. I have really reached out to industry. I must talk to an industry representative three or four times a day."

Selecting the Regulators

For the Office of Presidential Personnel, the selection of the regulators and their successful confirmation by the U.S. Congress is a continuing challenge. To gain confirmation, nominees to regulatory positions cannot be viewed as too close either to industry or to consumer interest groups. Recent administrations have run into difficulty getting their nominees confirmed for positions at the Consumer Product Safety Commission, the National Highway Traffic Safety Administration, and the Mine Safety and Health Administration.

Tenenbaum, Strickland, and Main were exceptions to the recent trend of highly controversial and contentious nominees. In the case of Tenenbaum, her state government experience had prepared her for dealing with stakeholders, but she had not had any direct experience in the consumer product safety field. In the case of Strickland, he had spent his career as a Congressional staff member dealing with automobile safety issues but had not worked for industry or a consumer group. Joe Main came to the position with a career-long background in working on mine safety issues, both as a miner himself and a staff member of the United Mine Workers.

The experience of Michael Bromwich is somewhat atypical. He was chosen because of his management and turnaround experience, not his expertise on energy-related issues. Because of intense interest in the events surrounding the Deepwater Horizon incident and its aftermath, future nominees to the successor agencies of BOEMRE are likely to receive close scrutiny both in the selection and confirmation process.

In selecting future nominees for regulatory positions, the following factors should be considered:

- **Prior experience in the field is highly useful, as is knowledge of industry stakeholders.** While experience and knowledge of the stakeholder community are important, the appointee must not be viewed as too closely aligned with either side of the regulatory spectrum (whose attitudes range from support of heavy regulation to support of lighter regulation). In the case of Joe Main, his prior experience in mining helped him to know exactly how to respond to the Upper Big Branch mine explosion. Main says, "I've lived through these experiences before, so I knew what to expect." As with all the positions described in this book, there is often no shortcut for relevant experience. There is also no shortcut for knowing many of the stakeholders in the arena before arriving. Strickland recalls, "I knew (the stakeholders) from my days on the Hill—the automobile manufacturers, the safety advocates ..."
- **Appointees to regulatory positions must be able to deal with conflict, handle controversy, and operate in a highly contentious environment.** Regulatory positions are not for those who like to avoid conflict. While often difficult to find, individuals who are well-respected on both sides of the regulated industry are needed to mediate the vast difference of opinions in any regulated arena.

Other Regulatory Agencies

In addition to the four agencies profiled in this chapter, there are other organizations throughout government which we categorize as regulatory agencies. While not comprehensive, the list and descriptions of each agency have been prepared to assist the Office of Presidential Personnel and Cabinet Secretaries in better understanding the unique nature of the regulatory agencies.

Other Federal Government Agencies Categorized as Regulatory Agencies

Department of Agriculture
Food Safety and Inspection Service

The Food Safety and Inspection Service (FSIS) is charged with ensuring that the nation's supply of meat, poultry, and egg products is safe for consumption and correctly labeled and packaged. FSIS engages in activities such as detecting and investigating food-borne disease outbreaks, conducting baseline studies on food-borne pathogens, inspecting catfish, and conducting public education campaigns about food safety. The agency had over 9,500 employees in FY 11, with a budget of over $1 billion.

Department of Health and Human Services
Food and Drug Administration

The Food and Drug Administration (FDA) is charged with ensuring the safety and effectiveness of $2 trillion worth of drugs, vaccines, medical devices, cosmetics, dietary supplements, and our nation's food supply. The FDA is led by a single agency head, the Commissioner. In FY 11, the FDA had a budget of over $4 billion and over 13,000 employees.

Department of Labor
Occupational Safety and Health Administration

The Occupational Safety and Health Administration (OSHA) is charged with preventing work-related injuries, illnesses, and fatalities. The agency creates mandatory safety standards for employers regarding construction, agriculture, maritime, and general industry work. OSHA also conducts workplace inspections and offers training and technical assistance to America's workplaces. In FY 11, OSHA had a staff of over 2,000 employees and a budget of over $550 million.

Independent Agencies
Commodity Futures Trading Commission

The Commodity Futures Trading Commission (CFTC), created in 1936, is charged with regulating derivatives, such as futures, stocks, swaps, and commodities, in order to protect market users from fraud and abusive practices such as Ponzi schemes. In FY 11, the agency had more than 650 employees and a budget of over $200 million. The agency requested a significant increase for FY 12 due to the Dodd-Frank Act of 2010, which expanded the role of the CFTC to also cover swaps and increased its role with agricultural and energy commodities. The Commission has five Commissioners, including the Chair.

Other Federal Government Agencies Categorized as
Regulatory Agencies (continued)

Federal Communications Commission

The Federal Communications Commission (FCC), established in 1934, consists of five Commissioners, including the Chair, each appointed for a term of five years. The purpose of the FCC is to regulate all radio, television, wire, satellite, and cable communication in the nation by developing and protecting the nation's communications infrastructure. The Commission is responsible for processing applications for licenses, analyzing complaints, conducting investigations, developing and implementing regulatory programs, and taking part in hearings. In FY 11, the FCC had a budget of over $400 million with nearly 2,000 employees.

Federal Trade Commission

The Federal Trade Commission (FTC), created in 1914, is charged with policing anticompetitive practices and protecting consumers from fraud and unfair practices. The FTC pursues vigorous and effective law enforcement; advances consumers' interests by sharing its expertise with federal and state legislatures and U.S. and international government agencies; develops policy and research tools through hearings, workshops, and conferences; and creates practical and plain-language educational programs for consumers and businesses in a global marketplace with constantly changing technologies. The Commission has five Commissioners, including the Chair, each serving a seven-year term. In FY 11, the FTC had a budget of over $300 million and over 1,100 employees.

Nuclear Regulatory Commission

The Nuclear Regulatory Commission (NRC), created in 1974, regulates the use of radioactive materials for civilian purposes. The Commission has five Commissioners, including the Chair. The NRC regulates the nuclear industry by developing regulations that it then enforces through an inspection program, issuing licenses to transporters and operators of nuclear materials, and decommissioning nuclear facilities. The agency also regulates hazardous waste disposal, and conducts health and safety inspections. In FY 11, the NRC had a budget of over $1 billion and a staff of 4,000 people in five primary locations across the United States.

Securities and Exchange Commission

The Securities and Exchange Commission (SEC), created in 1934, is charged with protecting investors, regulating markets, and facilitating capital formation. The agency has five Commissioners, including the Chair. The SEC oversees the key participants in the securities world, including securities exchanges, securities brokers and dealers, investment advisors, and mutual funds. In this role, the SEC is concerned with promoting the disclosure of important market-related information, maintaining fair dealing, and protecting against fraud. In FY 11, the SEC had a budget of over $1 million and over 3,700 employees.

Michael R. Bromwich
Director, Bureau of Ocean Energy Management, Regulation and Enforcement
Department of the Interior

The Beginning

"I was first contacted by the White House about taking this job just 11 days before I started," recalls Michael Bromwich. "I was on the job exactly one week after I said 'Yes.' In that week, I had to wind up a 10-year law practice. I arrived almost exactly two months after the Deepwater Horizon oil spill: the spill occurred on April 20, 2010 and I got here on June 21st. The Department was then focused on capping the well and stopping the flow of the oil."

"During my first week here, I went down to New Orleans because we have a lot of employees down there and the Gulf of Mexico regional office had been hit hardest in every way by Deepwater Horizon and its aftermath. Everybody wanted to see the new boss and take his measure. This was the first of many town hall meetings with employees in all of our offices, and with the public, during my first few months on the job. There were 400 people at the New Orleans meeting that first week. I answered all their questions. I also invited people to submit anonymous questions in case they didn't want to ask them for attribution in a public setting. I wanted people to ask difficult, tough questions. I am comfortable in that format and I thought it was important to show that I welcomed tough questions and that I would give them the best answers I could."

"For the New Orleans town hall meeting, we rented a screening room in a multiplex called the Palace Theater. So I now can say that I've played the Palace."

The Organization

The Bureau of Ocean Energy Management, Regulation, and Enforcement (BOEMRE) was created in May 2010 by a Secretarial order. Michael Bromwich was chosen to lead BOEMRE in June 2010, one month after its creation. Its predecessor agency, the Minerals Management Service (MMS), was also created by a Secretarial order in 1982. In 1983, Congress passed the Federal Oil and Gas Royalty Management Act with the stated purposes of managing all oil and gas originating on public lands and on the outer continental shelf. The then-Secretary of the Interior, James Watt, designated MMS as the agency responsible for implementing the new oil and gas royalty act.

Since its creation, MMS has had conflicting missions. One part of the agency,

Michael R. Bromwich

Tenure: Mr. Bromwich was selected to serve as Director of the Bureau of Ocean Energy Management, Regulation and Enforcement (BOEMRE) in June 2010.

Private sector experience: Prior to his selection as Director of BOEMRE, Mr. Bromwich was a Litigation Partner in the Washington, D.C. and New York offices of Fried Frank Harris Shriver & Jacobson, where he headed the firm's Internal Investigations, Compliance and Monitoring practice group. He has also been a Partner in the Washington, D.C. office of Mayer, Brown & Platt and an associate in the Washington, D.C. office of Foley & Lardner.

Federal government experience: From 1994 to 1999, Mr. Bromwich served as Inspector General for the Department of Justice. From 1987 to 1989, Mr. Bromwich served as Associate Counsel in the Office of Independent Counsel for Iran-Contra. From 1983 to 1987, Mr. Bromwich served as an Assistant U.S. Attorney in the U.S. Attorney's Office for the Southern District of New York. He served as Deputy Chief and Chief of the Office's Narcotics Unit.

Local government experience: In 2002, Mr. Bromwich was selected by the Department of Justice and the District of Columbia to serve as the Independent Monitor for the District of Columbia's Metropolitan Police Department (MPD). In 2009, he was selected by the Department of Justice and the Government of the Virgin Islands to serve a similar function for the Virgin Islands Police Department. He was also selected by the City of Houston to undertake a comprehensive investigation of the Houston Police Department Crime Laboratory.

Education: Mr. Bromwich received his undergraduate degree, *summa cum laude,* from Harvard College in 1976. He received his law degree from the Harvard Law School in 1980 and a master's degree in Public Policy from Harvard's John F. Kennedy School of Government the same year.

the Offshore Energy and Minerals Management office, was responsible for resource assessments and evaluation; environmental reviews, and leasing and permitting activities. The other part of the agency, Minerals Revenue Management, was responsible for collecting, accounting for, and distributing revenues associated with minerals produced on federal and Indian-leased lands. In 2008, the Inspector General of the Department of Interior found instances of improper conduct by employees of the Minerals Revenue Management office.

The life of BOEMRE was a short one. In response to the Deepwater Horizon explosion and the resulting oil spill in the Gulf of Mexico, the Obama Administration moved to reform the management of the federal government's activities related to offshore oil and gas regulations. The Administration set forth plans to divide the agency into three separate organizations:

- **October 2010:** The Secretary of the Interior created a new Office of Natural Resources Revenue (ONRR) and moved it out of BOEMRE to the Office of the Assistant Secretary for Policy, Management, and Budget. The new office was responsible for revenue collection activities. Over 600 staff members were moved from BOEMRE to ONRR in what Bromwich calls "a clean break."
- **October 2011:** The final two pieces of the reorganization were implemented and BOEMRE ceased to exist:
  - The new **Bureau of Ocean Energy Management (BOEM)** is responsible for managing the development of the nation's offshore resources in an environmentally and economically responsible way.
  - The new **Bureau of Safety and Environmental Enforcement (BSEE)** enforces safety and environmental regulations.

The Challenge

The challenges facing Bromwich are best described by him. Bromwich recalls, "The agency was suffering from years of negative publicity. There had been instances of corruption which had happened several years before. There had been the perception—and to some extent the reality—of a cozy relationship between the regulators and the regulated. There has never been any evidence to connect these problems to the oil spill."

"There was massive media attention given to the agency and many negative stories. Before I got here, there had already been discussions and plans for reorganizing the agency and separating the royalty function of the agency from its other functions. We wanted to create a separate office for royalty and revenue collection and split it off as quickly as possible. We were able to do that three months after my arrival."

"A significant part of my early time here was spent on the oil spill and its aftermath. We also faced some very substantial legal issues when the original moratorium on deepwater drilling was overturned by a federal judge the first week I was here. I then got swept up into that issue."

Responding to the Challenge

Bromwich was an interesting choice to lead BOEMRE in the aftermath of the

Deepwater Horizon oil spill. He had spent his entire career as a lawyer and had no energy expertise. "I think I was asked to take this job because I had substantial experience dealing with troubled organizations—both in the public and private sector—and had experience leading an agency in the public eye. I certainly wasn't hired for my knowledge of offshore energy issues—I didn't have any. I had to walk a difficult line after I got here. I didn't have substantive expertise in the area and people knew I had a reputation as a 'tough cop.' I had been an Inspector General and had a reputation for being tough when it comes to integrity issues and for being a no-nonsense enforcer. Because I didn't have a background in energy, people in the agency were naturally suspicious of me. There was concern about me tearing apart the place people knew and were comfortable with. All the employees were concerned about whether their job was at risk."

"I've found that it isn't healthy for an organization if people's dominant attitude toward you as the agency head is fear. That is not a healthy environment. I sent out e-mails early in my tenure and held town meetings, such as the meeting at the Palace. My initial thinking was not to replace people until I got to know the personnel, their strengths and weaknesses. I wanted to look around and get to know people."

"You have to gauge what the crisis really is. We were the most heavily criticized agency in government when I started in June 2010, which did create a crisis mentality in the agency and in Interior generally. We were being criticized in the media every day—every media outlet felt obliged to publish numerous critical pieces about the agency. Morale was as low as I've ever seen it in any organization. There was a lot of tension in the agency, and a stream of negative commentary about it, including from inside the government. There was no end in sight to the negative publicity. I was very careful not to reinforce all this negative feedback by jumping on the bandwagon of criticism, but on the other hand I could not defend past acts of misconduct or lack of competence."

"I had two major tasks. The first was to manage the crisis and the second was to manage the reorganization. Those are the reasons I was brought in."

When asked about his preparation for taking over an agency in crisis, Bromwich says, "I think I got the job in part because of the breadth of my experience. I had worked in various organizations and I know what good organizations look like. I had experience in law enforcement and an IG background. My law enforcement and IG background did include substantial experience with oversight and investigations—both of which were going to be part of the agency's future for some time. I had definite ideas about how things should be done. I felt prepared for this assignment. I didn't know the substance—offshore energy issues—but that was something I felt I could learn and I was eager to learn. My lack of substantive expertise did allow me to ask questions which had not been asked before about the rules, procedures, and processes of the agency."

Bromwich's analytical abilities proved helpful to him as the lead in figuring out the reorganization of BOEMRE. "We are now busy cross-walking the new organization and figuring out who will go where," says Bromwich. "The split

Mission
Bureau of Ocean Energy Management, Regulation and Enforcement

The Bureau of Ocean Energy Management, Regulation and Enforcement (BOEMRE) is the federal agency responsible for overseeing the safe and environmentally responsible development of traditional and renewable energy ocean and mineral resources on the 1.7 billion acres of the U.S. Outer Continental Shelf.

is taking up a lot of time. The spin-off of the royalty and revenue activities was pretty straightforward. The creation of the two new agencies is not as obvious and there are many tricky issues. The reorganization is clearly needed. All the studies on the oil spill, including the President's Commission, reported that the previous directors of MMS had spent most of their time on the revenue part of the job. The issue of balancing resource development demands with environmental considerations did not receive as much attention. The safety and environmental part of the job received little attention."

One challenging part of coming into a crisis situation is that you are never sure how long the crisis will last. Bromwich reports, "The crisis didn't end as quickly as I had anticipated. The external attention from the media and Congress continued. I expected it to diminish more quickly, in about 60 to 90 days after I arrived, but it continued for much longer. Then the issue of issuing new drilling permits in deepwater became a highly charged political issue, especially with the sharp rise in gasoline prices."

"I thought the crisis atmosphere would diminish, which would then give people more time for reflection and planning the best way forward," recalls Bromwich. "But it didn't happen. The legal controversies continued. The deepwater drilling moratorium was lifted on October 12, 2010, but we did not issue any deepwater permits until late February 2011 because industry had not yet developed the capacity to contain a subsea spill. Both before October 12 and after, there was a strong drumbeat to issue permits. The pressure began much more quickly than I would have thought."

In looking back on his first year at BOEMRE, Bromwich says, "We did a lot. We got the oil well plugged. We reorganized the agency. We started issuing permits again. We are putting the organization back on its feet and getting our employees back on track. But we aren't done yet. The battle for more resources is proving harder than I thought it would be. Among many other things, we need more inspectors for the more than 3,000 facilities we oversee."

Reflecting on Serving in BOEMRE

"This has been on the whole an extremely satisfying and enjoyable experience," reflects Bromwich. "In a career where I have spent 14 years in four very different public-sector jobs, I would say this has been the most satisfying single year of public service. I helped an agency that was in a very deep hole and helped to bring it back when many people—in and out of government—had given up on it. There is a lot of satisfaction in doing this."

In recruiting students at the University of San Diego, Bromwich told them, "You will be serving your country in an extremely important field right now. For all the benefits and virtues of private-sector jobs, which pay more, you don't get that." (Broder).

Epilogue

Michael R. Bromwich is now a litigation partner in Goodwin Procter's Washington, D.C. and New York offices, and a member of the firm's Securities Litigation & White Collar Defense Group. After the reorganization of BOEMRE, Mr. Bromwich served as the first Director of the Bureau of Safety and Environmental Enforcement.

Joseph A. Main
Assistant Secretary of Labor for Mine Safety and Health
Department of Labor

The Beginning

"I had been working with the agency since the 1970s, so I knew the place," states Joe Main. "I have worked with people in the agency for many years. On my first day in office, I was struck by the weight of my new responsibilities and the realization that I was going to have to run this place. I had used the time before my confirmation to get up to speed. I focused on the key issues and key challenges facing the agency. I asked the agency to send me over lots of information and reports which I could read before taking over."

"I had my own ideas about mine safety. I had been working in the field for over 40 years and knew a lot about it. So I had ideas about what needed to be done. But I first needed to work on the organization. When I got here, I found that nearly the entire senior staff was serving in acting capacities. The office had not had a confirmed head in five years. I went job by job to get all the positions filled on a permanent basis. I am happy with the people here but I wanted everybody to get into a permanent position."

The Organization

The Mine Safety and Health Administration (MSHA) is responsible for the safety and health of the nation's mines. The agency develops and promulgates safety and health standards, ensures compliance, assesses civil penalties, and investigates accidents. The federal government's role in mine safety dates back to 1891 when Congress passed the nation's first law regulating mining activities. In 1910, Congress established the Bureau of Mines within the Department of the Interior. Congress authorized federal inspectors to enter mines in 1941 and mandated federal regulations in 1947. In 1973, the Secretary of the Interior created the Mining and Enforcement Administration, an agency separate from the Bureau of Mines. The Federal Mine Safety and Health Act of 1977 transferred responsibility of the Mine Act to the Department of Labor and renamed the new agency the Mine Safety and Health Administration. In FY 11, MSHA had a budget of over $350 million and had over 2,300 employees.

Joseph A. (Joe) Main

Tenure: Mr. Main was nominated by President Obama as Assistant Secretary of Labor for Mine Safety and Health (MSHA) in July 2009, and confirmed by the U.S. Senate in October 2009.

Private sector experience: Prior to being confirmed as Assistant Secretary, Mr. Main was an independent mine safety consultant. Mr. Main began working in coal mines in 1967. In 1974, Mr. Main joined the United Mine Workers of America (UMWA) to be an Assistant to the International President. In 1976, he joined the Safety Division of the UMWA, serving as Safety Inspector, Administrative Assistant, and Deputy Director. In 1982, Mr. Main was appointed Administrator of the UMWA Occupational Health and Safety Department.

Education: Mr. Main attended the National Mine Health and Safety Academy.

The Challenge

Joe Main faced two sets of challenges at the Mine Safety and Health Administration. Upon arriving in October 2009, Main faced his first set of challenges. The first set of challenges is common to all regulatory agencies: fulfilling an ambitious mandate with limited resources, working with Congress to update and fine-tune existing legislation, and working with the regulated industry to develop initiatives.

The second set of challenges is a consequence of the Massey Energy's Upper Big Branch Mine explosion on April 2010 in Raleigh County, West Virginia, in which 29 miners were killed. This challenge involved both responding to intense Congressional and media interest in the explosion and conducting an agency investigation into the tragedy. Main says, "You have to ask yourself and the agency, 'What did we miss?' 'How did this happen,' 'What have we learned,' and finally, 'What changes do we need to make?'"

Responding to the Challenge

By April 2010, Main was making significant progress on his original agenda. "When I came in, a major issue facing us was reforming the Black Lung Disease

Program. There had been two prior attempts to reform the program but they had not worked. There had also been two reports on black lung disease which made recommendations on what needed to be done. I quickly developed a three-pronged approach to our black lung program. The first prong is education and outreach, the second prong is beefing up enforcement, and the third prong is revising the current law. One of the first things I did was to put together public events to launch the black lung program. I asked stakeholders to attend, some victims to attend, representatives from the National Institute for Occupational Safety and Health (NIOSH), and other public officials to attend the event. "

"Our initial agenda," recalls Main, "was also to reduce coal mining fatalities. We have too many mining deaths. So we again implemented a multifaceted program: an education program and a new compliance plan with enhanced enforcement. But I didn't want this to be just a gotcha program. I wanted to try to fix the problem. We knew that there were common causes to fatalities. So we identified and sat down with stakeholders, including unions and industry. We knew we had a strong training network among our stakeholders which we wanted to better use. We held events to launch the fatalities program. We first had our stakeholders at an event in February 2010." As part of this initiative, "Rules to Live By" focused on the 24 most frequently cited standards whose violations have caused or contributed to nearly half of the fatal accidents in the mining industry.

Another major problem facing the agency was the backlog in the agency penalty system. "I again adopted a multi-pronged approach," recounts Main. "I discussed with Congress shortcomings in the violations appeal process. We are adding additional resources so that we can hire judges, lawyers, and administrative support. We also launched a 90-day pilot program to test out new ways to reduce the backlog of contested citations."

On April 5, 2010, the mine explosion at Upper Big Branch occurred. Main recalls, "I've lived through these experiences before, so I knew what to expect. It is important to manage all the different groups involved with mine explosion. My experiences earlier in my career were crucial. I had been involved in the 2001 Jim Walter mine explosion and the 1984 Wilberg Mine explosion. You have to be careful not to let everyone run into the fire. I knew I had to leave some people here in headquarters in order to keep the place running."

"I was there from Tuesday to Saturday on the front line. I got there as fast as I could. I first found out about it at 5:30 p.m. on Monday. We set up a command center. I left for the mine at about 4 a.m. and got there about 9 a.m. on Tuesday morning. That day was hectic. We had meetings to decide what to get done that day. What were the pieces that needed to get done? We had Congress, the press, and the President all interested in what we were doing. We had to put together quality information for the President. You can't imagine the intensity of the situation. You can always do more in these situations than you think you can."

"I slept in a car at the mine. We had a mine emergency vehicle in which I slept. You can't expect to get much sleep in these situations. It is totally consuming.

Mission
Mine Safety and Health Administration

The purpose of the Mine Safety and Health Administration is to prevent death, disease, and injury from mining and to promote safe and healthful workplaces for the Nation's miners.

You can't think about sleep. You just have to keep going. It was my 40-year history with mine safety that equipped me for both the incident and the investigation after it was over."

"I had worked with many of our employees who were involved in responding to the Upper Big Branch mine disaster, so I knew the people I was working with. I also knew the decision-making process. If I had not had this experience before, it would have been much more difficult. There are many groups of people to respond to: the press, Congressional staff, and families. I had an idea of what each group needed from us. We had everybody apart. I knew how to avoid mishaps. I also knew how to manage the event. I knew what I (as an Assistant Secretary) should do and what I should stay away from. You didn't want too many people up front. Kevin Stricklin, Administrator of the Office of Coal Mine Safety and Health, had gotten there first. He was doing a good job and he told me, 'I need to do this.' So I let him continue as our lead spokesperson. I didn't need to do it. There were plenty of other things to do."

"You have to put yourself in the shoes of a parent, spouse, or child of a miner in an explosion. They keep hoping. You have to be as honest as you can under the circumstances. You have to respect their hope. I've been part of rescue teams where I had to participate in the decision to leave people in the mine. You have to do risk assessment and risk analysis. Risk assessment is hard. You have to be aware of family needs. But you also can't ask people to take greater risk. We had to pull out of the Wilberg Mine. You have to consider the families, but you also have to control the risk."

"After the incident, we had to figure out what went wrong and we had to make corrections. We did find that there was a computer error in the pattern of violations software. Upper Big Branch had a pattern of violations that we had not caught up with. They had many violations and were at the top of the list nationwide. All the violations did not show up because some of the violations were being appealed under the old process. We clearly had to improve our pattern of violations procedures which date back to 1977."

Reflecting on Serving at MSHA

"My goal has always been to make life better for miners," says Main. "Miners are our first priority, as are their families."

"I'm proud that I was able to keep the agency running in spite of Upper Big Branch. We had a successful strategy in place and we kept it going. We kept doing our work, while also responding to requests from Congress. We had to respond to all the issues raised by Upper Big Branch. The key thing is to stay focused."

"The job is tougher than I thought. It's been crisis after crisis. You constantly ask yourself 'How did this happen?' You have to find the confidence in yourself. It was quite an experience to go to the White House. I hadn't slept much in two weeks and I was at the White House to give the President news about the event. You have to be able to manage stress in these situations."

David L. Strickland
Administrator
National Highway Traffic Safety Administration
Department of Transportation

The Beginning

"I arrived on January 4, 2010," recalls David Strickland. "I got briefings all day long. I moved into my office, which I thought was big compared to my space in Congress. I had been doing oversight over NHTSA for nine years. I knew the agency, the structure, and the issues facing the agency. But I needed grounding on how NHTSA worked day to day. I knew a lot of the NHTSA senior staff. I knew Ron Medford, who is the Deputy Administrator. He had been Acting Administrator the year before I arrived. I needed to find out what I didn't know. I had many questions."

The Organization

The National Highway Traffic Safety Administration (NHTSA) was established by the Highway Safety Act of 1970 with the mission to reduce the number of deaths, injuries, and economic losses resulting from motor vehicle crashes. Its major activities include research, rulemaking, enforcement, collection of statistics and analysis, establishing fuel economy standards, and consumer outreach activities. NHTSA is the successor agency to the National Highway Safety Bureau, which was created in 1966. In FY 11, NHTSA had a budget of over $850 million and over 600 employees.

The Challenge

When David Strickland arrived in January 2010, the Department of Transportation was in the midst of intense Congressional and media scrutiny over the recall of Toyota vehicles due to unintended acceleration problems. Strickland and Secretary Ray LaHood were testifying frequently before Congress on NHTSA's oversight of this safety issue. In addition to the crisis atmosphere surrounding the Toyota recall, NHTSA was facing an ambitious agenda: issuing new Corporate Average Fuel Economy (CAFE) standards, issuing a rear-view visibility rule, working with Congress on updating vehicle safety legislation, and undertaking the ongoing activities of the agency.

David L. Strickland

Tenure: Mr. Strickland was nominated by President Obama to serve as Administrator of the National Highway Traffic Safety Administration on December 4, 2009, and confirmed by the U.S. Senate on December 24, 2009.

Federal government experience: Prior to being confirmed as Administrator, Mr. Strickland served from 2001 to 2009 as Senior Democratic Counsel to the Subcommittee on Consumer Protection, Product Safety, and Insurance of the U.S. Senate Committee on Commerce, Science, and Transportation.

Education: Mr. Strickland received his J.D. degree from Harvard Law School in 1993, and his B.S. degree in Communication Studies and Political Science at Northwestern University in 1990.

Responding to the Challenge

"When I got here in January, there had already been a significant amount of work in progress on Toyota," recounts Strickland. "There was much work underway, including a study by the National Academy of Sciences and a research initiative with the National Aeronautics and Space Administration. My first task was to determine whether NHTSA was broken. Some people were saying that we had a broken culture here. I decided that they were wrong and that NHTSA was not broken. That decision was a risk I had to take, but I believed it. It turns out that I was right. The final analysis showed that NHTSA had done a fantastic job on the Toyota recall."

In reflecting back on the Toyota perfect storm, as Strickland describes it, "I thought the Department did exactly the right thing in going to Japan and telling them that we were going to enforce the recall regulations. We were doing our job. It was the right call to stop selling the cars. It got people's attention." After the Toyota crisis passed, Strickland says, "I could finally turn my attention elsewhere."

A pressing item on Strickland's agenda was the issuing of CAFE standards. It is the responsibility of NHTSA to set the standards for fuel economy of cars and light trucks. Strickland was no stranger to CAFE standards. "I moved from being the architect of new CAFE requirements to being the one to administer and implement them. I had no idea that I would be the one implementing fuel economy standards I had worked on for almost 10 years. When I got here, we had to get this

Mission, Vision, and Values
National Highway Traffic Safety Administration (NHTSA)

Mission
Save lives, prevent injuries, and reduce economic costs due to road traffic crashes, through education, research, safety standards, and enforcement activity.

Vision
Global leader in motor vehicle and highway safety.

Values
NHTSA is dedicated to achieving the highest standards of excellence in motor vehicle and highway safety. The agency strives to exceed the expectations of its customers through its core values of Integrity, Service, and Leadership.

done," recalls Strickland. "I worked closely with our rulemaking staff on this. We had to develop enforcement standards as well. I wanted to keep the ball rolling on this. We were behind schedule. It was taking six months to elicit comments on some of our rules. We didn't have that long. We had to speed it up." In April 2010, five months after Strickland's arrival, NHTSA issued the CAFE Standards for light vehicles for model years 2012–2016. NHTSA also issued its Notice of Intent to prepare standards for Model Years 2017–2025. "My staff has been working pretty much nonstop for the past year," says Strickland. "We hit our milestones on the CAFE standards and other rules. We worked hard on our rulemaking activities and we had to borrow a few people from around the Department. We had a tight time line."

Like many of the regulators profiled in this chapter, Strickland spends much of his time working closely with his stakeholders, which include automobile manufacturers, equipment manufacturers, Congress, citizens and advocacy groups, and the states. Strickland says, "I knew a lot of them from my days on the Hill— the automobile manufacturers, the safety advocates. We all want a safer fleet of cars. It's our job to put out consumer alerts and narrow the safety gap. We understand the relationship between safety and costs and we want to work with manufacturers on safety. We want cars to be very safe but we are aware that we don't want them to be too costly for people to buy them. We don't want to price out the public. We want them to have choices."

There is another, lesser known group of stakeholders that Strickland meets with frequently. "I meet with families of individuals who die in car crashes. We lost over 33,000 people in 2009. Every one of these traffic fatalities had families. They come to meet with me. It gives me a sense of the importance of my job."

The impact of families can be seen in the history of a rule required by Congress in 2007 while Strickland was a committee staff member. Congress passed the Cameron Gulbransen Kids Transportation Safety Act. Two-year-old Cameron, for whom the bill is named, was killed when his father accidently backed over him in the family's driveway. NHTSA estimates that over 300 fatalities occur annually as a result of back-over crashes. In December 2010, NHTSA proposed a new safety regulation that would expand the required field of view to enable drivers to see directly behind the vehicle when it is in reverse. NHTSA believes that this rule will result in manufacturers installing rear-mounted video cameras and in-vehicle displays. "This is a rule that I'm very proud of," says Strickland, "because I think it will save lives. It will protect children and the elderly." As a result of initiatives such as this, Strickland says, "Every day, I walk out of here and think I may have improved safety in the years ahead. I'm especially gratified by the rear visibility rule."

State governments are also key stakeholders who play a crucial, lesser known role in automobile safety. "People don't realize," says Strickland, "that states have a big role to play in regulation. It is the states that govern many safety laws. We target our efforts with the states. There is a framework we use that has been successful in the past. First, we work with the states to get new laws passed. Second, the laws are enforced by state and local policy. Third, NHTSA supports this effort with an active media campaign. We followed this framework with seat belts and are now following it with the distracted driving initiative led by Secretary LaHood." As of October 2012, 39 states, the District of Columbia, and Guam had passed laws banning text messaging while driving.

Reflecting on the Next Set of Challenges at NHTSA

"We are going to have to devote more attention to pedestrian safety issues," states Strickland. "We have more bike riders and walkers now. We are developing regulations in this area. We are also doing some pedestrian pilot projects and are making progress in this area. I see this as a long-term issue and we have to increase safety awareness on this."

Looking ahead, Strickland predicts, "Our next big horizon is crash avoidance. We are working on evaluating the new technologies in this area. Electric cars will also be making a big difference. We will work with manufacturers on safer and greener products. A remaining question is how we go about updating the CAFE fuel economy standards."

Inez Moore Tenenbaum
Chairman
Consumer Product Safety Commission

The Beginning

Some political appointees might expect to have the red carpet rolled out for their arrival. Inez Tenenbaum's experience was different. "The physical office space was a real mess," recalls Chairman Tenenbaum. "The walls had not been painted. I found old furniture in my office that needed replacing. The building itself was run down. It was a pretty dreary place. We had very few supplies, and we also had no business cards or stationery. At the start, I just had one staff member who I brought with me from South Carolina. We have since improved the physical look of the building and created standard operating procedures."

The Organization

The Consumer Product Safety Commission (CPSC), created by Congress in 1972, is the independent federal regulatory agency charged with protecting the public against unreasonable risks of injury or death from consumer products. The Commission consists of five Commissioners who are appointed by the President with the advice and consent of the Senate for staggered seven-year terms. The President appoints one of the Commissioners as Chairman, with confirmation by the Senate. As with most regulatory commissions, the 1972 law stipulated that no more than three of the Commissioners should be affiliated with the same political party. Thus, the current Commission has three Democrats and two Republicans. One of the current Commissioners, Nancy Nord, served as Acting Chairman of the CPSC from July 2006 to May 2009. The agency was slowed in recent years by frequent lack of quorums due to vacant Commissioner positions.

The Commission's organizational structure has proven to be more difficult than Chairman Tenenbaum expected. "It's been harder than I thought working with the five Commissioners. I didn't come here to talk about the role of government. I'm here to enforce the statute. The agency should not be about ideology. Once something becomes a statutory mandate, you have to develop the rules."

While 87 percent of the Commission's votes are unanimous, the Commission is more partisan than Chairman Tenenbaum anticipated. "I was expecting a more positive environment. I wasn't expecting so much conflict. I initially viewed the Commissioners being more like administrative law judges than partisan commissioners. I thought that once a decision was made, we would all put the decision behind us and move on. It hasn't turned out like that."

Inez Moore Tenenbaum

Tenure: Ms. Tenenbaum was nominated by President Obama on June 9, 2009 to serve as the ninth Chairman of the U.S. Consumer Product Safety Commission, and confirmed by the U.S. Senate on June 19, 2009, to a term that expires in October 2013.

Private sector experience: Prior to being confirmed as Chairman, Ms. Tenenbaum served as Special Counsel to the McNair Law Firm in the area of public school finance. Ms. Tenenbaum practiced health, environmental, and public interest law with the firm Sinkler & Boyd, P.A.

State government experience: Ms. Tenenbaum was elected South Carolina's State Superintendent of Education in 1998 and completed her second term in 2007. Ms. Tenenbaum also served as the Director of Research for the Medical, Military, Public and Municipal Affairs Committee of the South Carolina House of Representatives. She carried out the Committee's responsibilities for all legislation relating to public health, the environment, child welfare, social services, adult and juvenile corrections, state military affairs, and local government.

Non-profit experience: Ms. Tenenbaum served as an attorney at the South Carolina Center for Family Policy.

Education: Ms. Tenenbaum received her B.S. degree in 1972 and Master of Education degree in 1974 from the University of Georgia and her law degree in 1986 from the University of South Carolina.

The Challenge

As is common with many incoming political executives, Chairman Tenenbaum did not start off with a clean slate when she arrived in 2009. CPSC was still operating in the aftermath of the 2007 recall of millions of Chinese-made toys that were found to be contaminated with lead paint. The issue of dangerous cribs then surfaced in 2008. The publicity surrounding these incidents led Congress to pass the Consumer Product Safety Improvement Act (CPSIA) in August 2008. The new legislation updated the 1972 law and expanded the agency's regulatory mandate. The CPSIA mandated new federal safety standards in numerous areas. The new law also increased the agency's budget and staffing levels. One provision of the law mandated the creation of a publicly searchable Web-based database of

Mission, Values and Goals
Consumer Product Safety Commission

Mission
Protecting the public against unreasonable risks of injury from consumer products through education, safety standards activities, regulation, and enforcement.

Vision
The CPSC is the recognized global leader in consumer product safety.

Goals
Goal 1: Leadership in Safety
Goal 2: Commitment to Prevention
Goal 3: Rigorous Hazard Identification
Goal 4: Decisive Response
Goal 5: Raising Awareness

reports of injury, illness, or death, or risks of injury, illness, or death associated with consumer products.

Challenges facing Chairman Tenenbaum during her first two years in office included implementation of the CPSIA and getting the mandated rules out, as well as working on the backlog of rules that had not yet been finalized and issued. In addition, Tenenbaum arrived at the CPSC when imports from overseas were continuing to rise dramatically. Four out of five consumer product recalls now involve imported products.

Responding to the Challenge

Chairman Tenenbaum's initial response to this set of challenges was to devote much of her time during her first year to the internal management of the organization. "I found that the agency had no standard operating procedures. So everything we did was brand new. I had to issue directives on internal operations, like our directive on travel. We set up a six-month matrix schedule. I had to start setting deadlines. I wanted to know where people were on all the things we had to do."

Like many of the political executives profiled in this book, Tenenbaum wanted to speed up the agency. Given the number of rules mandated by the CPSIA and pending regulations, there was much to be done. Tenenbaum recalls, "I told our staff and the Office of General Counsel to pick up the pace. Everything was simply taking too long. The delays were burdensome on industry. Industry needed to know what we were going to do, so they could be ready to respond." In reflecting on her experience at the agency, Tenenbaum says, "I think organizations respond to the speed of the leader. Agency personnel can see that my staff and I are working very hard. I try hard to let everybody know what is expected."

Speeding up the agency also required Chairman Tenenbaum to try to change the culture of the agency. "You have to work on the processes of the organization," reflects Tenenbaum. "We are trying to create a new culture here and get people to change the way they are doing business. We want to create a culture of excellence. We want to bring in new talent and get new people." Like many federal organizations, CPSC is facing a dramatic increase in staff retirements as over one-third of the agency has worked at CPSC for over 35 years. Replacing that experienced staff will be a major challenge to Tenenbaum over the next several years.

When she arrived, Tenenbaum also found an organization with very poor internal communications, including communication among Commissioners, and a visible lack of transparency. "I tried to 'open up' the agency," says Tenenbaum. "I started to meet with all my key managers about how we were going to operate. I started weekly meetings with the other Commissioners. I also started holding votes at our meetings and broadcasting those meetings on the Web. Previously, the Commission did its voting by ballot, with no meetings. I quickly changed that. I wanted people to be able to see what we are doing."

There was also a clear need to find better, more effective ways to communicate with the public. During her first year at the agency, Tenenbaum pushed for expansion of the agency's use of social media. The resulting initiative, CPSC 2.0, included the creation of an OnSafety blog, the @OnSafety Twitter, a YouTube Channel, a recall widget, and a Flickr page.

Tenenbaum also concluded that the agency suffered from a lack of strategic direction. In response to this problem, the agency hired a consulting firm to assist in developing a five-year Strategic Plan for the agency. The outside consultant interviewed 76 stakeholders to get their views on the agency and how the agency might more effectively interact with industry. The resulting Strategic Plan included the development of measurable goals against which the agency could be evaluated. The strategic plan initiative also addressed the issue of a potential reorganization of the agency, which is now under study.

In response to the increased need to focus on the safety of imported products, CPSC opened an office in Beijing. Chairman Tenenbaum also made numerous overseas visits, including visits to Vietnam, China, and Singapore. The trip to

Vietnam resulted in a training program for Vietnamese manufacturers. A new working agreement with China was developed. In addition, CPSC continued to work closely with the European Union on product safety issues. This focus also resulted in an increased number of partnerships between CPSC and the Customs and Border Protection agency in the Department of Homeland Security.

Reflecting on the Next Set of Challenges at CPSC

As the agency worked its way through the regulations process by issuing 26 sets of regulations in 2009 and 2010 (compared to its previous high of seven regulations in one year), Tenenbaum is increasingly shifting her attention away from rule-making toward greater outreach, education, and partnerships initiatives.

"I'd like to cut back on our rule-making activities," says Tenenbaum. "I want to spend more time now on developing partnerships and working with manufacturing groups. I want to expand our outreach. I want us to do more education and outreach. We want to do more prevention. We want to work closely with manufacturers because voluntary standards are the first step for the agency." The shift is clearly seen in the number of campaigns launched in 2010 by the agency, including campaigns on safe sleep, pool safety, and furniture tip overs.

Chapter Nine

The Scientists

Understanding the Job of the Scientist

While nearly every federal Department funds research and development projects, there is a group of federal agencies solely dedicated to research, statistics, and analysis in specific scientific disciplines. We call these organizations the science agencies, led by individuals whom we have termed science political executives. The science political executives profiled in this chapter all share two key characteristics. First, they are highly qualified for their positions. In fact, calling them immensely qualified is not an overstatement. All have Ph.D.s in their respective fields and all have had long and distinguished careers prior to their Presidential appointments.

Second, they all have deep knowledge of their fields. This deep knowledge enables them to communicate effectively both within and outside their organizations. In addition, several brought deep knowledge about their organizations to their positions as well. All five executives profiled had served in government previously, with Patrick Gallagher, Director of NIST, Marcia McNutt, Director of USGS, and Kathryn Sullivan, Deputy Administrator at NOAA, having prior experience in the agencies which they are now leading.

It is also important to note that science political executives tend to be one of the few political appointees in their agencies. In the case of Gallagher, McNutt, and Richard Newell, Administrator of EIA, they are the only political appointee in the organization. In the case of Rebecca

The Scientists

Rebecca M. Blank, page 195

Under Secretary for Economic Affairs, Economics and Statistics Administration (ESA), Department of Commerce

Patrick D. Gallagher, page 200

Director, National Institute of Standards and Technology (NIST) and Under Secretary of Commerce for Standards and Technology, Department of Commerce

Marcia K. McNutt, page 205

Director, U.S. Geological Survey (USGS), Department of the Interior

Richard G. Newell, page 210

Administrator, U.S. Energy Information Administration (EIA), Department of Energy

Kathryn D. Sullivan, page 215

Deputy Administrator and Assistant Secretary of Commerce for Environmental Observation and Prediction, National Oceanic and Atmospheric Administration, Department of Commerce

Blank, former Commerce Under Secretary for Economic Affairs, there were only two other political appointees in her organization.

Key Roles

The science political executives we interviewed all faced similar management challenges. In addition to their ongoing management roles, all define their positions as including the following:
- Guarding the scientific integrity of their organization
- Interfacing with the political leadership of their organization
- Making their organizations relevant to government decision-making
- Strengthening their institution

Guarding the Scientific Integrity of Their Organization
All five of the individuals profiled emphasize the importance of scientific integrity. They all tell us that there is no margin of error in this role. Marcia McNutt says, "You need a strong firewall between USGS and the political chain of command. There is tension between keeping our peer-reviewed scientific studies independent until they are ready to be released. We share these scientific studies with the political appointees. I need to keep them informed and give them a heads-up at the appropriate time." Richard Newell comments, "I have to be sensitive not to blindside any of our political people on EIA reports." While needed by all political executives, good judgment and a sensitive political antenna are crucial to the success of a science political executive in order to maintain their credibility in both the scientific and political communities in which they travel.

After discussing their concern about potential conflicts between the scientific integrity of their organizations and politics, none of the science political executives interviewed report any instances of political interference during their tenure. "I've been surprised," says McNutt, "at how rarely politics have intervened. We were involved in the Recovery Act. I didn't receive any requests for specific projects. We were doing what was right."

While government's science civil servants clearly recognize that politics is a component of life in government, there is great sensitivity to "too much politics." Gallagher recalls, "In administrations of recent years, the position of NIST Director seemed somewhat more political than in the past—which it had never been before. That was a little unsettling to folks here, so they are glad now to be back in the days when a career person was selected for the Presidential appointment as Director."

Interfacing with the Political Leadership of Their Organization
Given that Gallagher, McNutt, and Newell are the sole political appointees in their organizations, this responsibility adds an additional complexity to their

positions. "I'm the only appointee here," says McNutt, "which has been difficult at times. There are meetings to which only I can go. My Deputy can't replace me at these meetings." The role also requires the science political executive to know the Administration and their Secretary's agenda and to determine how their organization can help move that agenda along. In many cases, this requires the science political executive to make key connections to other political executives and to "work the process." McNutt says that she spends more than 60 percent of her time working closely with the Office of the Secretary and other political appointees in the Department of the Interior.

The job of the science political executive is also to know when there is a problem in the organization. The executive must then determine whether that problem needs to be brought to the attention of the Department's political team. Rebecca Blank describes her experience with the 2010 Census, "We have a good team on this. Nancy Potok, Deputy Under Secretary at ESA, has done the day-to-day oversight, so I've spent less time on this than I had imagined. I am brought in when there is a problem to deal with."

There is inherent tension in the relationship between scientific agencies and a Department's political leadership. Newell describes it well, "It is important to note that our vision statement says that we are independent. We want to be impartial, but not irrelevant."

Making their Organizations Relevant to Governmental Decision-Making

All the science political executives profiled made great efforts to increase the relevance of their organizations. In her position near the top of the Department of Commerce, Rebecca Blank spent much of her time talking with key individuals in the White House, the Council of Economic Advisors, and the National Economic Council to better understand their economic information needs. As a result of Blank's interactions with policy makers, the White House asked her organization to produce several key studies for them.

While wanting their organizations to be policy-relevant, science political executives walk a fine line between wanting to be relevant and helpful and not distorting their historic mission. This tension was clearly seen in Patrick Gallagher's participation in the Administration's review of cybersecurity and the development of new policies in this area. "I was concerned that the issue of cybersecurity might change the role of NIST," says Gallagher. "We have a clear role to play on the technology side of the issue. We did not, however, want to be put in the position of setting policy rules. That isn't the role of NIST. We need to continue to do what we do best. I worry about mission creep. I understand what my organization can add and I know our capabilities. Key is understanding your role."

Strengthening the Institution

At their core, the science organizations in government are about people. While many of the science agencies have world-class equipment and facilities, we were told many times throughout our interviews about the importance of people. "The Energy Information Administration is all about its people—federal employees and contractors," says Newell. "It is a people organization. We have 370 federal employees with about 200 contractors. We need to keep them and attract new people. I'm pleased that people in our community are asking me about whether there are any new positions at EIA."

Patrick Gallagher is very clear about his deep commitment to the institution, "I want to create an environment conducive for our scientists. We have world class scientists here. Our job is all about attracting people—hiring and then retaining them. Retaining people is always a challenge because they can make three or four times more money anywhere else, either in the academic community or industry. Not only am I impressed that NIST has three Nobel Prize winners here, I'm more impressed that all three have stayed."

One aspect of strengthening the institution is putting the agency on sound financial footing and receiving funding from Congress. Kathryn Sullivan, Deputy Administrator, NOAA, describes her experience working on the NOAA satellite programs, "Our joint satellite program had been progressing technically, but we were operating on a continuing resolution that provided less than half the funding needed to sustain that progress in FY 11. We had to move the needle. I met with stakeholders inside and out of government … This is a long ballgame. We are putting our satellite programs on firm footing. These are seminal programs which must be fielded on schedule. We had to strengthen our analytical capabilities, scrub our requirements and cost figures. We also needed to communicate much more, get NOAA on some key radar screens again."

Selecting Science Political Executives

We found that science political executives believe that the academic and non-profit sectors prepared them well for their present position. The common thread between universities, non-profits, and government science agencies is that all tend to be collegial and somewhat "flatter" than most organizations. In describing his transition from academic life to government, Richard Newell says, "I used the skills I gained in academia and non-profits to bring people together. My agency isn't like the private sector where I can just tell people what to do. Here, I have to use my interpersonal skills." Industry research and development laboratories often have the same collegial atmosphere, as do universities; these are institutions from which science political executives have been recruited in the past.

Sullivan believes that her experience running a non-profit organization prepared her well for her return to government. Sullivan says, "Running a non-profit was a good experience. It required focus and discipline, sound strategy and crisp execution, robust internal and external communications. We have to motivate people to invest precious time and money to visit a science museum. We built a new building during my tenure, which forced every facet of our operations to change. Our staff had to do things that they had never done before and do familiar things in altogether different ways. We had to invest on the front end and build new business processes. I had to make sure that we were having the right conversations—bringing all pertinent expertise and perspectives to bear—on each of these challenges during this transformation."

But most of all, science political executives need to be highly regarded and respected scientists with strong professional careers. The credential for receiving a Presidential appointment as an executive leading a government science agency is time spent in their discipline, not time spent on the campaign trail. In short, no amateurs need apply for a political appointment as an executive of a science agency.

Other Science Agencies

In addition to the five science agencies profiled in this chapter, there are also numerous other science agencies throughout government. While not comprehensive, the list and descriptions of each agency have been prepared to assist the Office of Presidential Personnel and Cabinet Secretaries in better understanding the unique nature of these agencies, which play a key role in the sciences.

Other Federal Government Agencies Categorized as Science Agencies

Department of Agriculture
Agricultural Research Service
The Agricultural Research Service (ARS) works to find solutions to the nation's agricultural problems. In FY 11, ARS had a budget of approximately $1.3 billion, with over 2,200 scientists and 6,000 other employees. The agency's research projects focus on ensuring high-quality, safe food that will meet the nutritional needs of Americans, while sustaining a competitive agricultural economy and enhancing America's natural resources.

Economic Research Service
The Economic Research Service (ERS) is the Department's primary source of agricultural economic information. The 400 employees at ERS conduct research and gather statistical data on food, farming, natural resources, and rural development, and convey this information to the public through reports, magazines, scientific journals, websites, and oral briefings. In FY 11, ERS had a budget of approximately $82 million.

Department of Education
Institute of Education Sciences
The Institute of Education Sciences (IES), established in 2002, is the research arm of the Department of Education, charged with funding and conducting studies on educational practices and outcomes, especially targeted at groups at high risk of failure. IES has four centers: the National Center for Education Research, the National Center for Education Statistics, the National Center for Education Evaluation and Regional Assistance, and the National Center for Special Education Research. In FY 11, IES had a budget of approximately of $650 million, with 185 employees.

Department of Health and Human Services
Agency for Healthcare Research and Quality
The Agency for Healthcare Research and Quality (AHRQ) invested approximately 80 percent of its $400 million FY 11 budget in grants and contracts to improve the safety and quality, effectiveness, and efficiency of health care. AHRQ's 300 employees provide information services to health care providers, patients, policy makers, insurers, and medical school faculty across the nation.

Centers for Disease Control and Prevention
The Centers for Disease Control and Prevention (CDC) strives to promote health and quality of life by monitoring health and detecting and investigating health problems. CDC also conducts research to enhance disease prevention, develop and advocate public health policies, implement prevention strategies, promote healthy behaviors, and foster safe and healthful environments. The CDC has a Center for Global Health and nine national centers focused on health issues such as birth defects, immunization, and epidemiology, among others. In FY 11, CDC's budget was

approximately $11 billion, with over 10,000 employees. CDC distributes approximately 14,000 separate grants and contracts to fulfill its mission annually.

National Institutes of Health

The National Institutes of Health (NIH) is a research agency focused on studying the nature and behavior of living systems and applying that knowledge to the realm of health care. In FY 11, the agency had a budget of approximately $31 billion which is spent on researching human diseases, human growth and development, biological effects of environmental contaminants, and mental and physical disorders. This research is conducted by more than 324,000 researchers at over 3,000 universities, medical schools, and other facilities, both domestic and abroad. NIH has over 18,000 employees and will support over 35,000 research project grants in FY 2012.

Substance Abuse and Mental Health Services Administration

The Substance Abuse and Mental Health Services Administration (SAMHSA) was established in 1992 with a mission of reducing the impact of substance abuse and mental illness on America's communities. In FY 11, SAMHSA had a budget of approximately $3.6 million, with nearly 550 employees. SAMHSA has four Centers: the Center for Mental Health Services, the Center for Substance Abuse Prevention, the Center for Substance Abuse Treatment, and the Center for Behavioral Health Statistics and Quality. The Centers develop and run almost a hundred different substance abuse and mental health programs and initiatives, awarding grants to benefit a wide range of individuals, including trauma victims, military families, the homeless and high-risk youth and communities.

National Science Foundation

The National Science Foundation (NSF), founded in 1950, is an independent federal agency that aims to promote discovery, learning, research infrastructure and stewardship. The NSF is the funding source for approximately 20 percent of all federally supported research conducted at colleges and universities, issuing about 10,000 new awards per year with an average duration of three years. An estimated 300,000 people are involved in NSF activities, including researchers, teachers, and students from elementary to graduate school. In FY 11, the NSF had a budget of approximately $6.8 billion, with over 1,100 employees.

Rebecca M. Blank
Under Secretary for Economic Affairs
Economics and Statistics Administration
Department of Commerce

The Beginning

The beginning, for all the political executives profiled in this book, was their initial conversation with the political leaders they would be working with in their Departments. These were two-way conversations: each assessed the other and made a judgment as to whether they could work effectively together. In the case of Rebecca Blank, the outcome of the conversation was a high comfort level. "I was impressed by the people on the fifth floor, the Secretary's office," recalls Blank. I was impressed with them when I interviewed for the job. And I continued to be impressed with them when I got here. It's a superior group of people. The quality of these folks is one of the reasons I took the job."

The Organization

Rebecca Blank is one of five Under Secretaries in the Department of Commerce. Each of the Under Secretaries is responsible for a group of line agencies that report to them. Each Under Secretary reports to the Secretary and Deputy Secretary of the Department. In the case of Blank, her office—the Economics and Statistics Administration (ESA)—oversees the U.S. Census Bureau, the Bureau of Economic Analysis, and the Office of the Chief Economist (see Figure 9-1). In addition, ESA has its own staff of economists and experts who produce in-depth reports, fact sheets, and briefings on policy issues and current economic events.

The Challenge

Like some of the other political executives profiled in the book, Blank found a somewhat sleepy organization in ESA when she arrived. "I was impressed with the career civil service. They are always right there to help you. They have excellent technical skills—first rate. They get you the information you need. We have 16 Ph.D. economists on staff and they had not been utilized very well in recent years." Unlike some agencies, where the new political executive found a workforce with

Rebecca M. Blank

Tenure: Dr. Blank was nominated by President Obama to serve as the Under Secretary for Economic Affairs at the Department of Commerce in April 2009, and confirmed by the U.S. Senate in May 2009.

Academic experience: Prior to being confirmed as Under Secretary, Dr. Blank was the Robert S. Kerr Senior Fellow in Economic Studies at the Brookings Institution from 2008 to 2009. From 1999 to 2008, she was Dean of the Gerald R. Ford School of Public Policy at the University of Michigan. She also served as co-director of the University of Michigan's National Poverty Center. From 1989 to 1999, Dr. Blank was a Professor of Economics at Northwestern University and Director of the Northwestern University/University of Chicago Joint Center for Poverty Research. Dr. Blank has also taught at Princeton University and the Massachusetts Institute of Technology.

Federal government experience: From 1997 to 1999, Dr. Blank served as a Member of the Council of Economic Advisers. She served as a Senior Staff Economist on the Council from 1989 to 1990.

Education: Dr. Blank received her B.A. in Economics from the University of Minnesota in 1976 and her Ph.D. in Economics from Massachusetts Institute of Technology in 1983.

either the wrong set or an inadequate set of skills, Blank found a highly skilled workforce in place. The challenge facing Blank was to more effectively deploy that expert staff. Her job as Under Secretary consisted of three other major challenges:

- Overseeing the data agencies reporting to ESA. As it turned out, Blank's tenure as Under Secretary coincided with the 2010 Census.
- Participating in establishing data policies for the government's statistical agencies. There are nearly 100 federal agencies with statistical programs. Working with these agencies, the Office of Management and Budget, and the academic statistical community, the Commerce Under Secretary for Economic Affairs is a key player in setting national statistical policy.
- Undertaking policy-relevant studies which will produce useful information for the White House on Administration priority issues.

Figure 9-1: Economics and Statistics Administration (ESA) Organization Chart

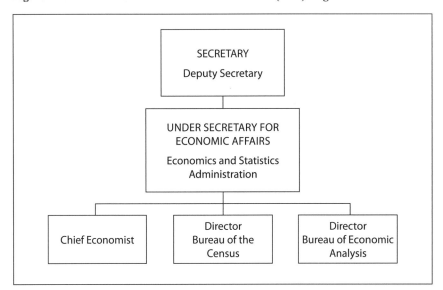

Responding to the Challenge

At the top of Blank's must-succeed list was the 2010 Census. The 2010 Census was on the Government Accountability Office high-risk list when Blank arrived at Commerce. "It's the biggest civilian hiring project in government—we hire about 850,000 Census takers. The Census had a lot of problems getting ready for the 2010 Census, including the cancellation of a contract to develop hand-held computers to conduct the Census. I'll be involved in overseeing management issues related to the Census, including the problems we already know about."

In reflecting back on her experience overseeing the Census, Blank says, "It was one of the most interesting things I have ever been involved in. All the pieces came together. It has been interesting from three perspectives: the management issues surrounding mobilizing for the Census, substantive issues regarding data collection, and the political overlay. I am proud of how well the Census Bureau handled the planning, execution, and follow-up of the 2010 Census. We were visiting almost 150 million households, so you can imagine the opportunities for problems. We had over 500 regional offices, one in every Congressional district. There were problems, as expected with undertakings of this size, but no major disasters. The news coverage of the Census changed significantly from the 2000 Census. For that Census, you could bring in a group of seven reporters and brief them. Today, there are numerous bloggers out there, including some of our own census takers. So there was more coverage and more interest than in the past."

Mission Statement
ESA

ESA's mission is to help maintain a sound Federal statistical system that monitors and measures America's rapidly changing economic and social arrangements; improve understanding of the key forces at work in the economy and the opportunities they create for improving the well-being of Americans; develop new ways to disseminate information using the most advanced technologies; and support the information and analytic needs of the Commerce Department, Executive Branch, and Congress.

Blank and the ESA staff learned from previous Censuses the importance of responding to misinformation or misleading stories about the Census. "We scheduled regular meetings with the public affairs office to go over any newsworthy events," recalls Blank. "We worked as a rapid response team. We had all the right people in the room. As a consequence, there were not as many inaccurate stories as might have been anticipated."

Like the other four science political executives profiled in this chapter, Blank's job is to manage the interface with political leaders in the Department. Upon arrival, Blank found intense interest in the Census from the Secretary and his staff. "I had meetings during my first week here on the Census with the Secretary and seven or eight other key decision-makers. We had a lot of the fifth-floor people (the Secretary's staff) in those meetings. There were a lot of different players involved in the oversight on the Census within our own Department—the General Counsel, Legislative Affairs, the Chief of Staff, Census Bureau staff, and others. You had to get everybody on board. And you then had to respond to questions from the Hill."

In addition to managing the interface with political leaders, all the science political executives profiled devote significant time and energy to making science (in Blank's case, economics) both communicable and relevant to top Administration officials. "Our job is to communicate to the political staff, none of whom are economists," says Blank. "We need to explain economics to them. We undertook economic briefings for the Secretary and his senior staff. The economy was obviously very important to them."

In reflecting on her accomplishments to date, Blank says, "We increased the visibility of ESA in the White House. The job and the agency had been relatively low visibility in the past." The increased visibility in the White House and other parts of the Administration were a consequence of Blank's finding opportunities in which economic analysis could contribute to policy making in the Administration. For example, ESA published two major studies in 2010 to assist the Administration. The first, *Middle Class in America,* was commissioned to assist the Vice President's Middle Class Task Force. The second, *Measuring the Green Economy,* was the first major attempt to measure the green economy using Census data. The Administration wanted to better understand the job components of a clean and energy-efficient economy. In 2011, ESA published *Women in America: Indicators of Social and Economic Well-Being,* which had been requested by the White House Council on Women and Girls. Between 2009 and the first half of 2011, ESA published 18 policy relevant studies (which do not include BEA or Census studies). This compares with the eight published studies in the 2005–2008 time period.

"We are now getting more requests to do studies," reports Blank. "The staff here is available to do this work and is enjoying getting involved in current issues and doing deep analysis. They like having new products and reports. These reports have generated requests from other parts of government to do similar studies but we are not able to undertake all the studies requested."

Reflecting on the Future of ESA

"Looking ahead, I think money is going to be a problem for our agencies in the years ahead," reflects Blank. "I see a flat budget with no increases. Keeping level will be an accomplishment. It will be hard to make anything new happen. If you have a great idea, something else will have to be cut to pay for the effort … It will be a different environment."

Epilogue

Rebecca Blank is now Acting Secretary of the Department of Commerce. She has served as Acting Secretary of Commerce twice, from August 2011 to October 2011 and once again starting in June 2012 after former Commerce Secretary Bryson resigned. She was confirmed as Deputy Secretary of Commerce in March 2012, after having served as Acting Deputy Secretary for most of 2011.

Patrick D. Gallagher
Director, National Institute of Standards and Technology and Under Secretary of Commerce for Standards and Technology Department of Commerce

The Beginning

There were really two beginnings for Patrick Gallagher. The first occurred in September 2008 when he was appointed Deputy Director while the Director position remained vacant. After carrying out the duties of Director for 13 months, he was nominated to be Director in October 2009 and confirmed by the United States Senate in November 2009. While he led the agency as Deputy Director, Gallagher recalls, "I didn't want to do the traditional caretaker role, but I also didn't want to make major decisions which might be binding on the new Director. But there were things that we could do. I knew that the next Director would need a management agenda," so Gallagher set the stage for organizational change by improving management in areas such as safety. "A new Director would want the organization to be organized and effective," says Gallagher. After being confirmed as the next NIST Director, he set out to create a plan for realigning the organizational structure of the agency.

The second beginning occurred after confirmation. "There was a greater sense of urgency about business after I got confirmed," says Gallagher. "There were more commitments, more media attention, and an increased level of activity. The confirmation impacted how I would spend my time and how I would manage."

The Organization

The historical origins of the current National Institute of Standards and Technology (NIST) date back to the writing of the Constitution of the United States, which assigned the federal government responsibility "to fix the standard of weights and measures" for the nation. The National Bureau of Standards was formed in 1901. In 1988, the Bureau was renamed the National Institute of Standards and Technology. In addition to its historical measurement role, the mission of NIST is to promote U.S. innovation and industrial competitiveness by advancing measurement science, standards, and technology. In Fiscal Year 2010, the agency budget was approximately $1 billion, consisting of about $850 million in appropriated funds, $50 million in service fees, and $100 million in funding from other federal agencies. NIST employs 2,900 scientists, engineers, technicians, and support and administrative personnel. In addition, NIST hosts

Patrick D. Gallagher

Tenure: Dr. Gallagher was nominated by President Obama to serve as Director of the U.S. Department of Commerce's National Institute of Standards and Technology (NIST) in September 2009, and confirmed by the U.S. Senate in November 2009. He also serves as Under Secretary of Commerce for Standards and Technology and as Co-Chair of the Standards Subcommittee under the White House National Science and Technology Council. The Under Secretary position was created by the America COMPETES Reauthorization Act of 2010 which was signed in January 2011.

Federal government experience: Prior to being confirmed as Director, Dr. Gallagher was Deputy Director of NIST. Dr. Gallagher joined NIST as an instrumental scientist in 1993. In 2004, he was selected to be the Director of the NIST Center for Neutron Research. Gallagher also served as the NIST agency representative to the National Science and Technology Council (NSTC). He also chaired the Interagency Working Group on Neutron and Light Source Facilities under the Office of Science and Technology Policy.

Education: Dr. Gallagher studied Physics and Philosophy at Benedictine College in Atchison, Kansas. He received his Ph.D. in Physics at the University of Pittsburgh in 1991. Gallagher did post-doctoral research at Boston University.

about 2,600 associates and facility users from academia, industry, and other government agencies.

The Challenge

When Gallagher was appointed Deputy Director in September 2008, NIST faced the following issues common to many government science agencies:
- It had a historically low profile.
- Its mission was not always clear to the Administration's political leadership and the agency's relevance was frequently questioned.
- It had not been reorganized in over 20 years, since the 1988 legislation which renamed the agency and added several functions.
- It was facing the continued challenge of recruiting and retaining a world-class workforce.

After being selected as Acting Director, Gallagher set out to respond to this set of challenges.

Responding to the Challenge

By being appointed as Deputy Director in September 2008, Gallagher had the unique opportunity to prepare for the Presidential transition to start in November 2008 and to then participate in the actual transition from November 2008 to January 2009. "I participated in all the transition activities and the change in administration," says Gallagher. "It was good to be starting at the same time as the new leaders. As a career person, I had good access to the new political leaders. I could interact with them on the major issues on their agenda. I felt comfortable with the political team. They viewed me as the 'career guy' with institutional knowledge. NIST had a clear role and an R&D agenda which I could communicate. But I also had to show people that the agency could execute."

Based on his previous 15 years as a career scientist at NIST, Gallagher had a clear sense of where he thought the organization needed to go. "I knew that the agency had to be better organized and more effective," reflects Gallagher. "I wanted to improve the stability of NIST. I thought it was unstable with a single Presidential appointee and a single Deputy Director. The previous NIST management structure had upwards of 18 line organizations all reporting to the Director or Deputy Director. In addition, NIST is like a national laboratory in many ways, but it wasn't organized that way. The Director of NIST was like a weak mayor. It wasn't working. We needed to remap the organization and we needed to improve customer service."

Gallagher undertook the reorganization as a series of steps. The first step was to eliminate the Deputy Director position and create three Associate Directors: for Laboratory Programs, for Innovation and Industry Services, and for Management Resources. The number of NIST laboratory organizations was reduced from 10 to six and placed under the Associate Director for Laboratory Programs. The reorganization of the labs was done to increase both the mission and multi-disciplinary focus of each laboratory.

Implementing the reorganization required approval by the Department of Commerce and Congressional appropriations committees. The reorganization was a top priority for Gallagher during his first year in office. "The organization was supportive of the change," he says. "It had been talked about for years and there was general recognition that the time had come to make the change. In the private sector, you can just come up with a plan, announce it, and then do it. Government is different. You need to invite participation. I shared our reorganization plan and met with NIST managers to discuss the reorganization. I invited everybody to comment on the plan. Things moved pretty quickly after this. I did learn the importance of engaging people on reorganizations. Nobody likes to be surprised. My

NIST

Mission, Vision, Core Competencies, and Core Values
NIST

NIST's Mission
To promote U.S. innovation and industrial competitiveness by advancing measurement science, standards, and technology in ways that enhance economic security and improve our quality of life.

NIST's Vision
NIST will be the world's leader in creating critical measurement solutions and promoting equitable standards. Our efforts stimulate innovation, foster industrial competitiveness, and improve the quality of life.

NIST's Core Competencies
- Measurement science
- Rigorous traceability
- Development and use of standards

NIST's Core Values
- **People:** We value and support an inclusive, engaged, and diverse workforce capable of fulfilling the NIST mission.
- **Integrity:** We are objective, ethical, and honest.
- **Customer focus:** We anticipate the needs of our customers and are committed to meeting or exceeding their expectations.
- **Excellence:** We expect world-class performance and continuous improvement in all we do.

rule was no surprises and we engaged people on it, including Congress which was very supportive."

The reorganization was not just an "add-on" activity for Gallagher. It was central to his strategy to change the culture of NIST and to strengthen the organization to survive in the 21st century. Because of his interest in management, Gallagher made a decision early in his scientific career that he wanted to move into management, which resulted in his serving four years as Director of the NIST Center for Neutron Research. "I really do enjoy my management activities. My reorganization initiative did help the organization. It amplified my message about the need to change the organization. Through my management activities, I am trying to make NIST a world-class destination for scientists. Being a world-class place for scientists involves a whole set of issues and activities. The reorganization was never just about organizational structure or who reports to whom. It wasn't about boxes. It was about getting the organization better aligned. We wanted to get the right people and align them in the new organization. Alignment was our larger goal. We need to reset the agency."

The resetting of the agency involved moving away from an activity-based approach in the labs, which were organized much like academic departments in a university. "In that structure, our managers," recalls Gallagher, "acted much like chairs of academic departments. We wanted to move toward a mission approach. Our historic mission is the metric system and we needed to align our activities with the mission."

The increased mission focus and reorganization was clearly related to Gallagher's goal to make NIST a good place to work and to enhance the organization's external image, both within the Administration and the research community. "NIST is a very special place," states Gallagher. "Researchers at NIST like their work and their mission. I wanted to restore the old sense of mission that the National Bureau of Standards had. Our efforts have brought more visibility to the organization. I'm pleased with the Administration's interest in NIST. That happened faster than I thought. They were eager to place increased expectations and enhanced responsibilities on us. This is a change from the past when we had to explain our relevance to an administration."

Reflecting on the Future of NIST

In the summer of 2011, three years after his appointment as Acting Director, Gallagher worked on two scenarios for the future—one a growth scenario and the other a retrenchment scenario. Resources will become tighter for NIST and government's other science organizations. "I've never managed in such a changing environment," says Gallagher. "Two years ago, everything was on the upswing. Our budget was increasing and innovation was receiving a lot of attention. That turned out to be a snapshot in time. It's hard to set direction when there is so much uncertainty." While all government organizations will face the same uncertainty, Gallagher is convinced that NIST is better positioned to face that future, given the organizational and cultural changes that have taken place during the past four years.

Marcia K. McNutt
Director, U.S. Geological Survey
Department of the Interior

The Beginning

The early days of a political executive are often difficult. Marcia McNutt's experience was no different. "It's the old story about finding your parking spot," recalls McNutt. "I came to the U.S. Geological Survey (USGS) from an Institute where we had 230 employees to an organization with nearly 9,000 employees. You can get lost in this building. It must have been designed by the CIA. You need friends to find your way around here."

McNutt's initial days were spent receiving briefings. "When I did find my way to this floor, I was overtaken by briefings in the first days and weeks," says McNutt. "My days were taken up by briefings. I had just gotten sworn in when I started to get briefings. There were lots of things that the agency wanted me to know about and there were conferences and Congressional testimony coming up on a variety of topics. But I felt that the agendas were being managed and I felt that I had other things to do. The person who controls the agenda controls the outcome of the meeting. My time was being chunked up into 15-minute components. I think the intent was good—the agency wanted to tell me as much as they could in a short amount of time. But I needed to have more time for myself so that I could figure out what needed to be done. I had to decide what I should focus on."

The Organization

The U.S. Geological Survey was created in 1879. The legislative mandate of USGS was to classify public lands, examine geological structure, and assess the energy, mineral, water, and biology resources and products within and outside the United States. Like the National Institute of Standards and Technology (NIST) discussed on page 200, USGS has in recent years moved away from being an agency organized around academic disciplines to an agency organized around problems. Today, the agency is organized around five key areas in which natural science can make a substantial contribution: climate and land use change; core science systems; ecosystems; energy and minerals, and environmental health; natural hazards; and water. USGS has over 8,000 employees and its annual budget is approximately $1 billion. The USGS campus is located in Reston, Virginia.

Marcia K. McNutt

Tenure: Dr. McNutt was nominated by President Obama to serve as the Director of the United States Geological Survey (USGS) and Science Advisor to the United States Secretary of the Interior in August 2009, and confirmed by the U.S. Senate in October 2009.

Non-profit sector experience: Prior to being confirmed as Director of the USGS, Dr. McNutt served as President and Chief Executive Officer of the Monterey Bay Aquarium Research Institute in Moss Landing, California from 1997 to 2009.

Academic experience: Dr. McNutt joined the faculty at Massachusetts Institute of Technology in 1982, becoming the Griswold Professor of Geophysics and serving as Director of the Joint Program in Oceanography & Applied Ocean Science & Engineering. She also was a Professor of Marine Geophysics at both Stanford University and at the University of California, Santa Cruz.

Federal government experience: Dr. McNutt worked at USGS in Menlo Park, California in the area of earthquake prediction.

Education: Dr. McNutt received a B.A. in Physics, *summa cum laude,* Phi Beta Kappa, from Colorado College in Colorado Springs. As a National Science Foundation Graduate Fellow, she studied geophysics at Scripps Institution of Oceanography in La Jolla, California, where she received a Ph.D. in Earth Sciences in 1978.

The Challenge

Like many leaders of government science agencies profiled in this chapter, McNutt faced three major challenges upon arrival at the USGS:

- **Financial resources:** "I was impressed with how USGS does a great amount of activity with a small amount of resources," said McNutt. "The agency has been sliced and diced very thin for several decades. The agency keeps on giving to the point that I don't know how much more I can give back to the Department."
- **People:** "The senior staff," states McNutt, "consists of very high performers. Forty percent are now eligible for retirement. I am concerned that we will be losing some good talent. We aren't doing very well on diversity. I'm not seeing an increase in the numbers that I'd like to see. We just don't have much

diversity among our earth scientists and biologists. They just aren't there which goes to the pipeline issue and reaching people when they are in school."

- **Status:** "I wanted to raise the status and prestige of the USGS," says McNutt. "My impression is that agencies that are self-standing, like the National Science Foundation and the National Aeronautics and Space Administration, receive somewhat more attention than agencies like USGS, NIST, and the National Oceanic and Atmospheric Administration, which are within Departments. Secretary Salazar does have an interest in USGS. In the past, USGS has often received little attention by departmental leadership. I want to increase the role of USGS in bringing science into decision-making."

Responding to the Challenge

The challenges described above are long-term and ongoing challenges faced by all directors of USGS and most heads of science agencies. In addition to these ongoing challenges, there were new challenges which were unexpected. While USGS is prepared to respond to a certain number of natural disasters annually, there were an unusually high number of incidents during Dr. McNutt's first two years at USGS. Well-known recent natural disasters included the Haiti earthquake in January 2010, the Iceland volcano in March 2010, and the Japanese earthquake of March 2011.

USGS's effective response to the increased number of natural disasters had positive impacts on the agency. McNutt states, "I think we increased the stature of the agency, increased our visibility and our name recognition. We received much attention in 2010 and were on the front pages of many newspapers. We made a diverse contribution in 2010. We were involved in responses to the earthquakes and volcanoes. It showed our diverse expertise in many areas. I think all the increased attention also helped inside the agency. It showed the relevance of the agency and it started people within the agency to think about things that we can do that they never imagined before."

Six months into her tenure, the unexpected happened. The Deepwater Horizon disaster occurred in April 2010, killing 11 men and triggering an environmental crisis. The gushing of crude oil into the Gulf of Mexico became an ongoing national story throughout the spring and summer of 2010. "I went to Houston to work with BP in May and didn't return to Reston full time until September," recalls McNutt. "Secretary Salazar wanted to place his top agency heads in places where the Department of the Interior had a major interest and a role in the recovery. The head of the National Park Service went to Mobile, Alabama to be involved in the cleanup, with a focus on Park Service lands. The head of Fish and Wildlife Service went to Louisiana to help out there."

"My job in Houston was to work with both the Coast Guard and the Department of Energy," describes McNutt. "I coordinated a group to work with

Mission and Vision
U.S. Geological Survey (USGS)

Mission
The USGS serves the Nation by providing reliable scientific information to describe and understand the Earth; minimize loss of life and property from natural disasters; manage water, biological, energy, and mineral resources; and enhance and protect our quality of life.

Vision
The USGS is a world leader in the natural sciences through its scientific excellence and responsiveness to society's needs.

BP. My role evolved over time as we worked with BP on what was known as the top kill to halt the gushing. By July, it became more a joint enterprise with BP and the Coast Guard making decisions. My Deputy Director, Suzette Kimball, was running the agency while I was gone. She knew how to run it. I did come up once or twice but my main focus was on the oil spill. I worked 17 hours a day, seven days a week."

On reflecting on her oil spill experience, McNutt says, "It was really quite an experience—a very wild ride—and I'm grateful that I got to participate and make a contribution. But it is something that I would not want to do again. After my work on the oil spill, I don't think I will do anything again that will have the same amount of impact. We got the relief well completed on September 16th. But thanks to the capping stack, the well was shut in after 87 days instead of the 100 days originally predicted." In describing her role and stay in Houston, Joel Achenbach writes in *A Hole at the Bottom of the Sea*:

> On the evening of May 6, U.S. Geological Survey director Marcia McNutt arrived, accompanying Salazar. For the secretary of the interior, this would be a … visit of the BP war room operation, but McNutt would not be so lucky. She happened to know a lot about taking hardware into the deep sea, having served as director of the Monterey Bay Aquarium Research Institute (MBARI), widely viewed as the NASA of deep-sea research. Anyone knowing about deep water was suddenly needed on the front lines of the battle. Salazar took off and left McNutt in Houston, and she set up shop in a windowless six-by-ten foot office. She had packed only a carry-on bag for her Gulf Coast trip (Achenbach).

In July, writes Achenbach, McNutt could "only dream of being back in her spacious office at the agency's headquarters in Reston, Virginia. She was still ensconced in her windowless office in the Houston headquarters of a company that, with its cowboy culture, struck her as a throwback to an earlier era" (Achenbach).

McNutt did return to Reston and resumed running USGS in September 2010. By then, Congress has signed off on the agency's 2012 plan for new activities based on the USGS strategic plan for the future. "USGS is 130 years old, so change is hard," reflects McNutt. "But the vast majority of our employees were positive. They wanted to give the reorganization a chance. There is a strong civil service here. I've found it very fulfilling to work with the staff here."

Reflecting on the Future of USGS

"We haven't made much progress on diversity at the agency level," says McNutt. "This is a tough problem. This is about the future of the organization. We also have retirements coming. This is not a good situation."

Financial resources continue to be a major challenge. "Budgets are going to be tight," forecasts McNutt. "I'm going to have to fight for USGS. This isn't going to be much fun. I think science is important, but we will have to work to prove it to the Office of Management and Budget."

Richard G. Newell
Administrator, U.S. Energy Information Administration
Department of Energy

The Beginning

Richard Newell arrived at the U. S. Energy Information Administration (EIA) with a plan to learn the organization before making any changes. "My first day was on a Monday morning after I was confirmed on a Friday," recalls Newell. "I had already planned to drive up since I knew my confirmation was coming. I didn't come in with an agenda. If I had, I think that would have turned people off. You have to learn about the agency and organization before you try to make changes. I took my time to learn and understand the agency."

The Organization

There were several prior iterations to the current EIA. In 1974, the Federal Energy Administration (FEA) was created with a mandate to collect, assemble, evaluate, and analyze energy information. Two years later, in 1975, the Office of Energy Information and Analysis was created within FEA. In 1977, legislation creating the Department of Energy established the current EIA as the single federal government authority for energy information. It gave EIA independence from the rest of the Department of Energy with respect to data collection, and from the whole government with respect to the content of EIA reports. Subsequent legislation mandated data collection in specific areas, as well as mandating specific inventories.

Today, EIA has 370 Federal employees and an annual budget of nearly $100 million. It has a comprehensive data collection program that covers the full spectrum of energy sources, end uses, and energy flows. Its products include a daily "Today in Energy," weekly reports on petroleum and natural gas storage and coal production, monthly electric power reviews, and long-term U.S. and international energy outlooks. The EIA website averages approximately 2.1 million visits per month.

The Challenge

Newell's early days were spent defining the challenge he faced at EIA. Newell recalls, "I had a positive impression of the agency. I thought EIA did good analysis and I had used their information previously. I thought the agency was

Richard G. Newell

Tenure: Dr. Newell was nominated by President Obama to serve as the Administrator of the U.S. Energy Information Administration in May 2009, and confirmed by the U.S. Senate in July 2009.

Academic experience: Prior to being confirmed as Administrator of EIA, Dr. Newell was the Gendell Associate Professor of Energy and Environmental Economics at the Nicholas School of the Environment, Duke University. He was also an Affiliated Professor of Business Administration and Corporate Sustainability at the Fuqua School of Business, Duke University. He joined the Duke faculty in 2007. He was also a Teaching Fellow at Harvard University.

Federal government experience: From 2005 to 2006, Dr. Newell served as the Senior Economist for energy and environment on the Council of Economic Advisers.

Non-profit sector experience: From 1997 to 2006, Dr. Newell was a Fellow and Senior Fellow at Resources for the Future.

Private sector experience: Early in his career, he was a Senior Associate at ICF Incorporated.

Education: Dr. Newell received a B.S. in Materials Engineering and a B.A. in Philosophy from Rutgers University. He also received an M.P.A. from Princeton University's Woodrow Wilson School of Public and International Affairs, and a Ph.D. from Harvard University in Environmental and Resource Economics.

deep in expertise. EIA undertook surveys which I thought were very important." The agency's agenda was also very clear to Newell. "We do three primary activities: collect data, analyze data, and disseminate it," he says.

While Newell had a very positive impression of the agency from both his personal experience as a consumer of EIA data and his early assessment of the agency after his arrival, he concluded that the agency would benefit from management improvements and potentially a reorganization. Newell says, "When I arrived, I saw a lack of coordination within the organization. There was too much stovepiping. I saw inefficiency in the agency and Department structure. In addition, there had been a long gap between my arrival and the departure of the previous Administrator so there were a lot of issues that had been put on hold until I arrived."

Newell also assessed the agency's website. "I thought the website could use improving," says Newell. "None of these problems were fully visible to outsiders. The website was perfectly usable. But it is critical because we use the website as our primary dissemination vehicle. I observed that we were also operating in stovepipes in how we ran the agency's website. Each office within EIA had their separate web operations. I decided we needed to focus on the look and feel and usability of the website. I wanted the agency to reexamine what kinds of software and programming they were using."

Responding to the Challenge

Based on his assessment of the agency, Newell reached several key conclusions about the organization and began to take steps in response to each of these challenges. First, he concluded that the agency's strategic plan wasn't going to work with the agency's current organization. "I started thinking and talking about what a new organization might look like," recalls Newell. "I talked to my Deputy Administrator, a career civil servant, who had years of experience in the agency. He thought the idea of a reorganization was good.

"I started thinking and talking to people about what a new organization might look like. The career staff thought it was feasible and would be helpful. I reached out to all the senior managers in the agency. I knew a number of the senior staff here which helped. I treated them with respect. Everybody realized that this needed to happen. If the senior staff had not bought in, it would have been really difficult to pull off the reorganization."

In describing his role in pushing the reorganization of EIA, Newell says, "My role was critical. If I had not been driving the change, I don't think it would have happened. If you don't get involved, an initiative will just chug along. So we proceeded with the reorganization. We went from eight direct reports to me to four. We created a new structure that has four Assistant Administrators, each focused on a main EIA functional area—statistics, analysis, communications, and resources and technology management. It was a well-thought-out reorganization. It was not motivated to get rid of anybody. It was all about a better structure." Previously the agency had been organized around type of energy source, such as oil and gas; coal, nuclear, electric, and alternate fuels; and energy markets.

Concurrently with proceeding to develop a plan to reorganize the agency, Newell also set out to improve other aspects of the agency's management. "I thought we needed to improve our budget tools," says Newell. "We didn't have the right codes and classification systems. Getting information sorted out was very difficult." Another problem was tracking information in and out of the Administrator's office. "The systems simply were not working when I first arrived and were not up to my expectations," he recalls. "We identified some new tools which could track incoming and outgoing information and correspondence." At the same time, the organization needed to beef up its procurement operations and replace its old

U.S. Energy Information
Administration

Mission
Energy Information Administration (EIA)

The U.S. Energy Information Administration (EIA) is the statistical and analytical agency within the U.S. Department of Energy. EIA collects, analyzes, and disseminates independent and impartial energy information to promote sound policy making, efficient markets, and public understanding of energy and its interaction with the economy and the environment. EIA is the Nation's premier source of energy information and, by law, its data, analyses, and forecasts are independent of approval by any other officer or employee of the U.S. Government.

procurement vehicle with a new one which would both save money and be more efficient. "I ended up spending more time on management than I had anticipated. I thought it was important to do," he says.

Like the other science political executives profiled in this chapter, Newell sought to encourage greater use of EIA data by the Department while avoiding any inkling of politicization of the data. "I want EIA to be viewed as independent," says Newell, "and we want to be a place where the Department can seek advice. I want EIA to do more analysis and help the Department more. We don't advocate, we analyze. I want us to provide input into policy making and provide higher quality analysis."

In reflecting back on the reorganization, Newell says, "The reorganization has been more successful than I had anticipated. The reorganization is raising many issues which had been submerged. It started us thinking about new ways to do things."

The reorganization and the agency's management improvements greatly assisted Newell when the organization faced budget cuts as a consequence of the final fiscal year 2011 budget. "When we had to make our FY 2011 budget reductions, we would not have been able to make them as wisely without having improved our budget process," said Newell. "The budget and procurement improvements helped us figure out what to do. So the good news was that we were able to make our budget reductions. We knew clearly what our base is."

Reflecting on Running EIA

"You have to walk a thin line between managing too much (micromanaging) and not managing enough," says Newell. "You have to know when to dig into detail and when not to dig in. But sometimes you have to dig in. You need to get your hands dirty and be willing to ask a lot of questions. You can't just go through the motions. You have to get into the details and 'go into the weeds.'"

Epilogue

Richard G. Newell is now the Gendell Associate Professor of Energy and Environmental Economics and Director, Duke University Energy Initiative, Nicholas School of the Environment, Duke University.

Kathryn D. Sullivan
Deputy Administrator and Assistant Secretary of Commerce for Environmental Observation and Prediction, National Oceanic and Atmospheric Administration Department of Commerce

The Beginning

"I have been confirmed twice for Presidential appointments," recalls Kathryn Sullivan. "The confirmation process was similar in both instances, but my pre-confirmation preparations were very different. Prior to my first appointment, my parent agency detailed me to the office of the National Oceanic and Atmospheric Administration (NOAA) Administrator. The projects I took on for Administrator John Knauss served as a great introduction to NOAA programs and issues."

"The second time (2010), I relied on the Internet for my preparatory research. The variety and volume of materials available online—budgets, program evaluations, independent review reports, and more—allowed me to become quite familiar with NOAA's current operations and challenges. A lot had changed in the intervening years, of course. The agency grew from a budget of roughly $2 billion to over $5 billion, technology programs that were just starting in the early 1990s were now in full service, and the frontiers of NOAA-relevant research had advanced considerably. Happily, something that hadn't changed was the level of talent and dedication all across the NOAA workforce. It's really very impressive."

After she was confirmed, Sullivan worked with NOAA staff to develop a detailed 90-day start-up plan. Recalls Sullivan, "I wanted to hit the ground running and become familiar with our operations and people as quickly as possible. I had countless briefings and made a point of getting out to meet with people in regions. I had been appointed to a newly created position, and felt it was important for our people to get to know me."

The Organization

Components of NOAA date back to the 19th century. The United States Coast and Geodetic Survey was formed in 1807, the roots of the National Weather Service go back to 1817, and the Bureau of Commercial Fisheries was formed in 1871. In 1970, these agencies came together to form the National Oceanic and Atmospheric Administration in the Department of Commerce.

Major components of NOAA now include the National Weather Service; the National Environmental Satellite, Data, and Information Service; the National Marine Fisheries Service; the National Ocean Service; and the Office of Oceanic

Kathryn D. Sullivan

Tenure: Dr. Sullivan was nominated by President Obama to serve as Deputy Administrator of the National Oceanic and Atmospheric Administration in December 2010, and confirmed by the U.S. Senate in May 2011.

Academic/Non-profit experience: Prior to being confirmed as Deputy Administrator, Dr. Sullivan served as the inaugural Director of the Battelle Center for Mathematics and Science Education Policy at Ohio State University's John Glenn School of Public Affairs. From 1996 to 2005, she served as the Chief Executive Officer of the Center of Science and Industry (COSI) in Columbus, Ohio.

Federal government experience: In 1993, Dr. Sullivan was appointed NOAA's chief scientist. Prior to joining NOAA, she spent 15 years in the NASA astronaut corps as one of the first six women to be selected for such a position. She flew three shuttle missions, including the Hubble Space Telescope's deployment, and holds the honor of being the first American woman to ever walk in space.

Education: Dr. Sullivan received her B.S. in Earth Sciences from the University of California, Santa Cruz, and a Ph.D. in Geology from Dalhousie University in Canada in 1978.

Atmospheric Research. NOAA has an annual budget of over $5 billion and over 12,000 employees.

The Challenge

When Sullivan arrived in 2010, NOAA faced a series of major challenges. In describing these challenges, Sullivan says, "We were facing some significant programmatic challenges and the prospect of a long stretch of flat or declining budgets. We had two big satellite procurements underway when I arrived, one of which was still working through a significant reorganization. The mission of NOAA had not changed, but the pressure points were now different."

NOAA develops and operates the nation's weather satellites. The agency's major satellite programs:

- The Geostationary Operational Environmental Satellite (GOES) is used for short-term weather forecasting and severe storm tracking.

- The Polar-Orbiting Operational Environmental Satellite (POES) provides surface and atmospheric information over the entire earth. NOAA is now developing its next generation of polar orbiting satellites, the Joint Polar Satellite System (JPSS), to provide continuity of polar-orbiting observations.

Sullivan also confronted a recent reorganization, in which the Office of the Administrator/Under Secretary of Commerce for Oceans and Atmosphere changed significantly. "Administrator Jane Lubchenco now has two Deputy Administrators," says Sullivan. "In addition, I assumed the role of Acting Chief Scientist not long after arriving. As Chief Scientist, I work with both Deputy Administrators and our senior career managers in a matrixed fashion." As Assistant Secretary for Environmental Observation and Prediction, Dr. Sullivan provides agency-wide direction for satellites, space weather, water, and ocean observations and forecasts.

Responding to the Challenge

Under the reorganization, Sullivan found NOAA to be different than the organization she had worked for in the 1990s. "Our headquarters organization had a different texture and different roles," says Sullivan.

"The budget formulation process had changed substantially; we have a very different planning and program analysis office. My primary goals for the first year were to establish the new Assistant Secretary role and stabilize our satellite portfolio. The environmental observation and prediction responsibilities of my office cut across all of NOAA. One of my challenges is to ensure that walls don't rise between these enterprise capacities and our mission areas."

In defining her job responsibilities, Sullivan says, "In setting my priorities, one question I always ask myself is, 'What are things that only the person in this job can do.' I play an important integrative role. It is my job to make sure we take the holistic view and to foster the connections that help us work as "One NOAA." When we do this, the whole of NOAA is truly greater than the sum of its parts."

Sullivan assumed strategic leadership for the two complicated satellite procurements. "Our joint satellite program had been progressing technically, but we were operating on a continuing resolution that provided less than half the funding needed to sustain that progress in FY11. We had to move the needle. I met with stakeholders inside and out of government. We have generally good relationships with our Congressional committees, especially on weather satellite issues, which still enjoy strong bipartisan support."

In working on the satellite programs, Sullivan says, "This is a long ballgame. We are putting our satellite programs on firm footing. These are seminal programs which must be fielded on schedule. We had to strengthen our analytical capabilities, scrub our requirements and cost figures. We also needed to communicate much more, get NOAA on some key radar screens again. There was plenty to do."

Mission and Vision
National Oceanic and Atmospheric Administration

Mission

Science, Service, and Stewardship
*   To understand and predict changes in climate, weather, oceans, and coasts,
*   To share that knowledge and information with others, and
*   To conserve and manage coastal and marine ecosystems and resources.

Vision for the Future
*   Resilient Ecosystems, Communities, and Economies
*   Healthy ecosystems, communities, and economies that are resilient in the face of change.

During summer 2012, Dr. Sullivan gave a progress report to two subcommittees of the House Science, Space, and Technology Committee in which she said:

> NOAA has stabilized the management structure, staffing, funding, requirements and oversights of these programs, leading to the completion of key program milestones. This gives us reason to have confidence in our ability to meet the cost, schedule, and performance milestones that lie ahead.
>
> We have worked hard over the past year to stabilize and improve the management of these vital programs and wish to work with you to ensure these satellite programs receive the stable and sufficient budget they need. We are confident that we now have solid life cycle cost figures and budget profiles for both programs, and we are committed to meeting them.
>
> These programs require stable budgets if they are to stay within their cost, schedule, and performance baselines. We must maintain schedule to ensure that each satellite is ready for launch before its predecessor satellite reaches its end of life; otherwise, we will have gaps in coverage that will erode the accuracy and reliability of the forecasts, watches, and warnings that our Nation has come to rely upon. (Sullivan)

Another major activity of Dr. Sullivan's was to reach out to stakeholders beyond the Hill. "We are engaging our academic and industry partners and scientific associations and general audiences across the country," says Sullivan. "We need to tell them what we are working on. We have found that professional organizations are good aggregators. They understand many of our issues and connect us to important constituencies. We are also getting out to the general public."

Like many of the political executives profiled in this book, Sullivan's background prepared her well for the NOAA Deputy Administrator position. While understanding NASA was helpful to her, Sullivan also found her non-governmental experience very useful. She says, "Running a non-profit was a good experience. It required focus and discipline, sound strategy and crisp execution, robust internal and external communications. We have to motivate people to invest precious time and money to visit a science museum. We built a new building during my tenure, which forced every facet of our operations to change. Our staff had to do things that they had never done before and do familiar things in altogether different ways. We had to invest on the front end and build new business processes. I had to make sure that we were having the right conversations—bringing all pertinent expertise and perspectives to bear—on each of these challenges during this transformation."

Reflecting on the Future of NOAA and Science

"I am concerned about the impact that tight budgets will have on the balance of science, service, and stewardship that is vital to NOAA's mission effectiveness," says Sullivan. "The necessary growth in satellite procurement accounts, coupled with the tight fiscal constraints facing the country, poses a real risk to this balance. It also jeopardizes our ability to invest in the scientific research that produces the new ideas and talents needed to ensure the agency's long-term viability."

Chapter Ten

The Collaborators

Understanding the Job of the Collaborator

While we believe that all political executives need collaborative skills, there are some political executives whose job requires a high degree of collaboration. In our interviews, we discovered a group of political executives whom we call the collaborators. These collaborators are found in three types of agencies:

Small agencies with limited funding and staff. Because their funding and staffing levels are limited, these political executives need to figure out how to leverage federal funds by creating partnerships with state and local government, the private sector, and non-profit organizations. Prime examples of this type of agency are the Minority Business Development Agency at the Department of Commerce, which has the significant mission of providing support to minority businesses; and the Veterans' Employment and Training Service at the Department of Labor, whose mission is to assist and prepare veterans to find jobs. Both agencies use their limited funding to find creative ways to further their agency's mission.

The Collaborators

Daniel M. Ashe, page 227

Director, U.S. Fish and Wildlife Service Department of the Interior

John Berry, page 233

Director, Office of Personnel Management (OPM)

David A. Hinson, page 238

National Director, Minority Business Development Agency (MBDA), Department of Commerce

Raymond M. Jefferson, page 243

Assistant Secretary for Veterans' Employment and Training Service (VETS), Department of Labor

Agencies whose mission requires collaborative and partnership activities with groups outside of government. An excellent example of this type of agency is the U.S. Fish and Wildlife Service (FWS). Because the vast majority of fish and wildlife habitat is on non-federal lands, FWS has created a variety of partnership programs to foster aquatic conservation and assist voluntary habitat conservation and restoration.

Central management agencies, with responsibility for working across government. A prime example of this type of agency is the Office of Personnel Management. While OPM is responsible for the direct delivery of some services (retirement and health benefits), the policy part of the agency requires collaboration across government.

The Small Agency Collaborator

David Hinson at MBDA and Ray Jefferson at VETS have adopted similar strategies in working toward achieving their missions. Hinson recalls, "I spent a lot of time during my first year on the road building relationships. You need to build good relationships with corporate America. Building these relationships is crucial." In describing his strategy for VETS, Jefferson says, "We want to create partnerships … to find employment opportunities for veterans." Both Hinson and Jefferson developed working relationships with the Chamber of Commerce, among many other organizations, in support of their different missions: assisting minority businesses and assisting veterans to find employment opportunities.

In addition to their work with the private sector and non-profit organizations, Hinson and Jefferson spend a significant part of their time working with other government agencies. Both MBDA and VETS were created to serve as "spurs" and leaders in government for their respective missions. Hinson and Jefferson had to carve out roles and activities in which their agencies could contribute in a crowded field of numerous agencies, all of whom have some "piece of the action" in their policy area.

For Jefferson, the veterans' field was indeed crowded. Other government agencies involved with veterans include the Office of Personnel Management (involved in the hiring of veterans within government), the Department of Veterans Affairs (involving in providing benefits to veterans via the Veterans Benefits Administration), and the Department of Defense (with its myriad offices related to veterans). There has long been a discussion as to whether VETS should be moved to the Department of Veterans Affairs or remain in the Department of Labor. In navigating between these various other government agencies, Jefferson recalls, "Sometimes I feel that I am conducting shuttle diplomacy."

The Partner Collaborator

As seen on page 231, the mission of FWS is "working with others to conserve, protect, and enhance fish, wildlife, plants, and their habitats for the continuing benefit of the American people." This mission is accomplished through a wide variety of partnerships. FWS notes that throughout its history, the agency has been committed to a collaborative approach to conservation. The agency has created partnerships with local municipalities, private landowners, school groups, corporations, state governments, federal agencies, and numerous other groups and organizations.

Like other collaborative agencies which need to create partnerships with organizations outside of the federal government, the FWS uses a variety of mechanisms to achieve its partnership activities, such as grants and cooperative agreements, memoranda of understanding, donations, and statutory partnerships.

In describing his outreach activities, Daniel Ashe, Director of the U.S. Fish and Wildlife Service, says, "We are now working to improve our partnerships with other organizations. We want to strengthen our relationships with professional communities. We reached out to our legacy partners. We wanted to know what they wanted and what they expected. We found that they wanted to be part of our team. They wanted a more consistent relationship. They are significant communities. We now have a more diverse set of communities with whom we interact. We need to develop more mechanisms for participation."

The Central Management Agency Collaborator

While John Berry might be able to give orders (when he chooses to do so) within the Office of Personnel Management, his influence across the government is based on his collaboration skills. In describing the unique challenge of getting interagency clearance on many of his initiatives and policies, Berry says, "This is a responsibility that most other agencies do not have to undergo. We have to get approval from OMB and then also get approval by agencies. We need 26 agencies to say 'yes.' Any of them can say no." Berry works hard to get input from his colleagues across government in the development of new policies and initiatives. By the time a document is ready for the clearance process, Berry has often touched base with all the key actors in Departments across government.

The interagency collaborative work is crucial to the success of OMB in its role as policy leader. Berry elaborates, "I work closely with the Chief Human Capital Officer's Council and the President's Management Council, as well as the Cabinet." In addition, it is crucial that OPM develop a close, working relationship with the Office of Management and Budget. Berry describes that relationship, "I wanted to develop a good relationship with OMB which I have done. I work closely with the White House on many initiatives, such as our activities on improving work life and veterans' hiring."

These collaborative skills are also clearly needed in government-wide leaders, such as the heads of the General Services Administration, or White House units, such as the Council on Environmental Quality. All have responsibility for shepherding government-wide initiatives. While all can use the power of their office to get desired results on occasion, most of their time is spent cajoling and sharing information with others across government regarding shared goals.

Other Collaborative Agencies

In addition to the four agencies profiled in this chapter, there are other organizations throughout government that we categorize as collaborative agencies. While not comprehensive, the list and descriptions of each agency have been prepared to assist the Office of Presidential Personnel and Cabinet Secretaries in better understanding the unique nature of these collaborative agencies. The key characteristic of the agencies listed on the next page is that all accomplish their mission by working in partnership with other government agencies (at the federal, state, and local level), the private sector, and the non-profit sector.

Other Federal Government Agencies Categorized as Collaborative Agencies

Department of Health and Human Services
Administration for Community Living

In 2012, the Department of Health and Human Services created the Administration for Community Living (ACL) with the goal of increasing access to community supports and full participation, while focusing attention and resources on the unique needs of older Americans and people with disabilities. ACL includes the Administration on Aging, the Office on Disability, and the Administration on Developmental Disabilities in a single agency, with enhanced policy and program support for both cross-cutting initiatives and efforts focused on the unique needs of individual groups such as children with developmental disabilities, adults with physical disabilities, seniors, and persons with Alzheimer's disease.

Administration for Children and Families

The Administration for Children and Families (ACF) is responsible for federal programs that promote the economic and social well-being of families, children, individuals, and communities. One of the main ways that it fulfills this mission is through partnerships with front-line service providers, states, localities, and tribal communities. The numerous programs that ACF participates in benefit children, youth, and families by providing services such as welfare, child support enforcement, adoption assistance, foster care, and child abuse prevention. In FY 11, ACF had a budget of over $50 billion and over 1,300 employees.

Department of Housing and Urban Development
Community Planning and Development

The Office of Community Planning and Development (CPD) seeks to develop viable communities by promoting integrated approaches that provide decent housing, a suitable living environment, and expanded economic opportunities for low and moderate-income persons. The primary means toward this goal is the development of partnerships among all levels of government and the private sector, including for-profit and non-profit organizations. In FY 11, CPD had a budget of $7.4 billion and over 800 employees.

Daniel M. Ashe
Director, U.S. Fish and Wildlife Service
Department of the Interior

The Beginning

"I was a known commodity to the Fish and Wildlife Service (FWS), having served many years in the agency, and I had been Deputy Director while I was being vetted for the position of Director. I really tried to take advantage of that familiarity to hit the ground running and introduce myself to the agency in my new capacity as Director," says Daniel Ashe, Director of FWS.

The agency developed a 90-day strategy designed to help Director Ashe communicate his priorities and give employees across the nation the opportunity to meet him in person—although Ashe says it took about six months to implement because of the demands of his new job.

The Fish and Wildlife Service is somewhat unique among federal agencies in that there is a tradition of selecting Directors (who are Senate-confirmed political appointees) from inside the agency. Four out of the past five Directors were career FWS employees, including both of Ashe's predecessors, Sam Hamilton and Dale Hall. "I support the selection of Directors from within the organization," Ashe says. "There are many unique aspects to being here, and it's an advantage to know the culture."

Knowing the FWS culture from the inside, Ashe emphasizes, gave him the knowledge and sense of urgency to push his transformative vision for the future of the agency from day one. This vision, as described by Ashe, is to become "an increasingly effective, relevant, science-driven organization that will accomplish the Service's mission as never before."

The Organization

The Fish and Wildlife Service's programs are among the oldest in the world dedicated to natural resource conservation. In 1940, a Department of the Interior reorganization consolidated the Bureau of Fisheries (created in 1871 in the Department of Commerce) and the Bureau of Biological Survey (created in 1885 in the Department of Agriculture) into one agency, then known as the Fish and Wildlife Service. The two bureaus had been transferred to Interior in 1939. Passage of the Fish and Wildlife Act of 1956 resulted in another reorganization establishing two separate bureaus: the Bureau of Commercial Fisheries and the Bureau of Sport Fisheries and Wildlife. In 1970, the Bureau of Commercial Fisheries was transferred to the Department of Commerce and renamed the National Marine

Daniel M. Ashe

Tenure: Mr. Ashe was nominated by President Obama to serve as Director of the U.S. Fish and Wildlife Service (FWS) in December 2010, and confirmed by the U.S. Senate in June 2011.

Federal government experience: Prior to being confirmed as Director, Mr. Ashe held a variety of key career positions within FWS, including Deputy Director for Policy, Science Advisor to the Director of FWS, Chief of the National Wildlife Refuge System, and Assistant Director for External Affairs. From 1982 to 1995, he served as a member of the professional staff of the former Committee on Merchant Marine and Fisheries in the U.S. House of Representatives. Ashe is a second-generation FWS employee. His father was a 37-year career employee, retiring in 1990 as Deputy Regional Director for the Northeast Region.

Education: Mr. Ashe received his B.A. degree in Biological Sciences from Florida State University, and a Masters of Marine Affairs from the Institute of Marine Affairs at the University of Washington in 1982.

Fisheries Service. In 1974, the Bureau of Sport Fisheries and Wildlife was again designated as the U.S. Fish and Wildlife Service.

Today, FWS has nearly 10,000 employees and a budget of $2.4 billion. It seeks to accomplish a mission to conserve, protect, and enhance fish, wildlife, and plants and their habitats by:

- Enforcing federal wildlife laws
- Protecting threatened and endangered species by administering the Endangered Species Act
- Managing migratory birds
- Restoring nationally significant fisheries
- Conserving and restoring wildlife habitat, such as wetlands
- Helping foreign governments with their international conservation efforts
- Distributing funds through the Wildlife and Sports Fish Restoration program

The agency manages the 150-million acre National Wildlife Refuge System, consisting of 560 National Wildlife Refuges. It also manages 70 National Fish Hatcheries, 65 fishery resource offices and 86 ecological services field stations. The agency has operations in every state and U.S. territory.

The Challenge

Like many agencies, FWS faces tight budgets in the years ahead. At the same time, the agency must address growing landscape-scale threats to wildlife such as climate change, habitat loss, invasive species, and water scarcity. The scale and intensity of those threats, Ashe notes, require the agency to become more effective and efficient. "Regardless of the specifics of our current and future budgets, we are not going to be able to do all the things we have done in the past, or even all that we do currently. With limited resources—from money to habitat—we will need to start making some hard choices," Ashe says. "We hear a lot of talk about waste and inefficiency in government, but I can say with absolute confidence that we get more out of the dollars we're given than just about any agency. If we have to make additional cuts, we're going to be eliminating highly successful, performing elements of our conservation capacity."

Comparing the agency's current position to triage at a field hospital, he says, "If we let ourselves be consumed with a crusade to save everything, then we'll save nothing. We have to work with our partners to identify and focus on the most strategically important species and actions in order to minimize our extinction losses and achieve the greatest conservation benefits for every dollar we spend."

Ashe also says that FWS seeks to respond to cultural trends, helping Americans understand why they should care about wildlife conservation. "We need to recognize that America is changing—becoming more urban, more diverse and less connected to the outdoors," says Ashe. "We need to do a better job of giving Americans a personal stake in conservation—whether it's by providing recreational opportunities, or by demonstrating the connection between healthy wildlife habitat and a healthy economy. At the same time, we need to recruit new voices and ideas into the agency and find new ways to reach out to nontraditional audiences."

Responding to the Challenge

Ashe was clearly no stranger to FWS, having grown up with a father who worked for the agency. "When I was a kid, our family vacations revolved around the Refuge System. We would follow my dad around during the summertime to places like Sanibel Island, Big Pine Key, Merritt Island, and Blackbeard Island, and while he worked, I'd be having fun with my brothers and my mom," recalls Ashe. These experiences shaped his positive feelings toward the agency, and he jumped at the chance to leave his job working for the House Merchant Marine Committee to join FWS in 1995. "I grew up admiring the Service and the work my father did. Getting the chance to lead this agency is a humbling experience, and the greatest honor of my professional life," he says.

During his time as a career employee, Ashe worked to secure the passage of organic legislation establishing the purposes and priorities of the Refuge System—long overdue for a system that began in 1903. He also led the push to increase the agency's scientific capacity and dedication to professional wildlife management, as well as its response to climate change.

Ashe says his primary goal is to use science and strategic partnerships to improve the agency's ability to deliver conservation. "The resource challenges we face are too big and too complicated for us or any other entity to tackle alone. But by using science to improve our collective understanding of what's happening on the landscape, we can align our efforts with those of state and federal agencies, conservation organizations and private landowners. If we do this, we can leverage our resources and have a much greater impact."

"We are very reliant on great partners to help us accomplish our mission. First among these partners are the state wildlife agencies, which have been so critical to conservation. We also have great working relationships with many organizations like Ducks Unlimited, the Nature Conservancy, Defenders of Wildlife, Trout Unlimited, and dozens of others. They can raise important funding and reach out to landowners and other partners in ways that we sometimes can't. They can also provide enormous contributions to research, land acquisition and protection, and other activities that help us do our jobs more effectively."

FWS is working with the states and other partners to develop a network of Landscape Conservation Cooperatives across the nation designed to coordinate biological planning, conservation design and delivery, monitoring, and research at a landscape scale.

In addition to the above programs, FWS is celebrating the 25th anniversary of the Partners for Fish and Wildlife (PFW) program, which was officially established in 1987. The Partners program has gained national recognition as a vanguard in the new era of cooperative conservation based on the premise that fish and wildlife conservation is a responsibility shared by citizens and the government. The program is using cutting-edge restoration and enhancement techniques, along with deploying proven methods of communication and partnership building (Filsinger and Milmoe).

Improving conservation delivery also requires cultural and structural change within FWS. "We have to simplify our management structure, creating a results-focused, flexible environment where decisions can be made more quickly by resource managers close to the field. This includes taking a strategic approach to the Service budget, linking funding decisions to explicit biological outcomes, and identifying representative species that we believe will be the best indicators of these outcomes," says Ashe.

Improving FWS' ability to communicate is another key component of successful conservation, especially in today's media-saturated environment. "If you look at our history, the employees who've truly had an impact on society, such as Rachel Carson, Olaus Murie, and Ding Darling—have been excellent communicators. Each

Mission and Vision
United States Fish and Wildlife Service

Mission
Working with others to conserve, protect, and enhance fish, wildlife, plants, and their habitats for the continuing benefit of the American people.

Vision
We will continue to be a leader and trusted partner in fish and wildlife conservation, known for our scientific excellence, stewardship of lands and natural resources, dedicated professionals, and commitment to public service.

of them realized that to have an impact beyond the agency, they needed to reach the public in a way that was visceral and real. We don't always live up to those standards, but we've placed a renewed emphasis on communicating with the public in recent years."

Based on his tenure at FWS and his observations of other organizations, Ashe concludes that trust is the key to a successful organization. "I want to build a trust-based environment," asserts Ashe. "Any person coming into this position has to have people trust you in order for them to hear you. You have to spend time on relationships."

A big part of building that trust, Ashe believes, involves standing up for the people in the organization. "Our work is becoming increasingly controversial, as resource conflicts and the nature of our political culture have been transformed by the 24-hour news cycle and the advent of social media. We are going to get criticism for the decisions we make. That comes with the territory. Pioneers like Rachel Carson and Olaus Murie were the target of vicious attacks in their day, so in some ways this is nothing new. But it is no less unacceptable. I strongly believe we need to push back with everything we have against efforts to target our employees for doing their jobs."

While he was very familiar with the issues facing FWS and much of his day-to-day work remained the same, moving to the position of Director did bring about major changes for Ashe.

"Most surprising to me," says Ashe, "is that as you move up in an organization, you would think you have fewer bosses. Instead, I now have many masters.

This was a revelation to me which I had not expected. We work closely with the Office of Management and Budget. I work with the Assistant Secretary for Fish and Wildlife Parks who oversees both FWS and the National Park Service. As a result, there are more constraints than I had anticipated."

Reflecting on Leading the U.S Fish and Wildlife Service

"You need to understand the agency," says Ashe. "If you want to get things done here, somebody once told me that you cannot use a command-and-control approach. You need to engage the organization and get employees invested in your vision for the future. They don't respond to command-and-control. The people here really care about the mission of the agency. They are very supportive if you can show them how they fit in with where you want to go."

John Berry
Director
Office of Personnel Management

The Beginning

"I wanted to convey to the agency that we were ready to go," recalls Berry. "I wanted all my team in place on the same day that I started. I worked with the White House in getting my team cleared. We were all sworn in on the same day—my General Counsel, Director of Congressional and Legislative Affairs, Chief of Staff, and the other key members of my team. This is the only time that the entire team has been sworn in on the same day. We wanted to get the team in place and get started."

After arriving at OPM, Berry settled on three priority areas for his first year in office: improving veterans' hiring and services, improving hiring and recruitment, and improving work life and the workplace. "I wanted everybody to know our priorities," recalls Berry. "We picked three things. We worked closely with OMB on this list and they agreed. We also came up with three longer-term priorities—diversity, federal employee health benefits, and performance appraisal. If an item isn't on my list of six priorities, I can tell people that it isn't on my list. This enables me to say 'no' to folks and to keep focused on priorities."

The Organization

The Office of Personnel Management has a long history. It was created as the Civil Service Commission (CSC) by the Civil Service Act of 1883 (also known as the Pendleton Act). The law stated that the CSC would be governed by three Commissioners. The original Pendleton Act structure lasted until 1978, when the organization was renamed the Office of Personnel Management by the Civil Service Reform Act of 1978. That 1978 Act replaced the Commissioner structure with a single Director of the Office of Personnel Management. The 1978 Act also moved three functions from the former CSC to independent agency status: the Merit System Protection Board, the Office of Special Counsel, and the Federal Labor Relations Board.

Today, OPM has a budget of over $2 billion and has over 5,000 employees. OPM has responsibility for the federal government's 1.9 million civilian employees nationwide. It performs a wide range of activities, including setting government personnel policy, delivering retirement payments, running the federal government's health benefit program, and managing federal investigative services. As part of the OPM reorganization described below, an Office of Veteran Services

John Berry

Tenure: Mr. Berry was nominated by President Obama to serve as Director of the U.S. Office of Personnel Management (OPM) in March 2009, and confirmed by the U.S. Senate in April 2009.

Federal government experience: Prior to being confirmed as Director of OPM, Mr. Berry was the Director of the National Zoo in Washington, D.C. from 2005 to 2009. From 1997 to 2000, Mr. Berry served as Assistant Secretary for Policy, Management and Budget at the Department of the Interior. As Assistant Secretary, Mr. Berry served as both Chief Financial Officer and Chief Operating Officer. Mr. Berry also served as Deputy Assistant Secretary and Acting Assistant

Photo: Tony Powell

Secretary for Law Enforcement at the Department of the Treasury. He also served as Director of Government Relations and a senior policy advisor at the Smithsonian Institution. Prior to his executive branch service, Mr. Berry served for nearly 10 years on the staff of Representative Steny Hoyer.

Non-profit sector experience: From 2000 to 2005, Mr. Berry served as the Director of the National Fish and Wildlife Foundation.

State and local government experience: Earlier in his career, Mr. Berry worked for the Montgomery County government. He also served as Staff Director of the Maryland Senate Finance Committee.

Education: Mr. Berry graduated *summa cum laude* from the University of Maryland with a Bachelor's degree in Government and Politics in 1980. In 1981, he earned a Master's degree in Public Administration from Syracuse University.

was created. Recent veteran initiatives include an executive order on employment of veterans in the federal government and a new Fedshirevets.gov website.

The Challenge

The federal government's human resource problems have a long history. "Strategic human capital management" has been on the Government Accountability Office's high risk list since 2001. In the GAO website on the GAO High Risk List and Other Major Government Management Challenges, GAO states that "agencies, with OPM's guidance, have made important strides toward improving aspects of human capital processes, such as recruiting and hiring" (GAOb). The federal government, however, continues to face the challenge of an aging workforce and a dramatic increase in retirement in the years ahead. GAO also pointed out the need for OPM to continue the modernization of the federal employee retirement system.

Responding to the Challenge

John Berry is classified as a collaborator because of the importance of successful collaboration to both his and OPM's success. While OPM is responsible for the direct delivery of services, such as retirement benefits and investigative services, much of its remaining and ongoing agenda involves gaining the support of agencies across government and the Office of Management and Budget. Berry says, "I wanted to develop a good relationship with OMB, which I have done. I work closely with OMB on all our initiatives. I've also engaged the White House on many initiatives, such as our activities on improving work life and veterans' hiring. We worked hard on building our relationship with the White House."

Unlike most other federal agencies, OPM faces the unique challenge of getting interagency clearance on many of its activities. "This is a responsibility," says Berry, "that most other agencies do not have to undergo. We have to get approval from OMB and then also get approval by agencies. We need 26 agencies to say yes. Any of them can say no." In addition, Berry says, "I work closely with the Chief Human Capital Officer's Council and the President's Management Council, as well as the Cabinet. So I get a lot of feedback and people do tell me what they are thinking." It is clear that collaborating with other agencies is a key to OPM's success in its role as a central management agency.

After working with the existing OPM organization for several months, Berry came to the conclusion that OPM needed to be reorganized. Berry says, "It's the last thing I wanted to do, but I think we needed to do it. We needed to fix the agency and I owed it to the organization to do it. I just couldn't look away from our organizational problems." He appointed a career OPM executive to lead the reorganization initiative.

In reflecting on the reorganization, Berry says, "Looking at our old organization chart, you see how difficult it was to communicate what we do. It was self-evident that it needed fixing. We also needed to create some new organizational capability. I wanted the reorganization to be clean, simple, and fill our capability gaps."

The reorganization was implemented in January 2010, and created five function-based organizations: Employee Services, Retirement and Benefits, Merit System Audit and Compliance, Federal Investigative Service, and Human Resource Solutions. In announcing the reorganization, Berry said, "Now, all of OPM's customers—both internal and external—will know exactly where to go for answers." In addition, the reorganization created four offices to provide OPM

Mission
Office of Personnel Management

The OPM mission is to "Recruit, Retain and Honor a World-Class Workforce to Serve the American People." We are committed to:

- Promoting the ideals of public service
- Championing the Federal workforce
- Achieving excellence in what we do
- Advocating for innovative human resources practices
- Attracting and developing the best people for Federal service
- Preserving merit system principles
- Encouraging professional development and recognition opportunities
- Spending taxpayer dollars wisely
- Valuing our customers
- Being accountable for our actions

with additional capacity in key areas: an Office of Planning and Policy Analysis, an Ombudsman office, a Healthcare and Insurance Office, and an Internal Oversight and Compliance Office.

Like several of the other agency heads profiled in this book, Berry concluded that the organization needed additional capacity. The creation of the OPM Healthcare and Insurance Office is a prime example of thinking ahead and anticipating future issues likely to be on an organization's plate. "I had an instinct," says Berry, "that we might get involved in the President's health care reform initiative. I decided to recruit two new health experts. OPM provides health benefits to nine million people, so we do know a lot here and I thought we should be able to help out on this issue. The persons we hired had no egos and just wanted to help out as experts and they were called upon for their advice." This is another example of both Berry and OPM as collaborators.

Another set of issues on which Berry worked were issues related to the gay, lesbian, bisexual, and transgender community. "As the senior gay person in government," says Berry, "I was obviously interested in these issues and had a responsibility to look at these issues. We have a senior group of leaders who work with the White House to make sure they are on top of these issues. We bring some issues to the White House's attention. As the senior gay official in government, I have a voice that goes to the White House. We were obviously pleased with the passage of the Don't Ask, Don't Tell Repeal Act of 2010. Twenty years from now, we will look back and recognize its full significance."

In an interview with the *Washington Post,* Berry acknowledged the weight of his history-making role. "The president asked me to wear two hats … Lead HR for the government and be the highest-ranking gay official … Anybody who is a first, they've got to do a good job … You're going against stereotypes, you're going against prejudice. You have to cut your grass twice as often as the rest of us for people to think your lawn is the same." (Rein)

Reflecting on Serving in OPM

In 2010, Berry told *Government Executive* magazine, "I'm having a ball. The opportunity to do good in government service is incredible—and humbling. And I'm working real hard to try to get as much good done as I can, knowing that the clock is ticking … Because I've got such a great team, I sleep well at night, and I'm pretty confident we're going to get some good points on the board" (Rosenberg).

In reflecting on his time at OPM, Berry describes one of his highlights, "We had a national conference on workplace life at the White House with private-sector leaders. I got to introduce the President. That was really neat for a boy from Montgomery County, Maryland."

David A. Hinson
National Director, Minority Business Development Agency
Department of Commerce

The Beginning

"I had never been in government before," says David Hinson. "I viewed this as an opportunity to apply business approaches to government and, in doing so, reenergize an agency critical to the long-term growth of the U.S. economy."

Before arriving, Hinson recalls, "I read everything that I could find about the agency. I developed a strategic plan to provide a foundation for decision-making and began executing on the plan upon arriving. I realized early on that the success of MBDA was contingent upon the ability of the agency to build a new level of strategic partnerships and collaborative relationships both outside and inside government. With this in mind, I was driven to move quickly to build the relationships necessary to achieve great success."

The Organization

The Minority Business Development Agency (MBDA) is the only agency in the federal government tasked with promoting the growth and global competitiveness of the nation's 5.8 million minority-owned and operated businesses. The agency was originally created in 1969 by Executive Order and named the Office of Minority Business Enterprises. A second Executive Order in 1971 expanded the scope of the agency by authorizing grants to public and private organizations to provide technical and management assistance to minority-owned businesses. In 1979, the agency was renamed the Minority Business Development Agency.

MBDA was created to assist the minority business community in overcoming the impediments that prevent these companies from growing to the same size and scale as the non-minority businesses. Currently, the minority business community contributes $1 trillion in annual economic output to the nation, creating nearly 6 million jobs for Americans. MBDA maintains a national network of 50 business centers and offices geared toward helping minority-owned firms to gain access to capital, contracts, new markets, and strategic relationships necessary to grow. Since 2009, MBDA has helped minority-owned firms gain access to nearly $7 billion in capital and contracts, creating nearly 12,000 new jobs. MBDA played a significant role in supporting federal government efforts to strengthen the economy under the American Recovery and Reinvestment Act of 2009. Finally, MBDA supports the federal effort to promote innovation and entrepreneurialism through various programs.

David A. Hinson

Tenure: Mr. Hinson was appointed by Secretary of Commerce Gary Locke as National Director of the Minority Business Development Agency in July 2009.

Private sector experience: Prior to joining the Department of Commerce, Mr. Hinson was President and CEO of Wealth Management Network, Inc., a financial advisory company. Mr. Hinson managed a 10-state sales region as Director of Advisory Services and Managing Director of Business Development for Envestnet Asset Management, a publicly traded, $70 billion financial advisory firm. Mr. Hinson has also held a variety of positions at Bank of America, Morgan Stanley & Company, First Chicago (now JP Morgan Chase) and the Village Foundation.

Education: Mr. Hinson received an M.B.A. in Finance from The University of Pennsylvania Wharton School, and a Bachelor's degree in Insurance and Finance with honors from Howard University.

The Challenge

When David Hinson arrived, he found an agency that needed to be energized. "While the agency has a long, rich tradition of support and advocacy for minority-owned businesses, there was a perception that in recent times the agency had lost its luster. There was a sense that the federal government, and the Department of Commerce in particular, did not fully appreciate the job creation capability and economic value the minority business sector brings to the U.S. economy." Hinson continues, "There is now a renewed commitment to the agency and the minority business community. For example, most people do not understand that minority-owned businesses are twice as likely to export as non-minority-owned firms are and are three times as likely to be pure exporters—that is, obtaining 100 percent of revenue from exports."

Over the last several years, agency performance has shown marked improvements. Hinson describes his assessment, "We have a sound core program. In 2010, MBDA generated $4 billion in contracts and financing, resulting in the creation of nearly 6,400 new jobs." Hinson continues, "By any measure, this is solid performance. We were able to take the Return on Investment (ROI) to 125-times in 2010 through focused efforts. While our current resources allow us to achieve targeted goals, current and projected demand from the minority business community may force a reduction in broad sector support at current funding levels. However, MBDA is committed to meeting the needs of this community."

MBDA's primary focus is to help the nation understand that minority-owned and operated businesses are not a tangential component of the U.S. economy, but are essential to the long-term maintenance and viability of our economy. Hinson says, "I think MBDA has been and continues to be a very good investment. Any agency or entity that promotes job creation should be widely supported. But it is still our challenge to make this case and if we don't, people will not understand our value. We have to communicate our value proposition better."

Responding to the Challenge

One of the first actions taken by Hinson was his decision that the agency would have to reemphasize its impact on the economy. "There was no other way for the agency to succeed," recalls Hinson. "We had to push the potential that minority-owned businesses add to the economy. We wanted to emphasize that the nation should not undervalue any part of the economy. The number of minority-owned firms is growing and according to the U.S. Census, they have the fastest job creation arc of any sector of the economy. We had to move away from people thinking of this agency as merely race-based, and help them understand that essentially, MBDA promotes companies in the fastest-growing communities in the nation. People really don't know how large a part of the American economy minority-owned businesses represent."

A major component of Hinson's strategy to emphasize the economic potential of minority-owned businesses is to focus on the export capabilities of these firms. Hinson recalls, "We wanted a greater focus on globalization and exporting. Our first effort in this regard was to develop the analytic foundation to support the agency's focus on exporting and build collaborative relationships with those entities within government that support export activities. We, therefore, developed partnerships with other agencies within government."

A second key action by Hinson was his decision to improve the agency's relationships with its stakeholders across the country. Hinson recounts, "There had been a decade of poor relationships with stakeholders. So I hit the road. I spent a lot of time during my first year on the road building relationships. You need to build good relationships with corporate America. Building these relationships in critical. You can't work in a box. You need to work with your stakeholders and you need to continue to build more partnerships. You have to work with cities and states and you have to build relationships with the Chamber of Commerce."

The goal of these outreach efforts is to get MBDA into the mainstream of the nation's economy. "I've been building relationships and working on access to capital," says Hinson. "We want to enter into new markets. We also want to get minority businesses out of minority business status. Once minority businesses

U.S. DEPARTMENT OF COMMERCE

MINORITY BUSINESS DEVELOPMENT AGENCY

Mission and Vision
Minority Business Development Agency (MBDA)

MBDA is an entrepreneurially focused organization committed to wealth creation in minority communities. MBDA actively promotes the growth and competitiveness of large, medium and small minority business enterprises (MBEs).

Mission Statement
The Minority Business Development Agency is an entrepreneurially-focused and innovative organization, committed to minority business enterprise and wealth creation.

Strategic Vision
MBDA's Vision is economic prosperity for all American business enterprises

get bigger, they get access to capital. We are increasing our strategic partnerships and devoting more effort to outreach." As part of the agency's outreach to stakeholders, Hinson formed a National Advisory Council for Minority Business Enterprises. The Advisory Council is the first council focused on promoting the minority business community since the early 1970s. The Advisory Council includes high-level private sector executives. A key MBDA goal under Hinson has been to increase private sector involvement in minority businesses.

Another major task for Hinson was improving the internal operations of the organization, as well as its image both inside and outside the Department of Commerce. Hinson says, "I had to build credibility for the agency. I wanted to show people what we were capable of doing. This required that we improve the skill sets of the agency. We had to make clear our expectations on training. I looked at everybody in the agency and decided what new capabilities we needed. I decided we needed a new head of business development and we went out and hired a terrific person for that job. I reorganized the organization to focus more on business development. We needed to grow in size and sell. We wanted to focus on expanding the economy by giving more people access to our agency."

As part of his focus on the internal operations of the organization, Hinson says, "I tried to get the agency more focused. I wanted to begin to quantify the results of the agency. I wanted to change the tone of the organization. I've been trying to get all of us to work together. We tended to work in silos before I arrived."

Hinson concluded that he had to build new relationships with Congress. "I needed to develop a legislative strategy for Capitol Hill. We had no legislative strategy in place when I arrived and we had no staff devoted to working with Congress. I wanted to start articulating our value proposition." As part of this outreach, Hinson testified more times before Congress than any other MBDA national director in the agency's history.

Just as he developed a strategy to work more closely with Congress, Hinson also developed an outreach effort to work with key agencies across government that have expertise in business development: the Overseas Private Investment Corporation, the Export-Import Bank of the United States, the United States Agency for International Development, and the Small Business Administration. "We want the support of these agencies and have begun piloting programs with them. We are seeking to increase our interagency collaboration and participation in government-wide task forces."

Hinson also increased his outreach initiatives to other agencies within Commerce: the Bureau of Industry and Security, the International Trade Administration, and the United States Patent and Trademark Office, to find opportunities to work together and support one another in their efforts to reach out to minority-owned businesses. Hinson says, "We are being more assertive in our relationships within the Department." Hinson also worked with Commerce's National Telecommunications and Information Administration (NTIA) in its implementation of the Recovery Act's broadband initiative.

Reflecting on Serving at MBDA

"We have increased the stature of the organization," says Hinson. "More people are paying attention to us now. I think the image of MBDA has improved. We are trying to get everybody engaged internally and are engaging more stakeholders and government agencies. We have a job to do—expanding the United States economy and creating more jobs. We want to do more. I believe we can go from $2.9 billion in minority business exports to $6 billion."

"It's been a great experience. I think we have moved the needle. I'm happy to be here. I think we have added value."

Raymond M. Jefferson
Assistant Secretary for Veterans' Employment and Training Service
Department of Labor

The Beginning

"I was nominated and quickly started developing a plan for what to do upon being confirmed," recalls Ray Jefferson. "I prepared a memo with my plans. I set out to meet experts in the field and learn about the best practices in management, adult education, and adult employment. My early assessment of the agency was a positive one."

"I worked on putting together my team. My military and West Point career influenced my thinking on the importance of creating a team. My new team members and I started to meet and we put together our tentative plan. Similar to what I used to prepare in the military, it was a preliminary plan from which we could work."

"During this period, I also went out and visited people, spending the days before confirmation learning more about VETS programs, opportunities, and challenges. I thought the job was a perfect fit for me, my military career and my interest in veterans and managing organizations all came together. I had a plan on what I wanted to do before I started. I refined the plan after getting here."

The Organization

The Office of the Assistant Secretary for Veterans' Employment and Training Service was established by Executive Order in 1981. The new position replaced the Deputy Assistant Secretary for Veterans' Employment which had been created in 1976. The Congressional intent for the program was to establish a leadership position in the Department of Labor for services related to veterans, including job and job training counseling programs, employment placement programs, and job training placement service programs.

In FY 11, the Veterans' Employment and Training Service (VETS) had a budget of over $250 million and over 200 employees. VETS also has responsibility for administering and enforcing the Uniformed Services Employment and Reemployment Rights Act of 1994.

Raymond M. (Ray) Jefferson

Tenure: Mr. Jefferson was nominated by President Obama to be Assistant Secretary for the Veterans' Employment and Training Service in June 2009, and confirmed by the U.S. Senate in August 2009.

Private sector experience: Prior to being confirmed as Assistant Secretary, Mr. Jefferson served as a Leadership Consultant with McKinsey & Company in Singapore.

State government experience: Mr. Jefferson served as the Deputy Director for the State of Hawaii's Department of Business, Economic Development and Tourism.

Federal government experience: Mr. Jefferson was selected as a White House Fellow and worked as a Special Assistant to the U.S. Secretary of Commerce. He served as an Army Officer with the infantry, Rangers, and Special Forces, with leadership positions in the U.S. Presidential Honor Guard, 3rd Ranger Battalion, and 1st Special Forces Group.

Education: Mr. Jefferson graduated from the U.S. Military Academy at West Point with a major in leadership. Mr. Jefferson attended Harvard's Kennedy School of Government, earning an M.P.A. in Strategic Management with Distinction as a Littauer Fellow. He also has an M.B.A. from Harvard Business School.

The Challenge

The challenge was clear to Jefferson—the organization needed to be both transformed and revitalized. One of its major programs, the Transition Assistance Program (TAP), was in need of modernization to meet the changing employment environment currently facing veterans. Jefferson says, "We did an assessment of the gap between what's current best practice and what we're doing. It became obvious that we needed to completely transform and redesign the program."

Jefferson was also faced with an increasing unemployment rate for veterans. Given the economic crisis facing the nation, Jefferson decided that the agency could no longer keep doing "business as usual." In an all-hands, town hall meeting with VETS staff, Jefferson said, "If we keep doing what we have done in the past, we'll keep getting the same results. To help our veterans we need to do better, and in order to do better, we must change and do things differently."

Responding to the Challenge

Within six months of his confirmation, Jefferson and his team concluded that they wanted to take a great leap forward by "speeding up" the organization to demonstrate what it was capable of achieving. On May 6, 2010, Jefferson acted directly on this speed imperative by launching a "100-Day Sprint." In describing the Sprint, Jefferson says, "The Sprint was a vehicle to transform our mindset regarding what we were capable of accomplishing. The Sprint was also a vehicle to transform our culture and programs, benchmark ourselves to best practices, and innovate to address gaps and produce the best possible outcomes."

The concept of the Sprint was inspired partly by Jefferson's experience as an Army officer and a West Point graduate, as well as a management consultant at McKinsey (Lawrence and Abramson, 2010b). The military is used to the concept of mobilizing to accomplish specific goals. The concept of mobilization is seldom used, however, on the civilian side of government. In many ways, the 100-Day Sprint is a mobilization of the employees of the Veterans' Employment and Training Service to move out quickly on four fronts:

- Improving current programs
- Launching new initiatives
- Improving management practices in the agency
- Developing talent in the agency

There were many components in each of the above four areas for which the agency focused on dramatic improvement within the 100-day time period, with specific deadlines and goals. A few of the major 100-Day Sprint initiatives include:

- Launching the transformation of the Transition Assistance Program's two-and-a-half day employment workshop to make it relevant for today's transitioning service member
- Beginning the modernization and automation of the case management process for all veterans having claims under the Uniformed Services Employment and Reemployment Rights Act
- Improving employer outreach to increase veteran hiring by launching a pilot program with the U.S. Chamber of Commerce and formalizing relationships with private sector and non-profit organizations
- Initiating more effective outreach to underserved veteran populations through the Rural Veterans Outreach Program
- Increasing career, credentialing, and training opportunities for young veterans (age 20–24) by launching a demonstration program with the Department of Labor Job Corps program

The 100-Day Sprint was a success. All of the goals were met. "It was an accelerator—a shot in the arm of the organization," says Jefferson. "We showed people what we could do. We energized our employees. Our challenge then was keeping up the momentum. The real work began afterwards and was the focus

Vision and Mission
Veterans' Employment and Training Service

Vision
"Meaningful and Successful Careers for All Veterans"

Mission
VETS Proudly Serves Veterans & Service Members! We Provide Resources and Expertise to Assist and Prepare them to Obtain Meaningful Careers, Maximize their Employment Opportunities, and Protect their Employment Rights.

on sustained execution. We took on five tough transformation initiatives. The Sprint established a 'new normal.' It showed the organization what we could be and do. It gave them insights into what they can do. It brought VETS to a new level of performance. It taught us a new way to do business and increased participation and commitment in the agency." In many ways, the 100-Day Sprint was similar to the experience of the Federal Railroad Administration, the Federal Highway Administration, and the Rural Utilities Service in their implementation of the Recovery Act. The tight time schedule for implementing the Recovery Act served to "up the game" of employees in those organizations. At VETS, the 100-Day Sprint had a similar impact.

Concurrently with the 100-Day Sprint to improve the internal operations of VETS, Jefferson continued to develop key relationships both within the federal government and across the private sector. Because of VETS' relatively small budget, it was crucial for Jefferson to create partnerships and to leverage the programs of VETS with activities in other agencies and in the private sector. As an example, one of the major goals that Jefferson set out for VETS was increasing awareness about veteran unemployment. This goal led to collaborations with *Fortune, Forbes, Business Week*, and *GI Jobs* to increase attention to unemployed veterans. Another key outreach initiative by Jefferson was to the private sector. "We have been meeting with the Chamber of Commerce, the Business Roundtable, the Young Presidents Organization, Business Executives for National Security, and CEOs of Fortune 500 companies," says Jefferson. "We want to create partnerships and to work with their staff to find employment opportunities for veterans."

In addition to reaching out to the private sector, Jefferson was also busy meeting with representatives from other federal departments, including the Department of Defense, the Office of Personnel Management, and the Department of Veterans

Affairs. "Sometimes I feel," recounts Jefferson, "that I am conducting shuttle diplomacy. We brought together agencies to work on developing an interagency, public-private, online National Platform and Program for veteran employment. This is a major initiative that would be the one-stop solution that the private sector and all employers would use to hire veterans and veterans would use to find employment. Nothing like it had been attempted before, and it has the potential to solve the high rate of veterans' unemployment—a true game-changer. We needed to get the involvement and support of other agencies to participate in this important initiative. We reached out to get White House involvement and they were very supportive."

Reflecting on Serving in VETS

"I've enjoyed being part of an organization that is passionate about their mission. I view our mission as a noble calling," says Jefferson. "Our team has brought energy and skill to our mission. Our goals are to assist and prepare veterans and service members to obtain meaningful careers, maximize their employment opportunities, and protect their employment rights."

"Being part of this team has been a great experience and very meaningful. It's been a robust and rich experience for me."

Epilogue

Raymond M. Jefferson resigned his position at the Department of Labor in July 2011.

Appendix

Dates of Interviews

Dates of Interviews

Jonathan S. Adelstein, Administrator, Rural Utilities Service, Department of Agriculture
April 8, 2010; October 15, 2010; April 7, 2011

Daniel M. Ashe, Director, U.S. Fish & Wildlife Service, Department of the Interior
April 4, 2012

John Berry, Director, Office of Personnel Management
July 30, 2009; June 21, 2010; March 15, 2011

Rebecca M. Blank, Under Secretary for Economic Affairs, Economics and Statistics Administration, Department of Commerce
December 4, 2009; June 1, 2010; March 9, 2011

Rafael Borras, Under Secretary for Management, Department of Homeland Security
April 25, 2012

Michael R. Bromwich, Director, Bureau of Ocean Energy Management, Regulation and Enforcement, Department of the Interior
November 30, 2010; June 28, 2011

William V. Corr, Deputy Secretary, Department of Health and Human Services
March 26, 2012

Patrick D. Gallagher, Director, National Institute of Standards and Technology and Under Secretary of Commerce for Standards and Technology, Department of Commerce
January 15, 2010; July 26, 2010; May 13, 2011

W. Scott Gould, Deputy Secretary, Department of Veterans Affairs
October 8, 2009; June 4, 2010; March 22, 2011

Seth D. Harris, Deputy Secretary, Department of Labor
December 22, 2009; June 25, 2010; April 11, 2011

David J. Hayes, Deputy Secretary, Department of the Interior
March 23, 2012

Allison A. Hickey, Under Secretary for Benefits, Department of Veterans Affairs
March 7, 2012; August 14, 2012

David A. Hinson, National Director, Minority Business Development Agency, Department of Commerce
June 25, 2010; December 20, 2010; June 29, 2011

Dennis F. Hightower, Deputy Secretary, Department of Commerce
November 11, 2009; July 6, 2010

Raymond M. Jefferson, Assistant Secretary for Veterans' Employment and Training Service, Department of Labor
June 16, 2010; December 3, 2010; July 5, 2011

David J. Kappos, Under Secretary of Commerce for Intellectual Property and Director, United States Patent and Trademark Office, Department of Commerce
March 30, 2010; August 25, 2010, April 26, 2011

Joseph A. Main, Assistant Secretary of Labor for Mine Safety and Health, Department of Labor
March 9, 2010; September 1, 2010; May 24, 2011

Arun Majumdar, Director, Advanced Research Projects Agency-Energy, Department of Energy
June 10, 2010; January 7, 2011; July 6, 2011

Marcia K. McNutt, Director, U.S. Geological Survey, Department of the Interior
March 30, 2010; September 16, 2010; March 24, 2011

Victor M. Mendez, Administrator, Federal Highway Administration, Department of Transportation
December 8, 2009; June 22, 2010; March 16, 2011

Kathleen A. Merrigan, Deputy Secretary, Department of Agriculture
November 4, 2009; May 25, 2010; March 8, 2011

Anthony W. Miller, Deputy Secretary, Department of Education
January 13, 2009; July 8, 2010; March 23, 2011

Richard G. Newell, Administrator, U.S. Energy Information Administration, Department of Energy
April 12, 2010; November 3, 2010; April 20, 2011

Thomas R. Nides, Deputy Secretary for Management and Resources, Department of State
March 7, 2012

John S. Pistole, Administrator, Transportation Security Administration, Department of Homeland Security
May 10, 2012

Daniel B. Poneman, Deputy Secretary, Department of Energy
February 25, 2010; August 3, 2010; May 18, 2011

David H. Stevens, Assistant Secretary for Housing and Commissioner, Federal Housing Administration, Department of Housing and Urban Development
December 16, 2009; June 22, 2010; March 21, 2011

David L. Strickland, Administrator, National Highway Traffic Safety Administration, Department of Transportation
June 21, 2010; December 1, 2010; June 15, 2011

Kathryn D. Sullivan, Deputy Administrator and Assistant Secretary of Commerce for Environmental Observation and Prediction, National Oceanic and Atmospheric Administration, Department of Commerce
April 4, 2010

Joseph C. Szabo, Administrator, Federal Railroad Administration, Department of Transportation
June 21, 2010; December 16, 2010; July 6, 2011
William J. Taggart, Chief Operating Officer, Office of Federal Student Aid, Department of Education
February 24, 2010; August 2, 2010; March 31, 2011
Inez Moore Tenenbaum, Chairman, Consumer Product Safety Commission
November 13, 2009; June 3, 2010; April 7, 2011

Index Of Profiles by Organization

References

Achenbach, Joel. *A Hole at the Bottom of the Sea: The Race to Kill the BP Oil Gusher.* New York: Simon & Schuster, 2011.

Broder, John M. "The Regulator: Answering a Call, Slowly." *New York Times,* April 20, 2011.

Clark, Charles. "State Department Executive: No 'Fantasy World' about Budget," *Government Executive* website, March 15, 2012.

Coons, Chris. "Statement from Senator Coons on Resignation of ARPA-E Director," May 9, 2012.

Department of Homeland Security, "Rafael Borras Confirmation Hearing to be Under Secretary for Management, U.S. Department of Homeland Security," April 7, 2011.

Department of State, 2011. "A Unified Security Budget for the United States," Remarks by Thomas Nides to the Center for American Progress, August 31, 2011.

Department of State, 2012a. "Rightsizing U.S. Mission Iraq," Special Briefing: Thomas Nides via Teleconference, February 8, 2012.

Department of State, 2012b. "Remarks to the Global Business Conference," Remarks by Thomas Nides, February 21, 2012.

DeSeve, G. Edward. *Speeding Up the Learning Curve: Observations from a Survey of Seasoned Political Appointees.* IBM Center for The Business of Government, 2009.

Filsinger, Matthew and Milmoe, Joe. "Restore & Enhance," *Fish & Wildlife News,* Summer 2012.

Government Accountability Office (GAOa). "GAO High Risk and Other Major Government Challenges: Department of Veterans Affairs." www.gao.gov/highrisk/agency/vad/.

Government Accountability Office (GAOb). "GAO High Risk and Other Major Government Challenges: Strategic Human Capital Management." http://www.gao.gov/highrisk/risks/efficiency-effectiveness/strategic_human_management.php.

Government Accountability Office (GAOc). "GAO's High Risk List: Implementing and Transforming the Department of Homeland Security," February 2011, GAO-11-278.

Government Accountability Office (GAOd). "Continued Progress Made Improving and Integrating Management Areas, but More Work Remains," March 1, 2012, GAO-12-365T.

Lawrence, Paul R., and Mark A. Abramson (2010a). *Analysis: Getting Appointees Up to Speed.* GovernmentExecutive.com, February 17, 2010.

Lawrence, Paul R., and Mark A. Abramson (2010b). *Speeding up Government: Responding to the Continuing Challenge.* Federal News Radio website, May 18, 2010.

Lederman, Doug. "So Far So Good." *Inside Higher Ed*, October 25, 2010.

Partnership for Public Service. *Ready to Govern: Improving the Presidential Transition.* January 2010.

Peters, Katherine McIntire. "Wasteland: Decades of Poor Management at the Energy Department Threatens Public Health and National Security," *Government Executive*, December 2010.

Pistole, John S. Statement of John S. Pistole before the United States House of Representatives, Committee on Homeland Security, Subcommittee on Transportation Security, June 7, 2012.

Rein, Lisa. "The Rights Man for the Job," *Washington Post,* September 19, 2012.

Rosenberg, Alyssa. "Charged for Change: OPM Director John Berry Taps Positive Energy to Push Through Telework, Hiring, and Pay Reforms." *Government Executive*, March 2010.

Rossotti, Charles O. *Many Unhappy Returns: One Man's Quest to Turn Around the Most Unpopular Organization in America.* Boston: Harvard Business School Press, 2005.

Sullivan, Kathryn D. Written Statement by Kathryn D. Sullivan before the United States House of Representatives, Committee on Science, Space and Technology, Subcommittees on Energy and Environment and Investigations and Oversight, June 27, 2012.

About the Authors and Contributors

Authors

Paul R. Lawrence is a Principal in the Advisory Services practice of Ernst & Young LLP, and a leader in its Federal Government Consulting Practice. He served as the Partner-in-Charge of the Ernst & Young "Initiative on Leadership," which resulted in the publication of this book.

Mr. Lawrence has more than 25 years of experience working closely with government leaders. Prior to joining Ernst & Young LLP, Mr. Lawrence was a Vice President with Accenture, an Executive Director with the MITRE Corporation, a Vice President with IBM Business Consulting Services, and a Partner at PricewaterhouseCoopers.

He has written extensively on technology, management, and government. He is the co-editor of *Transforming Organizations* and *Learning the Ropes: Insights for Political Appointees*. He has testified before Congress and several state legislatures. He serves on the Board of Advisors to the Economic Program at the University of Massachusetts and has served on the Board of Advisors of the Thomas Jefferson Public Policy Program at The College of William and Mary. He was twice selected by *Federal Computer Week* as one of the top 100 public service business leaders. He is a Fellow of the National Academy of Public Administration.

Mr. Lawrence earned his Master of Arts and Ph.D. in Economics from Virginia Tech. He earned his Bachelor of Arts degree in Economics from the University of Massachusetts, Amherst, graduating Phi Beta Kappa.

Mark A. Abramson is President of Leadership Inc. He served as Project Director of the Ernst & Young "Initiative on Leadership."

During his career, Mr. Abramson has served as Executive Director of the IBM Center for The Business of Government, President of the Council for Excellence in Government, and a Senior Program Evaluator in the Office of the Assistant Secretary for Planning and Evaluation in the Department of Health and Human Services. While at the Council for Excellence in Government, Mr. Abramson was instrumental in launching *The Prune Book* series in 1988, which profiled the toughest jobs in government.

Throughout his career, Mr. Abramson has published numerous books and articles. He is the co-editor of *The Operators Manual for the New Administration, Getting It Done: A Guide for Government Executives,* and *Learning the Ropes: Insights for Political Appointees.* Mr. Abramson serves as editor of the *IBM Center for The Business of Government Book Series,* published by Rowman & Littlefield Publishers. He is also the author or editor of 16 books and has published more than 100 articles on public management. From 2005 to 2008, he served on the editorial board of the *Public Administration Review* as Case Study Editor. He has also served as a Contributing Editor to *Government Executive* and as a member of the Board of Editors and Forum Editor for *The Public Manager.*

Mr. Abramson was elected a Fellow of the National Academy of Public Administration and is past President of the National Capital Area Chapter (NCAC) of the American Society for Public Administration. He received a Master of Arts degree in political science from the Maxwell School of Citizenship and Public Affairs at Syracuse University and a Bachelor of Arts degree from Florida State University.

Contributors

Marc Andersen is the Americas Markets Leader for Government and Public Sector for Ernst & Young LLP. In this role, he has overall responsibility for strategy, growth, development, and performance of the Ernst & Young member firm government practices in the Americas. Mr. Andersen created and launched the firm's U.S. Federal advisory business. Mr. Andersen also serves as the Global Coordinating Client Service Partner to federal and commercial clients of Ernst & Young LLP. In addition to practice leadership and client service roles, Mr. Andersen's prior experience also includes strategy, public policy, marketing and business development leadership.

Prior to joining Ernst & Young, Mr. Andersen was a Partner at Arthur Andersen LLP.

Mr. Andersen is active in the community, serving on a number of boards and donating his time and talent to make a difference in the community, with a specific emphasis on improving the lives of at-risk children. He is a board member of the Washington Redskins Charitable Foundation Board, the Tower Club Board of Governors, the Professional Services Council, the Fairfax County Boys and Girls Club, and the Great Falls Rotary Club. He has served as past Chairman of the Fairfax County Chamber of Commerce Government Contractors Council and a member of its Audit Committee. Mr. Andersen has a Bachelor of Arts degree in Economics from George Mason University.

Werner Lippuner is a Principal in the Advisory Services practice of Ernst & Young LLP. He has more than 20 years of experience in providing financial management and information technology assurance and advisory services to international and national clients. Mr. Lippuner works with federal government agencies on their evaluation and improvement of internal controls and risk management practices.

Within the Government and Public Sector practice, Mr. Lippuner leads the Ernst & Young LLP IT Risk practice. He also is the Coordinating Partner for services provided to the Department of Agriculture (USDA). He directs services to assist the USDA in complying with the Federal Manager's Financial Integrity Act, Office of Management and Budget Circular A-123, the Improper Payments

Information Act, and a variety of other federal initiatives, including the Open Government initiative.

Mr. Lippuner holds the following certifications: Certified Accountant (Switzerland), Certified Information Systems Auditor (CISA), Certified Information Security Manager (CISM), and Certified in Governance of Enterprise IT (CGEIT).

Aloha McBride is an Executive Director in the Advisory Services practice of Ernst & Young LLP, where she leads the Government and Public Sector Healthcare practice. Ms. McBride works closely with both the Military Health System and the Department of Veterans Affairs, as well as international health organizations. She has 18 years of commercial and federal management consulting experience and focuses on strategic planning, cost take-out, merger integration, performance improvement, and clinical transformation.

Prior to rejoining Ernst & Young LLP in 2010, Ms. McBride held management positions at PricewaterhouseCoopers and BearingPoint serving federal and commercial consulting clients. She also worked internationally for Ernst & Young LLP in South America.

Ms. McBride holds a Bachelor of Arts Degree in Psychology from the University of California at Berkeley and a Master of Business Administration from Thunderbird School of Global Management.

Robert Shope is the Assurance Leader for Federal Government services at Ernst & Young LLP. In his 35-year career at Ernst & Young, Mr. Shope has served a wide variety of positions in the areas of government services, manufacturing, real estate, and healthcare. He has extensive experience in serving clients undergoing significant transitions including the initial SEC filings, business acquisitions, and business sales.

Mr. Shope has extensive experience in financial management in the federal government. He served as the lead partner in the United States Postal Service financial statement audit. He currently leads the financial statement audit teams for both the Department of Health and Human Services (HHS) and the Centers for Medicare and Medicaid Services (CMS). In addition to his work with federal agencies, Bob has extensive experience in the managed health care, hospital, assisted living and biotech industries.

Mr. Shope is a Certified Public Account (CPA). He received his Bachelor of Sciences degree in Business Management/Accounting from Indiana University of Pennsylvania.

Linda M. Springer is an Executive Director in the Government and Public Sector Practice of Ernst & Young LLP. She serves the Federal advisory practice as coordinating and engagement partner for selected departments and agencies and leads Ernst & Young's Federal risk service line.

Prior to joining Ernst & Young LLP in August 2008, Ms. Springer was the Director of the United States Office of Personnel Management. Previously, Ms. Springer was Controller at the White House Office of Management and Budget (OMB) and head of the Office of Federal Financial Management.

Her public service involvements have included Fellow, National Academy of Public Administration; Principal, Partnership for Public Service; the President's Commission on White House Fellowships; Principal, U.S. Joint Financial Management Improvement Program; the President's Council on Integrity and Efficiency; and the President's Management Council Executive Committee. She also led the Federal CFO, CHCO and Senior Real Property Officers Councils.

Before her career in public service, Ms. Springer spent over 25 years in the financial services industry. She held positions of Senior Vice President and Controller at Provident Mutual and Vice President and Product Manager at Penn Mutual Life Insurance Company.

Ms. Springer received her Bachelor of Science degree, *cum laude*, from Ursinus College. She is a fellow of the Society of Actuaries and a Member of the American Academy of Actuaries.

Donald L. Thomas is an Executive Director in the Advisory Services practice of Ernst & Young LLP, where he leads the Government and Public Sector National Security practice. His primary consulting focus has been with senior executives in the federal sector in the areas of financial management, strategy, change management, organizational development, and business process reengineering.

Prior to joining Ernst & Young LLP, Mr. Thomas was a Vice President with Dell Services, a Principal at SRA International, the Director of

Consulting for Métier, Ltd, and a Product Manager for Thomson Financial.

Mr. Thomas is a certified Project Management Professional (PMP). He received his Bachelor of Arts degree in Economics from the University of Virginia, and received a Masters of Business Administration from the Fuqua School of Business at Duke University.

About Ernst & Young LLP

Ernst & Young

Assurance | Tax | Transactions | Advisory

About Ernst & Young

Ernst & Young is a global leader in assurance, tax, transaction and advisory services. Worldwide, our 167,000 people are united by our shared values and an unwavering commitment to quality. We make a difference by helping our people, our clients and our wider communities achieve their potential.

Ernst & Young refers to the global organization of member firms of Ernst & Young Global Limited, each of which is a separate legal entity. Ernst & Young Global Limited, a UK company limited by guarantee, does not provide services to clients. For more information about our organization, please visit www.ey.com.

Ernst & Young LLP is a client-serving member firm of Ernst & Young Global Limited operating in the U.S.

EYG no. FK0023